Contemporary
sociology of
the school
General editor
JOHN EGGLESTON

Readings on
interaction in
the classroom

CONTEMPORARY SOCIOLOGY
OF THE SCHOOL

PAUL BELLABY
The sociology of comprehensive schooling

PATRICIA BROADFOOT
Assessment, schools and society

BRIAN DAVIES
Social control and education

SARA DELAMONT
Interaction in the classroom
Second edition

Sex roles and the school

JOHN EGGLESTON
The ecology of the school

COLIN LACEY
The socialization of teachers

PETER MUSGRAVE
The moral curriculum

ROY NASH
Schooling in rural societies

PHILIP ROBINSON
Education and poverty

MICHAEL STUBBS
Language, schools and classrooms
Second edition

WILLIAM TYLER
The sociology of educational inequality

TOM WHITESIDE
The sociology of educational innovation

ed. SARA DELAMONT
Readings on interaction in the classroom

eds MICHAEL STUBBS and HILARY HILLIER
Readings on language, schools and classrooms

Readings on interaction in the classroom

edited by
SARA DELAMONT

METHUEN
London and New York

First published in 1984 by Methuen & Co. Ltd
11 New Fetter Lane, London EC4P 4EE
Published in the USA by Methuen & Co.
in association with Methuen, Inc.
733 Third Avenue, New York, NY 10017

Selection and editorial material © 1984 Sara Delamont

Typeset by Tradespools Ltd, Frome, Somerset

Printed in Great Britain
by Richard Clay (The Chaucer Press) Ltd
Bungay, Suffolk

British Library Cataloguing in Publication Data

Readings on interaction in the classroom.—
(Contemporary sociology of the school)
1. Teacher-student relationships
I. Delamont, Sara   II. Series
371.1'02   LB1033

ISBN 0-416-35220-0 Pbk

Contents

vi

Acknowledgements

The selection of articles in this reader is a personal one, but I am grateful to Louis Smith, David Hamilton, David Hargreaves, Martyn Hammersley, Martyn Denscombe and John Furlong for encouragement and suggestions for inclusion. I have not been able to act on all their ideas, but they helped me with a difficult task. Paul Atkinson was his usual supportive self while I worked on the selection, and his continuing scepticism and commitment are an essential part of my scholarly efforts. Anne Murcott deserves my thanks for being the best kind of colleague. Rhian Ellis, Gill Parsons, Odette Parry and Mary Darmanin have been the best kind of student, forcing me to clarify my own ideas.

Liz Renton, Sheila Pickard, Joan Ryan, Margaret Simpson and Val Dobie have typed bits of this book and dealt with my editorial vacillations. Myrtle Robins prepared the final version of the manuscript with her professional skill and efficiency. I am very grateful to all these people for their secretarial help.

The editor and the publishers wish to thank the following authors and publishers for permission to reprint the following extracts and articles: John Wiley & Sons, Inc. for Chapter 3; The Australian Council for Educational Research Ltd for Chapter 4; CBS College Publishing for Chapter 5; Croom Helm Ltd for Chapter 6; the President and Fellows of Harvard College for Chapter 7; Temple University Press for Chapter 8; The Scottish Council for Research in Education for Chapter 10; Teachers College Press and Women's Action Alliance, Inc. for Chapter 12; Cambridge University Press for Chapter 13.

General editor's introduction

Less than a decade ago the 'Contemporary Sociology of the School' series was conceived. Its purpose was to bring together the new and often complex sociological explorations of events in and around the school and its classrooms in a way in which they could be understood and made use of by teachers and other professional workers. An important part of the purpose was also to bring together, with similar clarity, the relevant range of theoretical orientations and research strategies, for without these any new understanding could only be incomplete. The enterprise has been an outstanding success. With the help of an able and enthusiastic team of authors, a group of books has been produced which has been used by tens of thousands of students. The distinctive red volumes have become key texts in their own right in universities and colleges throughout the world.

There is little doubt that the series has made an important contribution to sweeping away many of the misleadingly easy and often unexamined assumptions of the 1960s – such as those about the achievements of working-class children, girls and members of ethnic minorities. The books have illustrated the ways in which individual teacher's and student's definitions of situations can influence events, how perceptions of achievement can not only define achievement itself but also identify those who achieve; how expectations about schooling can help to determine the nature and evaluations of schools.

The books explore the main areas of the sociology of the school in which new understandings of events are available. Each introduces the reader to the new interpretations, juxtaposes them against the longer standing perspectives and reappraises the contemporary practices of education and its consequences. Each author in the series has worked extensively in his or her areas of specialism and has been encouraged not only to introduce the reader to the subject but also to develop, where appropriate, his or her own analyses of the issues. Yet though each volume has its distinctive critical approach, the themes and treatments of all of them are closely interrelated. The series as a whole is offered to students who seek understanding of the practice of education in present-day societies, and to those who wish to know how contemporary sociological theory may be applied to the educational issues of these societies.

A new development in the series is the introduction of 'readers' to accompany several of the volumes. They contain a range of papers which have been selected by the authors of the original titles to augment and develop their analyses and to help readers to extend their understanding of the fields. There was little hesitation in choosing *Interaction in the Classroom* as the subject of one of the first readers. Since the publication of the original volume the pace of research by sociologists, anthropologists and ethnographers has been rapid. Equally fast has been the diversification of patterns of interaction in the classroom. These have been brought about by new teaching methods, new curricula, changes in ethnic distribution and, above all, by the changing relationships between children and children and between teachers and children in modern society. All this has not only led Sara Delamont to revise and update her original text extensively (Delamont, 1976b/1983), but also to assemble this selection of important new writings in this field. Together they present the understandings needed by teachers if they are to work effectively in the interactions of the modern classroom – interactions that are the key to success, or failure, in teaching and learning.

John Eggleston

Introduction

This introduction is deliberately brief. The accompanying text – *Interaction in the Classroom* (Delamont, 1976 and 1983) – and the papers which follow are both self-explanatory. I want merely to explain the criteria used to select papers for inclusion here.

The choice of papers for such a reader is inevitably idiosyncratic. However, it is possible to explicate the bases on which the selection was made. The first decision taken was to divide the reader into the same sections as the text it accompanies. There are, therefore, sections on the intellectual context of classroom research; on the settings in which classrooms are embedded (time, space, institutional control, the curriculum); on pupils' views of schooling; and finally on classroom interaction itself. Once this framework was established, my main aim was to choose papers which were not widely available elsewhere. There are some 'classic' papers which have been anthologized often, and it seemed more useful to provide access to less 'public' works of equal merit. Some attempt has been made to include papers from different parts of the English-speaking world.

All the papers are ethnographic studies, and most are sociological. There are papers on very young children and on older pupils, on males and females, and on different racial and cultural groups. However, it is not possible to provide coverage of all the ethnic groups, religious minorities, types of school, and every subject in the curriculum in the UK, USA, Australia, New Zealand and Canada. I have simply tried to pick the best examples of research to illustrate the kind of work that I drew on in writing *Interaction in the Classroom*. Each paper is therefore one example of a research genre.

There is now a large amount of research published on classroom interaction. This book has deliberately excluded the literature on classroom language whether done by sociolinguists, conversational analysts or ethnomethodologists. This area has been surveyed by Edwards (1980) and in omitting it, I mean no denigration of it. It is the area of classroom research with which I feel least competent, and would have least confidence in selecting. The parallel collection of papers edited by Stubbs and Hillier (1983) will give some purchase on the field, and the two collections can, and should, be seen as complementary.

The first part contains only one paper, which is intended to provide the intellectual context for the collection. It has been substantially rewritten by the authors since the first publication, and so is tailored to its place in this collection. The paper co-authored with David Hamilton, gives the intellectual justifications for focusing the collection on ethnographic studies, rather than observational work done with coding schedules.

The papers in Part Two deal with aspects of the settings in which classrooms are embedded, paralleling Chapter 2 in the accompanying text. There are papers on time, on space, and on the knowledge framework which surround teaching and learning. One paper is British, one American and one Australian, but equivalent pieces of research can be found in all three countries.

Parts Three and Four again follow the equivalent chapters of the accompanying text. In Part Three there is a classic paper on the teacher's career, one on the institutional context in which she works, and one on how teachers in a pair of free schools operate without any of the attributes of the role common in 'ordinary' schools. In the section on pupils there is a paper on peer groups in American elementary schools, and one on West Indian boys in London Schools.

Finally, Part Five is made up of papers about classroom encounters. Like the text, the papers distinguish between *initial* encounters – when teachers and pupils meet as strangers – and *routine* ones; that is, teacher-pupil interaction where a relationship has been established. There are two papers on initial encounters, one by David Hamilton (1977) on the first days of schooling as experienced by four- and five-year-olds, and one by John Beynon, on how eleven-year-old boys 'suss-out' their teachers on arrival in the secondary school.

The two papers on established teacher-pupil routines are very different. Lisa Serbin's is a summary of five years' research in American nursery and infant classes showing habitual patterns of sexual inequality in the classrooms. The extract by Ball, by far the longest in the collection, shows the wide range of teacher-pupil interaction patterns across the curriculum in an English comprehensive.

Part one
The intellectual context

Revisiting classroom research:
a continuing cautionary tale

Sara Delamont and David Hamilton

> We took the challenge provided by our mentors to provide a
> mirror for educators. Our intent was to help educators look
> at themselves ... to turn their attention to what *actually*
> goes on in schools rather than to be so singularly preoc-
> cupied with what *ought* to go on in them.
>
> (Wolcott, 1982, p. 7)

All classroom researchers share Wolcott's goal. In this paper
we revisit a research area we surveyed together in 1972 and
examine some of the routes taken towards Wolcott's goal in the
last decade. In 1972 we were both research students in Liam
Hudson's (1977) Centre for Research in the Educational
Sciences at Edinburgh University, and participants in a series
of small conferences on classroom research run at Lancaster.
Responding to the prevailing orthodoxy we wrote a critical,
even polemical, paper, making a strongly worded attack on the
kind of classroom research which uses a prespecified coding
schedule ('systematic' observation) and a determined plea for
more attention to be paid to an alternative observational

strategy, the ethnographic (also called participant observation or anthropological observation).

The article was accepted by a journal and appeared within twelve months (Hamilton and Delamont, 1974). It was also included as a 'position paper' in a collection of essays on classrooms (Delamont and Hamilton, 1976). Our arguments were by no means unique, as others were making similar points elsewhere (Coulthard, 1974; Walker and Adelman, 1975a). However we had, apparently, produced a benchmark, mentioned in everyone's literature reviews and either lauded or vilified in later debate. In ten years it has been reprinted at least eight times, and it has continued to be attacked by exponents of the 'systematic' observational tradition throughout the decade (e.g. McIntyre and MacLeod, 1978).

Such a *succes d'estime* is flattering, but looking back it also produces discomfiture in the authors. In some respects the paper is badly dated. Since 1972, although the basic arguments still retain their relevance, there has been a major change of emphasis in the American systematic observation research, and in Britain classroom studies have taken a path different from the one we foresaw. There has also been a rapid growth of ethnographic research in the USA and the UK in both pure academic projects and in the evaluation of innovations. It seems to be both necessary and desirable to prepare a new version of our argument which takes account of these changes. The basic position we adopted in the early 1970s is still the same, but it is hard to disentangle the argument from the specific empirical examples.

Accordingly in this paper we do three things: (1) examine the current state of play between the two traditions in classroom research; (2) present our reasons for preferring the ethnographic approach ourselves; and (3) look forward to the next decade of classroom studies. This article replaces the 1974 version, including as it does the same basic theoretical position and methodological arguments, in the context of recent empirical material.

Our position in 1974 was a cautious one. We argued for

more attention to be paid to the then neglected ethnographic tradition, but also accepted that 'systematic' observation schedules had strengths. We concluded that researchers should be scrupulous in discovering the limits of whatever technique they adopted, and accepting those limitations explicitly. In 1984 we would wish to make the following general points about our position on classroom research.

Both of us are inclined towards the ethnographic approach to educational research, but not so fanatically or exclusively that we wish to dissuade other people using other methods. Part of our attachment to the ethnographic is a desire to treat educational research as an 'open-ended' endeavour, where premature closure is a dangerous possibility. Therefore we do not endorse views which treat research (i.e. ethnographic versus systematic observation; normative versus interpretive, etc.) as the equivalent of self-contained epistemological and theoretical paradigms. There is a tendency for educational researchers who advocate one 'method' or another to imply far too narrow and prematurely prescriptive views of what counts as legitimate enquiry.

Throughout this paper we draw a distinction between ethnographic and systematic classroom observation. However we wish to emphasize that any such distinction is not hard-and-fast. Differences between methods are often overplayed and the cleavage (complete in the minds of some researchers) is not absolute. We use the distinction to characterize the 'state of the art' and do not wish to endorse it.

Studying classrooms in the 1970s

David H. Hargreaves (1980) has suggested that the 1970s were a 'notable decade' for classroom studies both because of the number of projects and the wide range of theoretical and methodological approaches. Hargreaves hoped that the 'three great traditions' of studying classrooms – systematic observation, ethnographic observation and sociolinguistic studies – would cross-fertilize each other, and not waste time on squabbling from entrenched positions. Certainly the intellectual hostility between the various classroom researchers has lessened since we wrote in 1974. However, there is, at root, a real difference between the systematic observers and the ethnographers which cannot be glossed over. We address that difference, with empirical examples, and do not dwell upon Hargreaves's third approach: the sociolinguistic (but see Edwards, 1980). The underlying tension between the research done with a prespecified coding scheme and that done from an ethnographic perspective is the tension between positivism and interactionism which runs through all social science. It is a fundamental difference of approach to the study of humans and human society, and it cannot be done away with by calling for interdisciplinary *rapprochements*. More than a century of social science research exists, based on distinct conceptions of humankind, and it cannot be wished away by the pious hopes of classroom observers. This is not the place to rehearse all the debates about positivism (see, for example, Davies, 1976, p. 16); about normative and interpretive paradigms (Cohen and Manion, 1981); or about sociologies of 'order' and 'control' (Dawe, 1970). But we do believe that the different traditions of classroom research which we discuss in this paper are merely one empirical example of two distinct kinds of social science methodology. Classroom research may well benefit from the approach advocated by Hargreaves (1980) but a desire to improve teaching (McIntyre, 1980) will not, in itself, overcome deep fissures between schools of social science. Bearing this *caveat* in mind, we outline some recent developments in classroom research on both sides of the Atlantic.

In the USA the early part of the 1970s saw the dominant approach to classroom observation as a systematic one. This was the group of prespecified coding schemes focusing on verbal behaviour and using it to measure/assess the empathy of the teacher and warmth of the atmosphere. These coding schemes came from a social-psychological tradition with its roots in the 1939–49 period (Amidon and Hough, 1967) and the best known example, Flanders' Interaction Analysis

Categories (FIAC), dates from the late 1950s (Flanders, 1970). A directory of observational coding systems produced in the USA (as a researchers' 'pharmacopoeia') (Simon and Boyer, 1974) contained ninety-nine systems, 30 per cent of which were directly derived from FIAC. This domination was recorded in our paper, together with our concern about over-enthusiasm for such an approach. Even as we published our doubts about the field there was a change of direction in the USA (recorded by Rosenshine and Berliner, 1978). Rosenshine states that the emphasis on the socio-emotional climate of classrooms, and the 'warmth' of teachers which 'was a burning issue in the early 1970s ... doesn't seem worth debating today'. In America attention shifted from the teacher and her speech towards the pupils and their behaviour. The systematic classroom research undertaken in the USA since 1974 has focused more closely on pupils' behaviour, especially their 'academic engaged time' (Denham and Lieberman, 1980). Flanders and his colleagues are no longer the dominant influence in the field (Borich and Madden, 1977). During the 1970s American classroom researchers also became much more interested in ethnographic procedures (e.g. Tikunoff and Ward, 1980; Spindler, 1982; Popkewitz and Tabachnick, 1981).

In Britain the pattern of research has been rather different. Although there have been a range of projects funded using prespecified coding schemes – and the investment in them has been much larger than that in 'pure' ethnography – most of the projects have used homegrown schedules. Interaction analysis did not, as we had feared, sweep all before it. The British version of 'Mirrors' (Galton, 1978) looks different from its American foster parent. The large, and the influential, projects in the UK did not follow the Flanders' pattern in the second half of the 1970s. Hobbs and Kleinberg (1978), Bennett (1976), Rutter *et al.* (1979) and the ORACLE project (Galton, Simon and Croll, 1980) used principles very different from interaction analysis. Ethnographic studies have also prolif-erated in Britain since 1972 (Hammersley, 1980), although there are still many aspects of education in the UK for which such data are lacking.

In summary, the development of classroom studies since 1972 has been very different from the future we feared. Many of the changes are along the lines we hoped to see. However, we feel that there are valid points in our 1974 argument which we made specifically in relation to interaction analysis research, but have *general* application to the systematic observation schedules used since FIAC fell from favour.

The continuing critique of systematic observation

Our criticisms of the prespecified coding schedule as a research tool in the classroom are illustrated here with reference to two recent British systems: that of Boydell used in the ORACLE project (Galton, Simon and Croll, 1980) and that of Rutter and his colleagues (1979) (see appendix).

Our main criticisms of prespecified coding schedules are for their exponents strengths, and we, in making the following seven criticisms, are not insensible that each of our flaws will be seen by others as a source of potency. We set out our general points and then give particular illustrations of them from the two studies.

(1) The aim of coding schemes using prespecified categories is to produce numerical and normative data. The findings are similar in kind to those produced by tests and questionnaires. Suitable for statistical treatment, the data produced tell the reader about 'average' or 'typical' classrooms, teachers and pupils.

(2) Systematic observation schemes typically ignore the temporal and spatial context in which the data are collected. Thus although this is not made explicit in the description of the schedules, most systems use data gathered during very short periods of observation (i.e. measured in minutes and single lessons rather than hours or days); and the observer is not expected to record information about the physical setting like that discussed by Hamilton (1976), Delamont (1976a, 1976b)

8

or Bullivant (1978). For example, only ten of the ninety-nine systems in Simon and Boyer (1974) record any information about the physical environment at all. Divorced from their social and temporal (or historical) context in this way, the data collected may gloss over aspects relevant to their interpretation.

(3) Prespecified coding systems are usually concerned only with overt, observable behaviour. They do not take directly into account the differing intentions that may lie behind such behaviour. Where intention is relevant to the observational category (as in Flanders's Category 2, 'Teacher praises or encourages') the observer has himself to impute the intention, making no attempt to discover the actor's actual or self-perceived intention. Thus by concentrating on surface features, interaction analysis runs the risk of neglecting underlying but possibly more meaningful features. A comprehensive understanding of classroom life may, for example, depend upon the translation of 'silent languages' (Smith and Geoffrey, 1968) or the uncovering of 'hidden curricula' (Snyder, 1971). The papers by Walker and Adelman (1976) and Pollard (1980), and books by Hargreaves *et al.* (1975) and Swidler (1979) are examples of the kinds of analysis which may be necessary to understand the underlying features of verbal interaction in the classroom.

(4) Prespecified coding systems are expressly concerned with 'what can be categorized or measured' (Simon and Boyer, 1974, p. 4). They may, however, obscure, distort or ignore the qualitative features which they claim to investigate by using crude measurement techniques or having ill-defined boundaries between the categories.

(5) Prespecified coding systems focus on 'small bits of action or behaviour rather than global concepts' (Simon and Boyer, 1974, p. 4). Thus, inevitably, they have a tendency to generate a superabundance of data which, for the purposes of analysis, must be linked either to a complex set of descriptive concepts – customarily the original categories – or to a small number of global concepts built up from these categories (e.g. Flanders's

9

'direct/indirect ratio' built up from combinations of categories 1, 2, 3, 6 and 7). But since the categories may have been devised in the first place to reduce the global concepts to small bits of action or behaviour, the exercise may well be circular. The potential of these systems to go beyond the categories is limited. This circularity and lack of potential to generate fresh insights necessarily impedes theoretical development.

(6) The systems utilize prespecified categories. If the category systems are intended to assist explanation, then the prespecification may render the explanations tautological. That is, category systems may assume the truth of what they claim to be explaining. For example, if a set of categories is based on the assumption that the teacher is in the same position as the leader of a T-group, any explanation of 'teaching' in other terms is not possible.

(7) Finally, we feel that, by placing arbitrary (and little understood) boundaries on continuous phenomena category systems may create an initial bias from which it is extremely difficult to escape. Reality frozen in this way is not always easy to liberate from its static representation.

All these limitations inherent in interaction analysis systems are implicitly or explicitly acknowledged by their originators (e.g. Flanders, 1970, Chapter 2). However, they are not usually acknowledged by other researchers and soon slip from view even in the writings of the originators themselves. We believe that if such systems are to be used, these limitations must not be allowed to become implicit, but must be openly acknowledged all the time. The methods must not be seen as something they are not. To be valid as methods for studying the classroom, the techniques must be constantly scrutinized, not once accepted and then taken for granted. In 1972/3 we used the Flanders system to illustrate these points. However, they are general criticisms, equally applicable to the systems under scrutiny here.

Normative data are often interest-catching and attention-arousing, but they frequently raise more queries than they can solve. For example, Karweit (1981) reports a study of fifth-grade maths classes in which the amount of 'non-instructional time' varied from 3 per cent to 18 per cent of maths time. This is interesting, but in itself only tantalizing. We believe such findings are chiefly intriguing because they raise the issue of why teachers decide to do things so differently, and one strategy would be to ask participants for their accounts. Systematic observation precludes taking notice of such data.

In the first ORACLE book (Galton, Simon and Croll, 1980, p. 110) the authors, having spent two long chapters giving all the normative results obtained with two schedules disarmingly admit: 'most of the teachers differed in some respects from the typical profile.' They move on to separate six teaching styles which are the main topic of the project. Again the tantalizing question is *why* the teachers chose to act as they did. The ORACLE data cannot inform us about that.

In the interests of objectivity, many systematic research studies feel compelled to survey large numbers of classrooms. It is argued (correctly) that small samples may fail to provide statements relevant to the population at large. Such an approach (even if it can achieve true randomness) may, however, fail to treat as significant local perturbations or unusual effects. Indeed, despite their potential significance for the classroom or classrooms to which they apply, atypical results are seldom studied in detail. They are ironed out as 'blurred averages' and lost to discussion.

Perhaps the most infuriating normative finding comes from the Rutter (1979) study. The authors report (p. 112) a negative correlation between observed pupil behaviour and the head-teacher's emphasis on pastoral care reported in interviews. They offer various speculations about reasons for this, but there is nothing of the subtlety of the similar problem as examined by Metz (1978). Equally tantalizing is the Rutter team's finding (p. 118) that schools where lessons finished early had worse pupil behaviour than those which used up the whole lesson.

Lack of contextual data characterizes most research using coding schedules. Karweit (1981) discusses appropriate obser-

11

vational periods for 'the detection of time-on-task effects on achievement', and seriously suggests that five periods of ten minutes each can give a reliable estimate of the amount of engaged time. At another extreme Wolcott (1973) spent two full years observing one elementary school principal.

Galton and Simon (1980, pp. 190–1) report that the teaching styles they isolated using the Teacher Record were age-related. Older (and more experienced?) teachers adopted different classroom styles from younger (less experienced?) ones. This finding can only be understood if data are gathered on teacher careers and life histories of a kind eschewed by ORACLE. Similar criticisms about the lack of attention paid to context and meaning variables have been made about the Rutter (1979) research by at least three reviewers (Reynolds, 1980; Hargreaves, 1980; and Blackstone, 1980). The detailed study of 'progressive' Leicestershire primary schools by Ann and Harold Berlak (1981) shows the importance of observation in depth. They found that what, in a short period of observation, appeared to be unstructured classrooms were actually tightly controlled in ways not immediately visible to a visitor. The history of the class had to be built up in order to understand it.

Emphasis on overt behaviour

Our doubts about the undue emphasis on overt behaviour is echoed by Harry Wolcott's (1981) comment on the systematic observers' efforts to achieve inter-observer reliability:

> If I am directed to observe eye movement, gait, proximity etc., then we can talk about reliability, but when you so direct me, I become your observer, an extension of your senses or your system. With Flanders, I floundered, wondering how a whole generation of 'trained' classroom observers could abide with so few categories for sorting everything that goes on in classrooms.   (Wolcott, 1981)

The emphasis on overt behaviour is revealed as problematic in the American Beginning Teaching Evaluation Study

12

(Denham and Lieberman, 1980) and in the ORACLE project (Galton, Simon and Croll, 1980) when the researchers studied pupils' academic engaged time. As the researchers admit, observers have to 'guess', or 'impute' whether pupils are working, when, for example, they stop writing and look out of the window. 'Thinking' is not observable, yet is crucial to the observers' codings of pupils' work habits in both studies. A parallel example, pointed out by Andrew Hargreaves (1980) is the coding of pupil 'lateness' in the Rutter research. The Rutter team (1979, p. 236) offer an unproblematic definition of a 'late' pupil, for the observer's instruction states:

> The number of pupils in the class and the number who arrived after the start of the lesson is to be recorded.

Andrew Hargreaves points out that:

> 'being late' is subject to negotiation between teacher and pupil and dependent upon the criteria employed by the teacher, the reasons provided by the pupil and so forth.

The complexities and subtleties of such negotiations are examined in the work of Stebbins (1975) and a comparison of the two sets of data reveals the threadbare nature of the Rutter team's concept.

Crude measurement techniques

There is no doubt that observers can be trained to use complex coding schedules with considerable reliability. However, some of the categorizations and distinctions which underlie such systems may do violence to classroom reality. In the Rutter research, teachers' actions were separated into those 'on the topic' and those related to pupil behaviour. We accept observers were able to do this, but argue that it is a pointless distinction in most schools. Similarly the Rutter coding 'Personal' (the observer is told to 'score for specifically personal comments, which would usually indicate some background knowledge of, or interest in, the child, home, or activities') strikes us as a clumsy and crude categorization. The ORACLE project's Pupil Record includes a category 'RIS' which is 'not coded because the target is responding to internal stimuli' which we feel cannot but be arbitrary. In the BTES (Denham and Lieberman, 1980) learning is defined as a student getting a high number of correct responses on tests. The reader is told that 'If a student did not understand the task and made correct responses at about chance level, the situation was labelled low success rate' (p. 75). Defining successful and unsuccessful learning in such a way seems to us to be a violation of educational norms.

CIRCULARITY/TAUTOLOGY/REALITY-FREEZING

Our three final points all deal with the way in which prespecified coding schemes are self-limiting. Boydell's Teacher Record makes a distinction between interaction with the whole class, with a small group, and with an individual. The ORACLE team (Galton, Simon and Croll, 1980, pp. 120–1) subsequently produced six teaching styles, three of which – individual monitors, class enquirers, and group instructors – are chiefly distinguished by the proportion of interaction they have with the three audience categories. Yet Group Instructors only spent 17.7 per cent of their time interacting with groups and 52.3 per cent with individuals.

The BTES and the Rutter works seem to us to be circular in the same way. Both studies assume that academic task involvement produces school achievement. That is, they take it for granted that what the school does affects the pupils. They set up the research with the assumption that the causal relationship runs in one direction, i.e. good teachers maximize pupils' learning time and hence their mastery, less effective staff lack this ability and pupils learn less. We do not know of any clear evidence that the reverse is not the case. Perhaps anti-school pupils prevent the teacher from engaging them? The research by Rutter and the BTES studies do not allow that argument to be examined. Research with prespecified coding schemes is governed by preordained descriptive categories (e.g. 'verbal', 'non-verbal', 'teacher', 'pupil') and does not allow and encourage the development of new categories. The ethnographic research can freely go beyond the *status quo* and develop new and potentially fertile descriptive languages, yet *Mirrors for Behaviour* (1974) failed to acknowledge that there are (or even can be) '"metalanguages" for describing communication of various kinds' (p. 1) that are based on anything other than measurement or *a priori* categorization.

Two other criticisms of the systematic observation approach need to be made. We feel that all the systems used deny the observer the reflexivity needed to handle the role of classroom observer. It is naive to assume that there is no effect (Samph, 1976) from an observer's presence, but those using coding schemes either ignore the issue, or rely on coding it as a sufficient resolution. With one exception, all the systems in *Mirrors for Behaviour* make a rigid distinction between the observer and the observed. The former is considered a 'fly on the wall', detached from the classroom events. For example, in an observational study of English infant classrooms, Garner (1972) devotes no discussion to the impact of the observer. More particularly, his checklist makes no reference to infant behaviour directed towards the observer, though it is reasonable to assume that it did (or could) occur. This is remedied by Boydell's Pupil Record which has categories for pupils' interacting with the observer, although the books (Galton, Simon and Croll, 1980; Galton and Simon, 1980) have no reflexive discussion of the topic.

By maintaining a strict 'distance' from those being observed, interaction analysis may again promote an incomplete appraisal. As Louis Smith has pointed out, teaching must be viewed as an intellectual, cognitive process:

The way (the teacher) poses his problems, the kinds of goals and sub-goals he is trying to reach, the alternatives he weighs ... are aspects of teaching which are frequently lost to the behavioural oriented empiricist who focuses on what the teacher does, to the exclusion of how he thinks about teaching.   (Smith and Geoffrey, 1968, p. 96)

In much of interaction analysis these aspects are rarely considered. They are labelled 'subjective' and placed beyond the bounds of the empirical world. This lack of reflexivity is part of the systematic observation tradition's claims to be objective. Its proponents argue that, compared to other forms of observation their systems provide unambiguous data uncontaminated by observer 'bias'. However, the price paid for such 'objectivity' can be high. We believe that by rejecting as invalid, non-scientific or 'metaphysical' data such as the actor's ('subjective') accounts, or descriptive ('impressionistic') reports of classroom events, the prespecified coding approach risks furnishing only a partial description. Furthermore, in justifying the rejection of such data on operational rather than theoretical or even educational grounds, the systematic approach may divert attention from the initial problem towards more 'technocratic' concerns such as the search for 'objectivity' and 'reliability'. In the instructional handbook of the Flanders system, ten pages deal with observer reliability, but only two with how to understand classroom phenomena (see Flanders, 1966). In Galton and Simon (1980) an eighteen-page Appendix deals with replication, no space is made for participants' accounts.

These are our main reservations about the research tradition of observation of using prespecified coding schedules. Many of these objections centre on these systems' premature closure, a drawback we feel is avoided by the ethnographic alternative.

The ethnographic tradition

In 1972/3 it was necessary to explain to an educational audience in Britain what we meant by 'anthropological' observation, or ethnography. Even the latter term was relatively unfamiliar, whereas it is now well known enough to be used not only here but also as an entry in the new encyclopedia of educational research (Louis M. Smith, 1982) and in the series edited by Rist (*Studies in Ethnographic Perspectives on*

16

American Education). Further reviews of British and American work can be found in Hammersley (1980), Borman (1981), Smith (1978, 1982) and Wilcox (1982). There are now many more texts of a methodological type (e.g. Hammersley and Atkinson, 1983). Indeed ethnography has grown in popularity and acceptability to the extent that one of the founding fathers Spindler (1982) could write:

> it is a rare research project today that does not have somewhere in the table of operations at least one ethnographer and somewhere in the research design some ethnographic procedures.

With the growth and proliferation of studies has come what Louis Smith (1982) calls 'zesty disarray' among different groups of ethnographers. We do not attempt to map or evaluate these here, instead we have summarized the 'common core' of ethnography.

Most of the earliest ethnographers were either anthropologists – who lived in alien cultures – or social scientists focusing on 'strange' ethnic groups in their own society. They suffered 'culture shock' and were forced to rethink their *own* preconceptions about everyday life by living among people who saw 'the same' phenomena differently or indeed, did not even 'see' the same things at all. The most crucial difference between those using prespecified coding systems and ethnographers is that the former take for granted many aspects of school life, which the ethnographer struggles to make problematic. The ethnographer may not succeed in this aim, and the best admit this quite openly. For example, Wolcott (1981) says that it took a colleague from outside educational research:

> to jolt me into realizing that the kinds of data teachers gather 'on' and 'for' each other so admiringly reflect the dominant society and its educator subculture. 'At Task' measures particularly intrigued my friend. 'How incredible', he observed, 'that teachers would measure classroom effectiveness by whether pupils appear to be busy. How like teachers to confuse "busy-ness" and learning.'

The attempt to challenge one's own sense of familiarity in classrooms is usually made by the observer immersing himself/herself in the 'new culture'. Ethnographies involve the presence of an observer (or observers) for prolonged periods in a single or a small number of classrooms. During that time the observer not only observes, but also talks with participants; significantly, the ethnographer calls them informants, rather than subjects. Also, the anthropologist does not make such a strong category distinction between observer and observed as the interaction analyst does. Gussow and Vidich put the anthropological case most clearly:

> When the observers are physically present and physically approachable the concept of the observer as non-participant though sociologically correct is psychologically misleading. (Gussow, 1964, p. 240)

> Whether the field-worker is totally, partially or not at all disguised, the respondent forms an image of him and uses that image as a basis of response. Without such an image, the relationship between the field-worker and the respondent by definition does not exist. (Vidich, 1955, p. 35)

In addition to observing classroom life, the researcher may conduct formal interviews with the participants and ask them to complete questionnaires. Usually, to record his observations, the observer compiles field-notes or, more recently, field-recordings. Compared with the results produced by coding interaction with one of the published schedules the initial data gathered by the ethnographer are open-ended and *relatively* unstructured. The degree of openness varies between 'pure', 'exploratory' ethnographies (e.g. Bullivant, 1978) and 'applied', 'evaluation' ethnographies (e.g. Popkewitz *et al.*, 1982).

The ethnographer uses a holistic framework. He accepts as given the complex scene he encounters and takes this totality as his data base. He makes no attempt to manipulate, control or eliminate variables. Of course, the ethnographer does not claim to account for every aspect of this totality in his analysis. He reduces the breadth of enquiry systematically to give more concentrated attention to the emerging issues. Starting with a wide angle of vision, he 'zooms' in and progressively focuses on those classroom features he considers to be most salient. Thus, ethnographic research clearly dissociates itself from the *a priori* reductionism inherent in the prespecified coding systems. In a very real sense, then, it operates with an open and 'unfinished' methodology.

It is often argued against anthropological studies that their results cannot be generalized to other settings. This criticism refers only to statistical generalization. To an anthropological researcher, the development of generally or universally applicable statements is quite a different task, one that is never achieved merely by carrying out a survey. Despite their diversity, individual classrooms share many characteristics. Through the detailed study of one particular context it is still possible to clarify relationships, pinpoint critical processes and identify common phenomena. Later, abstracted summaries and general concepts can be formulated, which may, upon further investigation, be found to be germane to a wider variety of settings. Case studies, therefore, are not necessarily restricted in scope. This issue has been addressed by Hamilton (1981) and Delamont and Atkinson (1981) and is not elaborated further here. However, we do feel that the kinds of generalizations produced from good ethnography are just as useful to both researchers and practitioners as those available from systematic observation. The prespecified coding systems, as we stated above, are often concerned with generating normative data, that is, in extrapolating from sample to population. It should be remembered, however, that statistical norms (e.g. the 'teacher-talk percentages' of Flanders, 1970) apply to the population *taken as a whole*, not to its individual members. They apply to individual settings only in probabilistic terms. And since settings are never equivalent, such statistical generalizations may not always be relevant or useful.

In our view the great strength of the ethnographic research is that it gets away from the simplistic behavioural emphasis of the prespecified coders.

We feel that much classroom description has been simply behavioural. It has tended to disregard the meaning(s) that behaviour entails. As already suggested, such an approach may miss important differences that underlie the behaviour. To the extent that classroom research claims to illuminate the processes associated with classroom life, it cannot afford to divorce what people do from their intentions. If it treats teachers and students merely as objects, it can only obtain a partial analysis, one that falls short of explanation in terms of the subjective processes that inform a teacher's or student's actions.

To inquire into subjectivity or relative truth is not, as is sometimes imagined, to accept solipsism or relativism. It can still be a central theme for empirical research, as Harré and Secord (1972, p. 101) point out,

> to treat people as if they were human beings it must still be possible to accept their commentaries upon their actions as authentic, though revisable, reports of phenomena, subject to empirical criticism.

This is related to the successful use of interaction analysis systems as teacher training rather than research tools (e.g. Wragg, 1974). As training instruments, they are used to give information back directly to the people being observed. Indeed, when audio-visual systems are employed, the observer and the observed can be one and the same person. Clearly, when interaction analysis is used in this way, the observer is more aware of the intentions and subjective processes involved and, at the same time, is sensitized to their temporal and social context. Thus, he or she has the necessary data to reach a more powerful understanding of the interaction. In this respect, interaction analysis as 'research' is fundamentally different from interaction analysis as 'training'. In that it necessarily incorporates a phenomenological understanding as well as a behavioural description of the situation, its use in training is much closer to the ethnographic research model.

Classroom research in the future

In this final section we make a few points about the way we would like to see classroom studies develop.

(1) There is still a danger that research will cease to consider the wider educational and social context of the classroom. To contrast 'classroom' with 'society' is to construct a false opposition. While it is possible, for research purposes, to regard the classroom as a social unit in its own right, it is only with considerable difficulty that it can be regarded as self-contained. An adequate classroom study must acknowledge and account for both the internal and external aspects of classroom life. In particular, classroom research should not be treated as a substitute for studies which look at the broader societal aspects of education. As Walker (1970, p. 143) has warned,

> any description of classroom activities than cannot be related to the social structure and culture of the society is a conservative description.

(2) Development of audio-visual techniques has meant that much classroom research can work from recorded rather than 'live' data, that is, at one remove from the classroom. While this allows for *post hoc* analysis, it has the disadvantage that much of the (usually implicit) contextual data normally made available to the on-site observer may be lost. It is significant, we suggest, that at least some studies which have used visual and/or audio recordings still consciously supplement them with the physical presence of an independent observer (see Walker and Adelman, 1976; Erickson and Mohatt, 1982). In our view, while an elaborate technology can facilitate description of behaviour, it cannot furnish *explanations* for that behaviour. The methods themselves do not provide such a link, nor do they supplant the conceptual processes needed to generate explanations. In the past, classroom research – particularly the interaction analysis tradition – has poured

forth an endless stream of comparative studies, hoping presumably that some conceptual clarity would mysteriously emerge. Technological sophistication is no substitute for conceptual vigour.

(3) We recognize that, like all other research, every classroom study develops from certain premises, suppositions and interests held by the researcher. Typically, these reflect the ethos, especially the intellectual ethos, of his or her time. As we have noted, there is an insidious danger of an uncritical acceptance of techniques developed from different (and often forgotten) standpoints. As the history of mental testing amply illustrates, research methods and statistical techniques just as much as the theoretical constructs with which they are sustained, may bear the hallmarks, if not the scars, of earlier and possibly rejected assumptions. (See, for example, Smith and Hamilton, 1980.)

(4) Research in classrooms, both using prespecified codings and using ethnographic methods, would be improved if researchers read the literature more thoroughly, covering both existing empirical work and the literature on research methods. We concur with the position taken by Marten Shipman (1981), who argues that

> curriculum evaluators have not acknowledged with sufficient force that the wheel has already been invented ... The mainstream research literature has come to be neglected ... Those who launched the particular research perspective, and those who attacked them, did so from a knowledge of social science ... many of those who practised evaluation (are) unaware of the long tradition on which they were drawing.

While Shipman writes about the evaluation of curriculum innovations the same points apply to studying classrooms. Classroom research is part of social science, and that means that there is a literature to be assimilated before, during, and after any particular research project.

(5) There is one final issue on which we wish to dissociate ourselves from the prevailing pattern of educational research.

22

This is the congenital and manic optimism with which much educational research is suffused. Absolute truth is heralded as lying just beyond the horizon. For example:

> A revolution in teaching is being fomented. If successful it will overthrow the hegemony of the centuries-old pattern whereby one teacher and 20–40 pupils engage for most kinds of instruction in a teacher-dominated discourse ... If the revolution succeeds the teacher will spend much less time each day with groups of students in time-honoured ways ... In short, a spectre is haunting research on teaching – the spectre of programmed instruction.
>
> (Gage and Unruh, 1967)

This optimism and its essentially nineteenth-century belief in rational man and the power of science (with its implicit denial of the historicity of truth) has been of considerable consequence, not least for classroom research. In a field where instant solutions are at a premium, this belief, surely, is unlikely to bear much fruit. Rather, it can often lead to premature closure (when an exploratory or heuristic stance would be more useful), to the presentation of cautionary notes dressed up as 'conclusions', and to the pursuit of short-term reliability at the expense of long-term validity. One sobering example here is the original publication by Neville Bennett (1976) of his findings on primary schools which were substantially modified when further analysis was carried out by Aitken, Bennett and Hesketh (1981). In summary, this belief can produce 'tunnel vision', a mental state where a clear view ahead is achieved at the expense of a fading appreciation of the past and an ignorance of what is taking place close by.

Since we first reviewed this research area several bandwagons have been and gone. At the time of writing, ethnography is booming in ways which disconcert such old hands as Spindler (1982) and Wolcott (1981, 1982). We sought in 1972, and are still seeking for a new, open-ended attitude towards research, in which eclectic combinations of research methods can be used and in which different problems can be tackled by different, and mutually appropriate, methods. Instead of looking for one solution to all problems, we suggest that more consideration be given to the nature of the specific problems being faced and, hence, to choosing a particular research strategy, appropriate for that problem.

Acknowledgements

The authors were financed by the SSRC, SCRE and the SED in the earlier phases of their careers when the preliminary research for this paper was conducted. The material for this revised version was gathered with the help of the Inter-Library Loan Service at University College, Cardiff.

Val Dobie, Sheila Pickard and Myrtle Robins typed this version of the paper and we are grateful to them for their speed and skill.

This appendix contains the schedules used by the ORACLE project (Galton, Simon and Croll, 1980) and *15,000 Hours* (Rutter *et al.*, 1979).

1 Boydell's observation schedules

Table 1.1 The observation categories of the pupil record

Category	Item	Brief definition of item
Coding the pupil–adult categories		
1 Target's role	INIT	Target attempts to become focus of attention (not focus at previous signal)
	STAR	Target is focus of attention
	PART	Target in audience (no child is focus)
	LSWT	Target in audience (another child is focus)
2 Interacting adult	TCHR	Target interacts with teacher
	OBSR	Target interacts with observer
	OTHER	Target interacts with any other adult such as the head or secretary
3 Adult's interaction	TK WK	Adult interacts about task work (task content or supervision)
	ROUTINE	Adult interacts about routine matter (classroom management and control)
	POS	Adult reacts positively to task work (praises)
	NEG	Adult reacts negatively to behaviour, etc. (criticizes)

Category	Item	Brief definition of item
	IGN	Adult ignores attempted initiation
4 Adult's communi-cation setting	IND ATT	Adult gives private individual attention to target pupil
	GROUP	Adult gives private attention to target's group
	CLASS	Adult interacts with whole class
	OTHER	Adult gives private attention to another child or group or does not interact

Coding the pupil–pupil categories

Category	Item	Brief definition of item
5 Target's role	BGNS	Target successfully begins a new contact
	COOP	Target cooperates by responding to an initiation
	TRIES	Target tries unsuccessfully to initiate
	IGN	Target ignores attempted initiation
	SUST	Target sustains interaction
6 Mode of interaction	MTL	Non-verbal, mediated solely by materials
	CNTC	Non-verbal, mediated by physical contact or gesture (with or without materials)
	VRB	Verbal (with or without materials, physical contact or gesture)
7a Task of other pupil(s)	STK	Same as target's task
	DTK	Different from target's task

Category	Item	Brief definition of item
7b Sex and number of other pupil(s)	SS	Target interacts privately with one pupil of same sex
	OS	Target interacts privately with one pupil of opposite sex
	SEV SS	Target interacts publicly with two or more pupils having same sex as target
	SEV OS	Target interacts publicly with two or more pupils, of whom one at least is of the opposite sex to target
7c Base of other pupil(s)	OWN BS	From target's own base
	OTH BS	From another base

Coding the activity and location categories

8 Target's activity	COOP TK	Fully involved and cooperating on approved task work (e.g. reading)
	COOP R	Fully involved and cooperating on approved routine work (e.g. sharpening a pencil)
	DSTR	Non-involved and totally distracted from all work
	DSTR OBSR	Non-involved and totally distracted from all work by the observer
	DSRP	Non-involved and aggressively disrupting work of other pupil(s)
	HPLY	Non-involved and engaging in horseplay with other pupil(s)
	WAIT TCHR	Waiting to interact with the teacher

Category	Item	Brief definition of item
	CODS	Partially cooperating and partially distracted from approved work
	INT TCHR	Interested in teacher's activity or private interaction with other pupil(s)
	INT PUP	Interested in the work of other pupil(s)
	WOA	Working on an alternative activity which is not approved work
	RIS	Not coded because target is responding to internal stimuli
	NOT OBS	Not coded because target is not observed for some reason
	NOT LIST	Not coded because target's activity is not listed
9 Target's location	P IN	Target in base
	P OUT	Target out of base but not mobile
	P MOB	
	P OUT RM	Target out of room
10 Teacher activity and location	T PRES	Teacher present with target through interaction or physical proximity
	T ELSE	Teacher privately interacting elsewhere with other pupil(s) or visitor
	T MNTR	Teacher not interacting but monitoring
	T HSKP	Teacher not interacting but housekeeping
	T OUT RM	Teacher out of room

*While it was recognized that the term 'Silence' was in some instances a misnomer, its use for everyday purposes was preferred to the cumbersome term 'silence or interaction other than by question or statement'.

Table 1.2 The observation categories of the Teacher Record

Questions	Task	Q1 recalling facts
		Q2 offering ideas, solutions (closed)
		Q3 offering ideas, solutions (open)
	Task supervision	Q4 referring to task supervision
	Routine	Q5 referring to routine matters
Statements	Task	S1 of facts
		S2 of ideas, problems
	Task supervision	S3 telling child what to do
		S4 praising work or effort
		S5 feedback on work or effort
	Routine	S6 providing information, directions
		S7 providing feedback
		S8 of critical control
		S9 of small talk
	'Silent' interaction, i.e. interaction other than by question or statement	Gesturing
		Showing
		Marking
		Waiting
		Story reading
Silence*		Not observed
		Not coded
	No interaction between teacher and any pupil in the class	Adult interaction
		Visiting pupil
		Not interacting
		Out of room
	Audience Composition	Class, group of individuals
		Identification of pupils involved
	Activity	For example, creative writing, practical maths, etc.

Observational Schedules used in *15,000 Hours*

1 Teacher section

The principle throughout this section is that the predominant activity in which the teacher has been engaged during the observation period should be selected and recorded, and that all likely sorts of behaviour should be covered by one or other of the categories.

The focus in this section should be the person principally in charge of instructing the class, i.e. if someone other than the class teacher takes the children for a time, the focus would be on this person.

(A) Interaction categories

If interaction of any kind constitutes the major activity during the observation period, one of the 'interact' categories, together with one of the 'type' categories, must always be scored.

(i) *Individual*

Score when the teacher interacts specifically with one individual, either by, for example, calling the child out to his desk, or by positioning himself next to the child, or speaking in a way which is clearly primarily directed to one individual. In mixed schools, enter M or F according to the sex of the child. If the teacher continues to interact with the same child during a second or subsequent observation period, mark these later entries $\sqrt{}$ (or M+).

(ii) *Class*

For use in all other instances of interaction with the children, i.e. for all chalk and talk sessions directed to the whole class, for question and answer sessions only involving individuals as representatives of the class (note: taking registers would also be marked 'Class' on these grounds) and when the teacher is going round the class, or looking at the class, whilst they are working.

(B) Type of interaction

In all cases where interaction is scored, one and only one of the following categories must also be scored:

(i) *Topic categories*

(a) *Equipment* Score for setting up of equipment, writing on board, distributing and collecting materials, etc., or for instructions to children on distribution of resources – but not, note, imparting of skills re use of equipment, which would be coded 'Topic'.

This category can also be used alone (i.e. with no interaction category) if appropriate.

(b) *Topic* Uninterrupted interactions focused on the subject matter in hand, on earlier or related work, and the children's acquisition of the skills necessary in executing the work, including methods of using equipment, laying out work and so on.

Positive comments on a child's work should be scored as 'topic' and 'praise'.

Negative comments on a child's work should be scored as 'topic' and 'punishment'.

Note: topic can also be scored alone, without any of the interaction categories, if the teacher is clearly engaged in work related to the instructional context of the lesson, but is not interacting with the children, e.g. marking their books, consulting registers or records, listening to tapes, or generally surveying the children while they are working.

(ii) *Behaviour categories*

In all cases, score only for non-task related references to behaviour or dress (i.e. references to appropriate behaviour in laboratories would be coded as topic).

(a) *Management* Score when the teacher gives initial instructions, or directions to prevent trouble occurring.

(b) *Control* Directions initiated to ensure compliance with previous management instructions which have failed to produce the desired result, or to curb unacceptable behaviour – i.e. score only when the directions given are contingent upon the children's behaviour. If any verbal rebuke is included, score also 'Punishment'.

If comments are made about the children's *good* behaviour, these should also be scored as control (i.e. as contingent on behaviour), but qualified by 'Praise'.

(iii) *Other*

(a) *Personal* Score for specifically personal comments, which would usually indicate some background knowledge of, or interest in, the child, home or activities. On these grounds include also references to other non-school activities which seem to have no relationship to the task, e.g. discussion of football teams would probably be rated as 'Personal' in a maths lesson (but could be topic in a games lesson!).

(b) *Admin* Score for points of school administration, outside the immediate requirements of the particular classroom – e.g. collection of school fund money, announcing general notices, etc., and for taking of attendance registers.

2 *Individual children*

In this section, certain behaviours only have been selected as of interest, and thus the principles to be applied in scoring entries are in some cases different from those in the 'Teacher' section, as any instances of the selected behaviours, however brief, may be coded.

(i) *Task categories*

Always score one, and only one, of these, relating to the predominant activity during the period:

(a) *On* Score when there is clear evidence that the child is on task, or, if only listening is required, that he is not doing anything which could preclude this. Score also if no task is prescribed.

(b) *?* Score when it is not clear whether the child is on task, e.g. if he is engaged in an activity which does not absolutely preclude being on task, but may make it unlikely.

(c) *Off* Score when there is evidence that the child is engaged in an alternative activity which would preclude his completing the task prescribed.

(ii) *Chat, etc.*

The remaining categories are not mutually exclusive, and any instances, however brief, should be scored (but note definition of chat).

(a) *Chat.* Exclude brief whispering, but include extended or easily audible chat.

(b) *Informal – mild.* Exclude fidgeting, but include, for example, rhythmic tapping on desk, chewing gum, sitting on desk/feet on desk, quiet singing/humming, and the use of swearing in general conversation or as mild expletives. As a general guide, the behaviours should be such as to be noticeable in a fairly ordered classroom, but not apparently disrupting others.

3 Class

Once again, any instances of the selected behaviours should be scored here or a score of 0 if none has occurred. Otherwise, ratings should be made in all cases on the following basis:

0 (i.e. blank) = no examples
1   = 1 or 2 children
2   = up to and including quarter of class
3   = between quarter and half class
4   = over half class

Definitions as for individual children above.

Procedures for checking inter-observer agreement

Twenty-two lessons were observed by pairs of observers to check levels of agreement. Some of these checks were made before the main series of observations, and others in the weeks intervening between the main data collection weeks. Total scores per lesson for each category (i.e. the units used in the analysis) for each observer were correlated to provide a measure of agreement. As three observers were involved, three series of corrections were made – A with B and C, B with A and C, and C with A and B. The probabilities given for the individual items ... relate to these product-moment correlations. The mean scores of each observer on each category were also examined for possible variations. Certain behaviours occurred too infrequently during the check lessons to allow for adequate assessments of inter-observer agreement.

DEFINITIONS FOR BEGINNINGS AND ENDINGS OF LESSONS

Initial sheet

Entries in each of the main sections have been coded in one of two ways:
(a) Items with mutually exclusive alternatives: 0–9: circle the appropriate coding.
(b) Single items which may be present or absent: circle 0 for absent, 1 for present.

(i) To lesson
Lost = fewer children in the current lesson than the previous one, where the number should be the same.
Fight = involving members of the class being observed.

(ii) Start
Resources = select the coding which seems to be the norm for the majority of resources.
Time to start of lesson: enter the time after the pips at which the majority of the class has settled to work, or the teacher has control of the class to start the lesson.
Late: enter the number of children arriving after the time entered above.

34

CHECKLIST FOR BEGINNING AND ENDING OF LESSONS

T O   L E S S O N

33	Start/after break/NK		0
	same room/double		1
	V. slow		2

34	Lost	0	1
35	Fight	0	1
36	750 yards	0	1

S T A R T

37	Outside:	mill		0
		enter room		1
		line up		2
	Inside:	muddle		0
		sit		1
		stand		2
39	Off-task chat to T		0	1
40	Silence		0	1
41	Greeting		0	1
42	Register		0	1
43	Ritual		0	1
44	Seating:	chosen by children		0
		T directs some		1
		T directs all		2
		N/K		9
45	Resources:	brought by children		0
		on desk		1
		distrib. by T		2
		distrib. by monitors		3
		collected by children		4

46–7 Time to start of work:

48   No. Late:

E N D

49	Timing:	long		0
		good		1
		short		2
		dismiss before bell		3
50	Stand behind chairs		0	1
51	Silence		0	1
52	Farewell		0	1
53	Line-up		0	1
54	Off-task chat to T		0	1
55	Tidy room		0	1
56	Dismiss by row/group/sex		0	1
57	Reports:	individual	0	1
58		class	0	1
59	Resources:	collected by T		0
		collected by monitor		1
		replaced by children		2
		kept by children		3

C H E C K L I S T

60	Homework set	0	1
61	Homework returned	0	1

Outings/trips:

Formal punishments:

Formal rewards:

Jobs of, for example, monitors:

35

(iii) End

Timing: short = teacher finishes early, and there is time to fill before the pips, but the children are kept until then.
long = teacher does not finish in time, and the lesson overruns the pips.
dismiss before bell = teacher finishes early, and allows children to go.

Resources: as above.

(iv) Checklist

Complete entries for any of the listed items which occur (and add notes on any other points of interest not otherwise recorded).

(a) *Outings/trips*

Note details, and whether subject or school-based.

(b) *Formal punishments*

Note types of punishment given, numbers of children involved, and, if possible, relevant 'offences'.

(c) *Formal rewards*

Again, note types of reward, number involved, and relevant standards of work or behaviour.

(d) *Jobs*

Note details of any jobs referred to during the lesson.

CLASSROOM OBSERVATION SCHEDULE

1 Number		Late				
2 Pencils						
3 Uniform						
4 Overcoats						
5 Chairs						
6 Windows						
7 Condition:	clean					
	tidy					
	plants					
	posters					
	pictures					
Total						
8 Work on walls	0	1	2	3	4	
9 Graffiti	0	1	2	3	4	

36

Classroom observation schedule – definitions

This observation schedule was used during the series of classroom observations of the third year and during the administration of the pupil questionnaire.

1 The number of pupils in the class and the number who arrived after the start of the lesson.
2 The number of pencils borrowed from the researchers during the administration of the questionnaire.
3 The number of children not in correct school uniform (as defined by the school).
4 The number of children in outdoor coats or anoraks.
5 The number of broken chairs in the classroom.
6 The number of broken or cracked windows.
7 The decorative condition of the room. One point was given for each of the five items and a total score assigned to each room.
8 The amount of children's work on the walls, coded from 0 to 4. 0 = none
   1 = one-quarter of available wall space
   2 = one-half of available wall space
   3 = three-quarters of available wall space
   4 = all available wall space.
9 the amount of graffiti, coded as item 8.

Classroom observation schedule – procedures for checking inter-observer agreement

The reliability of the items in this schedule was assessed by comparing the ratings given by the three observers in thirty-three lessons when all three were present. . . .

Part two
Classrooms in their context

This part parallels Chapter 2 of the accompanying text, *Interaction in the Classroom*. Three of the themes introduced there are highlighted here: the temporal context of classrooms; the physical setting of teaching; and the impact of the hidden and manifest curricula on teachers' and pupils' work. In 'The tyranny of the devil's mill' Stephen Ball and a group of students from Sussex provide an interesting account of one of the most neglected constraints upon teaching, the social organization of time. This paper has not been previously published elsewhere, although it draws on data from Corrie *et al*. (1982). The interrelationship between the physical setting in which teachers and pupils work and their social interaction is sensitively captured by Lou Smith and Pat

Keith in the extract from their book, *The Anatomy of Educational Innovation*, about an architecturally novel elementary school. This book has been out of print for far too long, and its insights deserve attention. Finally, Bullivant's work on an Orthodox Jewish boys' school shows how sociologists have analysed the curriculum. While both the Smith and Keith, and the Bullivant articles use data on unusual schools, their conclusions are directly relevant to more conventional ones.

2

The tyranny of the 'devil's mill': time and task at school

Stephen Ball, Robert Hull, Martin Skelton and
Richard Tudor

A modern industrial conception of time is strongly present in schools, where timetabling symbolizes the finite, ordered and scarce nature of 'school time', although this essentially industrial attitude towards time is set within an archaic, traditional annual cycle of work with fixed points set for the completion of tasks. Task-orientation (Thompson, 1967) is rarely to the fore, except in the most general sense of completion of the syllabus. But even here the coverage of the syllabus is normally subordinate to the teachers' estimate of 'what we can get through in the time'. School time is divided into equal, discrete and uniform units by the timetable, in the short term, and in the long term, according to the closeness of 'the exam' or 'the end of term' – which are fixed points. Either way it is time that is the determining factor in the organization and structuring of tasks. The present is always seen to be a matter of progress in relation to time passed and the time remaining measured against these fixed reference points. Consciousness in the present is tied to a fixed horizon of the future, time is limited but can be saved, made up and used wisely. The experience of the activity, the task, is subordinate to the 'pace' set by the teacher. Class lessons are frequently punctuated by urgent enquiries from the teacher as to 'who has not finished?'; 'how many of you have not got on to question 5?'; 'hurry up you three the rest of us are waiting'.

Concern is predominantly with the future, the exam – and the implications that follow from passing or failing it – the end of term, the end of year, leaving school. And the achievement-orientated, individualist ideology of the school suggests to the pupil that the future can be controlled, it's 'up to you' if you 'work hard', 'revise sensibly', 'do your homework', 'plan your time carefully'. It could be argued, if one allows for the functionalist weaknesses of a correspondence theory, that the experience of subordination in school, to time controlled by authoritative others, is in certain respects a preparation for work-life, where time is money. According to Willis the ideological effect of the capitalist linear time is to 'suppress a notion that different social groups may have different times, or some no times, or others attempt to pull time violently forward' (1977, p. 135). Willis argues in his account of 'the lads' that one aspect of the conflict between them and the school, and a further point of differentiation between 'the lads' and 'the ear 'oles', is their opposition to and subversion of the school's ordered and sequential time. Many of the strategies employed by 'the lads' to free themselves from the surveillance of their teachers involved 'directly freeing space for cultural time' (p. 135). 'In a sense', Willis says, 'the lads' events and adventures are hidden from bourgeois time' (p. 135). 'The lads' and many other counter-cultural groups like them appear to reject the future orientation of the use of time in school. For 'the lads' time is something they want to claim for themselves now as an aspect of their immediate identity and self-direction. In part at least, it would seem that 'the lads' rejected the distinction between school time and their 'own' time and thus their subordination to the timetable and the bell. However, 'the lads' are future-orientated in at least one respect – in regard to leaving school.

Clearly, it must also be recognized that the further away from the statutory school leaving age then the greater the latitude which exists in breaking down the strict time-relatedness of school work. In the context of integrated-day, open-plan primary schooling – an invisible pedagogy – the school day may no longer be divided into discrete subject-related units, pupils may be invited to make their own judgements about the length of time to be devoted to particular tasks. Although studies of open classrooms suggest that the extent of weakening of frame may, in some cases, be more superficial than real (Hargreaves, A., 1977 and 1979). And here too, apart from the constraints of resources and order, the teacher's managing of their class still has to be articulated with various organizational timetables for assembly, games, lunch, hall-time, television bookings, etc.

For the vast majority of school pupils, in contrast to Willis's 'lads', school time is experienced passively and unquestioning-ly. Their personal timetables are subordinated to the standard period, school day, school week and term; and the synchronization and sequencing of the timetable. The organization and structuring of educational knowledge are also in part determined by the segmentation of school time. Time is a boundary condition that imposes its own logical pattern upon social action.

> The critical nature of time, as ruler of content, is often conveyed by teacher comment to pupils, perhaps filling a space in one lesson by talking about the next subject which 'will take us up to half-term' or, by, inversely, talking about the compartmentalization of knowledge and how it is geared to time. (Woods, 1978, p. 320)

School life is organized by and into complex temporal sequences. The daily institutional reality of the school takes its experiential form from these sequences, and it is their finite length which constrains activity and provides the basis for the setting of priorities and making of allocations. Thus continually and immediately in school the conformist pupils' experience is that described by Berger and Luckmann:

> The temporal structure of everyday life confronts me as a facticity – which I must reckon, that is, in which I must try to synchronize my own projects. I encounter time in everyday reality as continuous and finite. All my existence in the world is continuously ordered by its time, and is indeed enveloped by it ... I have only a certain amount of time available for the realization of my projects, and the knowledge of this affects my attitude to these projects.
>
> (Berger and Luckman, 1967, p. 41)

Time as a profound phenomenological component of school life enters into the 'taken for granted' paramount reality of these pupils' experiences of schooling. Thus, Berger and Luckmann maintain, 'temporality is an intrinsic property of consciousness. The stream of consciousness is always ordered temporally' (p. 40). Time is seen as a continuous, flowing quantity; a basic and real aspect of the 'natural order of things'. Our lives are superimposed on an underlying, fundamental structure of time, and since we all know that 'time waits for no man', our practical activities are much influenced by the coercive constraining effects of time.

Schutz and Luckmann (1974) take up the description of the 'temporal structure (in) the natural attitude' by looking at the 'temporal structure (given in inner duration) of the meaning of experiences' (pp. 52–6). They state that:

> The unity of the stream of consciousness rests ... upon time's character as a form of lived experiences. In the fixed succession, a Now is transformed into a just-past-Now and becomes a past-Now. The actual impressionable phase of an experience is nothing but a limiting phase of continuous retensions and protensions. Every actual lived experience necessarily carries a horizon of the past and a horizon of the future. (Schutz and Luckmann, 1974, p. 52)

If one extends this account to an examination of the school,

44

one might say that the temporal structure of the school reflects a common sense, everyman's, everyday conceptualization of time and an orientation towards that conceptualization. It is almost a commonplace in the sociology of education that schools, as a human product, take up and reflect the constructions of the world that are held by their producers. In a manner typical of the way in which we construct and bring into play our sociologies, psychologies, epistemologies, and pedagogies, so too do we bring in our commonsense conceptualizations of time and space in the structuring of the school. We would like to suggest that, with regard to time, schools (like people) are seen as being carried along by the flow of absolute time, and that the flow of absolute time is likewise seen as a real coercive facticity with which we must continually reckon (for schools, as they reflect man, are merely elaborate ways of organizing collectively a more or less distinct portion of man's practical activities). But for schools, as for man, absolute time is important primarily in so much as it is seen to lie at the very base of our cosmology; as one of the basic external structures of reality around which all else must revolve. Of greatest significance for schools, as for man, is *finite time* or that portion of 'forever', or that section between antiquity and eternity, that we actually occupy – and the quality of finite time's duration and passage. In everyday life world time is seen as a continuous quantity; though as we have seen, time for me personally is finite. It is 'in the nature' of continuous quantities to be divisible – the possibility for which is exemplified by my own finitude and the historicity of others and of the world; and the motivation for which lies in our attempts to come to terms with their implications for my own practical activities.

In the commonsense apprehension of time lies a neglected, felt-but-unnoticed aspect of the backdrop against which teachers' organization of school activities are made. Time and space are both something to be filled or occupied. We are concerned with time as some sensible and external measure of duration, measurable by means of relative or common motion. Somehow, in the limited amount of time we have for our

45

projects, we gear our activities to a corresponding breakdown – time is that portion of duration which consists of definite periods; and that which we set out to accomplish over 'the duration' is broken down in an orientation towards that which is 'accomplishable' within the time available. We then judge the passage of time, the finite duration, by establishing systems aimed at assessing the quality and extent of motion through that time.

In somewhat typical fashion an alternative perspective to that presented here is taken by Sorokin and Merton (1937), in their 'functional analysis' of 'social time'. They see no discontinuity between the nature of time designation in primitive societies and that in modern societies and suggest that, in both cases, 'time expressions, both of duration and indication, are made in reference to social activities or group achievements' (p. 619). Furthermore, they present the social determination of time 'with its intimate nexus of a common and mutually understood rhythm of social activities' (p. 619) as consensual and communally based, 'with distinctly localized meanings' (p. 628), rather than as conflictual and related to the power of certain classes or groups to impose their conception of the appropriate social periodicities upon others.

Aspects of school time[1]

Finitude is of relevance to the temporal phenomenology of the school in a particular way and in a sense different from that originally intended by Schutz. Schools as people-processing institutions encompass fixed, objective social careers of limited duration. In British schools this means that pupils may leave at sixteen years of age, or must leave sometime soon after. Thus 'in time' the pupil passes through and beyond the world of school. To paraphrase Schutz, 'knowledge of finitude stands out against the experience of the schools continuance'. Others become older and leave but the school continues on, when each pupil is 'old enough' he will also leave and the school still continues. In other words there is an institutional finitude.

46

Certainly this notion of institutional finitude is of relevance to both teachers and pupils in their conception of, or realization of, concrete projects and life-planning. Many pupils hope to leave school with 'good qualifications' etc., and in their latter years at school they are daily reminded by their teachers of the necessity of preparing themselves for 'when they leave'. Although, as noted already, pupils vary in their attitudes to the possibility of 'passing examinations', expectations come to be tempered by *subjective degrees of probability* and *grades of ability*. Thus pupils' biographical situations and the plans and hierarchy of plans that follow from the subjective probabilities that are conjoined therewith, lead to 'leaving school' having significantly different meanings for different pupils.

The institutional finitude of schooling is a part of the inevitable and self-evident reality of the world of school for the pupil, but the long-term project-planning that is related to 'leaving school' is heavily overlain by the day-to-day planning that is related to the immediate experience of the organization of the school day. As Schutz and Luckmann suggest, 'the imposed, fixed course of the temporal structure affords a plan for the day alongside the life plan determined by my finitude' (p. 48). As noted already, the most immediate and obvious aspect of the 'fixed course of the temporal structure' of the school is the regular, fixed and regulated sub-division of school into lessons, breaks, lunchtime etc. In particular, lesson time is 'partitioned into quantitatively homogenous units' the beginning and end of which are normally signified by the ringing of the bell. This is as much the case for teachers as it is for pupils. It is clear from Corrie *et al.* (1978) data that for many teachers in two schools studied, this temporal arrangement of school time into 'periods' was a taken-for-granted and relatively immutable feature of their work lives, 'they were either not aware of them or had become so accustomed to a particular division that they could not imagine any other' (Corrie *et al.*, 1978, p. 49).

'It's fine, I don't suppose it's perfect but it's difficult to imagine in this particular situation, in this particular school, something else that would work any better.'

'Em . . . I've never really thought that about it em to tell you the truth. It just was there, you know . . . it may just be being used to it and not having experienced anything else but I find it very difficult to imagine, you know, what the physical aspect of another time scale would be.'

'Um, I can't say I've given much thought to it. It's just what I've been used to at school, and all the schools I've been at during training, they've all been organized the same way.'

'It's one of those mechanical things that I don't really consider very much.'

'Well, I haven't had much experience at other schools. This is the only secondary I've been in.'

'I've not thought an awful lot, very deeply about this, I must say, because the chances of having a change is so remote that it's just sort of a pipe dream.'

Here then, apparently, the 'fixed course of time' is experienced by those teachers as inevitable, the organization of the school day provides the fundamental temporal structure of their work lives.

But clearly in some respects 'the bell' is of most significance to the pupil. For its sounding often not only signifies the end of one period and the beginning of another, but it signifies the end of French and the beginning of maths, the end of games and the beginning of science, etc. Furthermore it also normally constitutes a sanctioned imperative upon their physical presence in a particular place at a particular time, the constant problem of 'not being late for the bell'. Clearly, in school, time 'belongs to', is the property of, the teacher. The end of French and the beginning of maths is also the end of Mr Enavant's lesson and the beginning of Mr Algebra's.

Teacher: Where have you been?
Corna: Mr Dawson kept me behind.
Teacher: What for?
Corna: To talk to me.

48

Teacher: Well this is my lesson now you should be on
time.   (Ball, 1981, p. 27)

What is more the pupil always runs the risk of 'wasting the
teacher's time'. And it is also evident from lesson transcripts
that the passing of time is frequently related to the imminence
of 'the bell'.

'It's almost time for the bell.'
'The bell's about to go we can't start another exercise.'
'The bell's about to go and we've achieved almost nothing
today.'
'Perhaps a couple more people before the bell.'

We hope to indicate later that this is only one aspect of
the way in which the passing of time in lessons is marked.
But we cannot leave consideration of the significance of
'periods' in the school day without taking account of the
experiences of lesson time reported by Corrie's teachers. It is
clear from many of the comments reported, which are concerned with the length of periods, that the teachers do not
experience all their lessons as temporally equal and equivalent.
Again, this is anticipated by Schutz and Luckmann (1974,
54–5).

inner duration cannot be partitioned into qualitatively
homogeneous unities . . . temporal articulation is concerned
with exhibiting the temporal frames of reference which are
the basis of the constitution in consciousness of well-
circumscribed experience and of our grasping of its
meaning.

Thus the teachers tend to characterize lessons according to the
constitution in consciousness of their inner duration. 'A double
period can flag a bit. It can be very lengthy'; a double period
can 'just last for too long'; but a single period may be 'a bit too
short' or 'short and snappy'. But the important point here is
that these expressions of inner duration, are only meaningful in
relation to the particular situations of their use. That is to say
the character of time as a lived experience is made meaningful

for the teachers in relation to what, when, how and who they are teaching. For example Corrie *et al.* (1978, p. 54) note that:

> it was teachers who taught no-language band classes at Western who were more likely to say that they would like less, or at least no more double periods, than they already had, whereas teachers of classes from other bands were more likely to be satisfied with the number of double periods that they had or said that they would like more.

Evidently double periods with no-language band classes were experienced by the teachers as 'too much time'.

> 'We have two doubles and two singles with them, they're a reasonably good class and they can take the double periods but you have to timetable for further down. And this is why I asked for two doubles and two singles, because with a bottom second-year class of very limited children, a double period is a strain for them and it's a strain for the teacher. So I've asked for this all the way up with the English classes, that you have a certain number of doubles but you must have a couple of singles. To make it easier for the staff.'

> 'I think some kids find it very difficult to take the span of forty minutes, you know, especially, well, not forty minutes, a double period, you know. I think forty minutes is fine, you know, but when you get two forty-minute periods, you know, something like . . ., who, you know, they find it very difficult to concentrate for any length of time really, you know. I think a shorter time would do them a lot of good.'

It should be noted that these comments refer to the length of individual social encounters within the temporal arrangements of the school, not to overall contact time. As one teacher notes, in reference to these 'very limited children' of the no-language band classes, 'a double period is a strain for them and it's a strain for the teacher'. Thus it is that these circumstances are accounted for in the teacher's use of tacit knowledge of human behaviour and practical solutions to assign meaning to and find meaning in the pupils' behaviour. 'They've got a limited span of attention, very limited'; 'They find it very difficult to concentrate for any length of time really, you know.' Here the teachers interpret and identify and 'explain' the pupils' behaviour in terms of a reference schemata based on a stock of previous knowledge concerning the typical behaviour of typical no-language band classes. The explication of the temporal experience of these classes is thus constituted in the social typification of the pupils.

But it is not only the pupils who influence the teachers' experiences of the temporal arrangement of the school; their subject and the nature of the task at hand are also factors. Here the allocation of time, through timetabling, is experienced as an overt constraint.

> 'I would quite like one extra. At the moment I have to cut back on class reading because although the top of the class is good, the bottom I have two or three who are struggling and I have to spend a lot of time on mechanical work. I wouldn't mind an extra period and I would use it for class reading.'

> 'I would like all of them as part of the English curriculum to have some face drama and expressive work to make it seven periods. I feel we should do, and perhaps more time for oral work, because these children, I don't know whether it's because I come from London and London children are a little more outgoing. I don't know. I might be wrong, but I find the children here, you know, very poor at standing up and talking, expressing themselves in formal language.'

> 'I'd love to have six periods with them but I don't think they suffer because they do work em and I work them. Em I'm missing out on some of the frills I would like to do with them. There are things I would like to do which I simply haven't got the time to do because there are other things that I've got to get through.'

Even here though it is not simply a straightforward problem of articulation between the syllabus and the timetable but the expenditure of time, in terms of numbers of periods, is related to the identity and behaviour of particular classes.

'I think that a shorter time with the younger ones is probably enough for them.'

'With this class I would prefer more. I would like to do more work with them. I find in the time I'm often shoving to cover certain aspects, and just for sheer teaching value I would like them to have an extra period. Plus the fact they are the section whom I think need to be pushed and shoved, and I think they could profit from an extra period. They are the bottom of the two language, well, not bottom because that's the wrong word, they're not really graded. They're very mixed. They're very mixed. There's a good top, a middle and a tail. The top will do it for themselves . . . from dropping and the tail need hard pushing.'

'It's enough for 2B. It's too much, I think for OA . . . You come back to the way, you always come back to the way OA mathematics is taught, you know, and I think if I had the time, you know, to research into a different way of teaching OA, you know, I mean you tend to be taught how to teach academic, you know, for the academic child and em when you get something like who are the, they aren't academic, you know, you have to sort of, to spend a lot of time getting concepts over, and you don't ever really, you know, you're taught just tell 2B something and they take it in, they do the cognitive processes and understand it, whereas with OA they can't do the cognitive processes. I think.'

'Em 2A are a good class. And I think they'll all get their 'O' grade, and most of them will, eventually, get the 'Higher'. They quite enjoy maths, em, an awful lot in OB need to learn, like basic arithmetic, maths, etc. em, I don't think they'll learn all that much because they don't like the subject and because they can't do it. And they just seem to shut their minds off. And I think if we get away from the academic approach to them it would be much better. Cut down to about two or three periods a week academic and then arrange something outdoors.'

'Well, I think, personally, they get too much maths. For that class, they're not very mathematical and they are not very promising pupils either and so I'm sure they could be educated in other ways ... Em, I would perhaps take on, maybe three pupils out of the class and put them into a higher class and I'd give the others arithmetic only.'

Corrie *et al*. (1978, p. 59) note that at Easton school where the allocation for second-year maths had been cut from seven periods to six the teachers 'considered this reduction increased the pressure they felt was placed on them to get through the work, *particularly in respect of pupils who could subsequently be following an "O" grade course*' (our emphasis). Then again this portrayal of the teachers' experiences of the temporal arrangement of the school is complicated further by the significance of methods of teaching as well as what is taught. Some of the teachers interviewed by Corrie *et al*. were engaged in teaching a second-year modular mathematics course. It is reported that

Five of the seven teachers who taught modular maths in the second year who were interviewed were amongst those teachers who preferred double periods to single periods and would have preferred to have all double periods. One teacher said that he chose which of his two maths classes to give modular maths to on the basis of the fact that one class was timetabled to have two double periods and the other class was timetabled to have one. (pp. 55–6)

Here it would seem there is a relationship between the teachers' curriculum planning and the 'limits' of action, the teachers here refer to the *province of the practicable*, which has been built up in the stock of their knowledge from experience in previous actual zones of operation. Thus

'I think it's when you are trying to get over a difficult point suddenly the bell rings in mid-sentence and you think if I just had another five minutes they would have grasped that and now I'll have to go back and start all over again the next time they come . . . Eh, I think with the module class, that's the second-year module class, I would prefer double periods all the time. Because by the time they get in, because of the system they don't take their books home with them, they have all to be dished out at the beginning, everything has to be arranged and eh, it takes up quite a long time.'

The final structural element in this complex equation which represents for the teachers the character of school time as a form of lived experience concerns the meaning-constitution of experience which inheres in the organization of the school week. That is to say, 'it did seem as though some teachers had reasons for preferring to teach their second-year pupils at particular times of the day rather than others and on certain days of the week rather than others' (Corrie *et al.*, 1978, p. 67). In particular these teachers attributed difficulties to those lessons situated on Monday mornings and Friday afternoons.

'Perhaps not to the kids but to us, yes. Monday is the day that I loathe. It takes me a long time to wind up enthusiasm. It's usually about after the morning interval before I begin to feel as though I'm with it. That might just be me.'

'Friday, well, you know, the next day's Saturday. The afternoon, the last couple of periods in the afternoon, tend to drag. I know this is ridiculous but this is just a subjective viewpoint. No matter how good the class is or how bad the class is you're still looking for the bell at a quarter to four. You become a clock watcher and, of course, the clocks here are not anything like accurate. I watch my watch.'

'Eh, Monday, when they're coming together for the first time, that's not a good day.'

'Not to such an extent. I think if they've had a Monday holiday then they're not very keen to work on the Tuesday, or if they're expecting a Monday holiday they're not very keen on the Friday. But normally I don't think it makes that much difference. Last two periods on a Friday are difficult.'

Furthermore, there was a general consensus that the pupils worked better in the mornings than in the afternoons.

'The best time for getting them started and working is definitely early forenoon. As you approach lunchtime their minds seem to be centred on their tummies and the afternoon, "Och, well, there's only four periods to go. It's near the end of the day."'

'I think, the last two periods, for example, they're tired, they want to get home. You can't get nearly as good work out of them as you can in the morning.'

'The class is a different class first period in the morning compared with the last period in a day. It's more noticeable with young children . . . It's just what you would expect of children who'd been sitting for far too long and are tired of academic education, especially when they're not very able. It's a slight rebellion, I think, probably, deep down, you know. They're tired really, just tired. I never teach them anything new unless it's entertaining. That's not too easy in maths.'

As a result of the meanings attributed, in reflection, by the teachers to their experiences in working with the pupils at particular times of the day and the week further 'limits' are imported into the practicabilities of curriculum and lesson planning. 'Allowances' are made for the time of the day or the week and particular activities are deemed more or less appropriate according to the time of the day or the week.

'I think to ask them to write for two whole periods, last thing on a Friday, is a bit much.'

'I begin to become aware of time in the second period, as it gets nearer to quarter to four, inevitable last period on a Friday, in that sometimes, if they've been working, we stop at say half three and I allow them to sit and talk until quarter to four.'

'In the morning if you get them the first two or three periods they're very docile. I think they're half asleep, some of them, and you can usually get down to it fairly quickly and quietly. In the afternoons they're jumpier. Eh, it's more difficult to read anything, it's more difficult to do anything which is silent. They're prepared to do drama, to act out and to have quizzes and things, anything which is lively but it's, it's impossible to work. I mean, I do, I work it along these lines. They do all the hard work in the morning and they do lighter things in the afternoon. But it's unfortunate if you have the same class all the time in the afternoon.'

One of the implications of this structure of meanings is that time emerges as a factor of some importance in the definition of situations; the teachers would appear to interpret the behaviour of their pupils and react to that behaviour differently, according to *when* the behaviour is manifested. The rule frames of lessons differ according to the time of the day and time of the week, as do the teacher's expectations of what are reasonable, that is practicable, activities.

The subjective structure of school time is built up for the teacher upon a number of non-simultaneous dimensions. The order and practical limitations of events are imposed in the social calendar of temporal arrangements – the school day, the school week and the school year. This dimension of lifeworldly time intersects with the constraints of 'biological time' that is pupils' speeds of working, of learning, spans of concentration, and with the organization of curriculum knowledge; the content and coverage of the syllabus and teaching methods. As we have seen these various constraints upon practical action, upon the possibility of actualizing plans and projects, are more or less important in different contexts. With 'good classes' the problems of curriculum knowledge ('getting through the syllabus') predominate: time usually passes too quickly. With 'poorer classes' the problems of time ('getting through the lesson') predominate: time usually passes too slowly. Woods recognizes this is a notable feature of school life:

There is a great deal of time-passing and time-filling not as

an adjunct to a larger purpose, but as an overall end in itself.
... The term, day, period is there, inevitably, and it is more
necessary that it be 'got through' than it is the syllabus,
especially with regard to non-examination classes.

(1978, p. 319)

Clearly, we have gone only a little way here in illuminating
the nature of school time. It is a feature of institutional and
classroom experience which requires the attention of empirical
study. So far, empirically, conceptually and theoretically time
has been virtually ignored by sociologists of education as a
phenomenal aspect of school. And yet it is a fundamental
organizing principle of the everyday life world of schooling; it
penetrates deeply into the organizational and curricular experience of the pupil and of the teacher and is a crucial factor in the
shaping and ordering of the curriculum in action at every level.
Also, as we have seen, time may constitute an important issue
of conflict between teachers and pupils. And it has been
suggested that the experience of time as a regulator of activities
in school may provide a basic socialization into subordination
to time regulation in other institutional contexts.

Note

1 The extracts quoted in this section are taken from Corrie *et al.*
(1978) by kind permission of the authors.

3

Kensington School: unique
physical facilities

L. M. Smith and P. Keith

The next paper is an extract from a long chapter in Lou Smith and Pat
Keith's (1971) major ethnography of an open-plan elementary school,
Anatomy of Educational Innovation (Chapter 6, New York: John Wiley
& Sons, Inc.). To follow Smith and Keith's discussion of the
relationship between architecture and social interaction, and of the
contrast between the architects' dreams and the educational practices,
a few brief points are necessarily clarified below.

The School Smith and Keith studied is in the American mid-west,
and they protect it with the pseudonym Kensington. It is an
elementary school, taking pupils from six to twelve years old. Instead
of putting them into single-age classes (grades 1 through to 6) the
children were divided into three broad groups, each to be team taught
in one area of the building. The three groups were called Basic Skills
Divisions (BSD), Transition and Independent Study Division (ISD).
These abbreviations appear in the text. The aim of the school was to
get *all* the pupils working independently in a self-directed way. So
ISD should have been the most important teaching team once the
school was open.

Throughout this paper Smith and Keith contrast the idealized
proposals for the various areas within the school building made by the

58

Architectural Design Institute of America (ADI) with the actual use made of those spaces by teachers, aides and children. They progress through the architectural proposals for various facilities presented in an ADI glossy brochure called the *Sketch*, contrasting rhetoric and sombre reality.

Kensington had a principal (Eugene), six teachers in BSD, three in Transition, and eight in the ISD. One man was in charge of curriculum materials, and there were five teachers' aides. These people are only referred to by their first names in the paper.

* * *

Our experience with the nature and conceptualization of material props, physical facilities, and school architecture has been quite limited. However, as we heard people talk about the possibilities inherent in building designs like Kensington's, and as we read glowing accounts of anticipated outcomes in similar new structures, a bit of skepticism began to mount. . . .

The physical structure of the school, as any other 'item', to use Merton's concept, is an element of the total system. As any element of a system it has its antecedents and consequences. Earlier we clarified the 'mandate', the people's wish and the superintendent's action in designing and erecting the building. This physical structure, as with the social structure, has its visible or facade components, which are presented to the varying publics, and its 'real' or working components, with which the members of the system, staff and pupils, must deal. . . . Where possible we treat both the physical facilities and their expected behavioral concomitants as specified in the Architectural Design Institute (ADI) document [the *Sketch*], an account purporting to present 'the educational life' within the innovatively designed structure. . . . On page 4 of the ADI document 'a Spirit of the old Northwest Territory' and 'another expedition into unchartered educational territory, new and dramatic approaches' are noted. Ten aspects of the new building are described:

Nothing here is absolutely new and untried, but the startling array of new structural approaches to old educational problems is enough to make even the casual observer ask for reasons – and the answers on why the school is significant. . . .

The classical shape

The first of the ten items concerns the classical Greek design. The pamphlet characterizes this shape as modern on the one hand, and then compares it to

> A Parthenon whose qualities contribute to an effect of organically articulated form rather than mere massiveness, of subtle refinement rather than gross power whose shape is, in fact a prototype of evolutionary progress in educational growth.

They continue to accent the classical yet modern idea with the following comment:

> It is a facility offering facility and speed, mobility and flexibility to a non-graded, organic, fluid approach to inquiry.

Once again, without question, it seems to me that the paragraph captures the major thrust of the school. The accent on what came to be called 'process' as opposed to 'content' has been a major part of the belief system or formal doctrine throughout the year. It also, as our notes will attest, has been a major point of conflict and discussion throughout the year. This probably, as much as anything, represents the major problem of translating ideals into specific, concrete programs of action. The only 'real process' that seems to have come to fruition is in the area of reading in the Basic Skills Division. At that point, reading process is so equivalent to content of curriculum that it is very difficult to separate the two and it is perhaps not an appropriate example. More specifically, the processes involved in inquiry in science are, perhaps, the classic case for the school. For some children, and a small number in ISD, there has been a considerable amount of emphasis and actual work in a variety of what might be labelled 'interest catchers' or what might be more appropriately called beginning experimentalism in physical and biological science.

In the spring our notes will attest to the ISD teachers' disillusionment with Jack, who provided again what might be called an excellent illustration of this program in science for, in their estimate, 15 per cent of the ISD kids. They were never able to make workable the program for the large majority of the children. In social studies, the process notions are perhaps best illustrated in Kay's unit on the stock market and Liz's unit on communism. The most telling critique probably lies in the issues discussed in the last few days of the notes concerning the inability to make use of the local tax campaign and the significance it possesses in the lives of the pupils, as they deal with their families and the community.

It seems noteworthy to comment that such glowing words as 'facility and speed, mobility and flexibility', while rallying cries for emotional appeals, the actuality is more akin to lack of facility and speed, immobility and inflexibility. Confusion and disarray characterize many events as they occurred.

Teacher work center

The next section is entitled 'The teacher work center'. In effect, this name has not been used; more typically it is called the Curriculum Center. As the *Sketch* comments,

> The area was designed to give the staff room to work individually in small groups in preparation for classes ... from this 'gut' section will come a continual flow of learning materials, varied and unique and limited only by the demands of students' needs and by the capacity of machines and technical specialists employed by the program.

In actuality, the work center is much more a gathering place for people to have lunch, drink coffee, and talk informally. The area also has been widely used in the community for a multitude of meetings. The staff, committee, and team meetings, almost always utilize this area. Occasionally, one will see teachers grading papers or preparing materials. The images that come to mind are Alec with his stack of arithmetic papers and Jean or other people from Basic Skills team 4 who often will be checking materials as they sit chatting and drinking coffee. Very little intensive class preparation is done here.

The area contains several other features that deserve comment. First, there are the trapezoidal tables, which have perplexed the staff all year in terms of readily shaping them into a design that will be useful to sit around. On a number of occasions they have served very well to illustrate Eugene's desire to have everything 'just right'. Second, the area contains the school's professional library, which consists mostly of Tom's books. Very seldom have they been used in any functional way. Only on a rare occasion have I seen anyone with one of the books checking a position or trying to amplify a point of view. Third, the problem of built-in facilities and storage space is also well exemplified. There is no built-in blackboard because this would cut down on the 'flexibility' of the area. There are no cupboards except brief space in some of the movable lowboy cabinets. The filing cabinets jut out at an awkward angle and yet are very necessary. Fourth, this area, and the Nerve Center below, has been the one part of the building that has been kept inviolate from the students' access. I do not believe that I have ever seen a pupil up here.

Fifth, this has been the area for congregating in the informal activity of the school. Seldom in the course of the day can one not find a conversation there. John and Tom and more recently Alec are there frequently. They are the ones with the flexible schedules and the ones who can come and go at greater will. Eugene also is a frequent habitué of the place. To tie this point down, one can note that Mary and Carla are practically never there. I do not think that I have seen them there informally during the course of any day. The BSD team 4 are there quite frequently, usually in singles or doubles. They, as we have indicated, perhaps more than any other group, have themselves well enough organized so that somebody has free time someplace almost all of the time. That's a bit too strong. The kindergarten teacher very infrequently is there. Among the Transition teachers there is less use than with Basic Skills team

62

4. However, Claire and Meg particularly are frequently there. Dan is about mostly at lunch time. In ISD the most infrequent use comes from David, although there was almost no occasion for him to be there in the last couple months. During this interval he has literally withdrawn almost totally from the school staff. Linda, Liz and Kay, particularly the latter, frequently come up for breaks during the course of the day. Invariably they just 'leave' their children. Irma does not use the area to a very great degree, and Jack also does not frequent the place. His absence from school in the last month or six weeks makes that interpretation a little harder to make. The real habitué is John. He is there almost as much as I am.

Another interesting point apropos of this concerns the teaching aides who are almost never up here unless they are working. Until now I had not really thought about that, but Arthur, Joan, Helen, Marjorie, and Inez drink their coffee down below or in the conference part of the office. . . .

The perception core

The *Sketch's* statement is a vivid picture of unreality. Although fragments of it are part of the vision that once existed, almost none of it is a part of the reality of it now. Specifically, the *Sketch* says this:

Out of this grew the perception core concept which represents an advancement over the instructional materials centers and the resource and research centers just as they were an advancement over the older library concept. Where conventional learning patterns are conceived to begin in the homeroom or the classroom and to proceed to the library and back, the pattern here begins in the perception core area, expands and overflows into what were once called the classrooms but which we must call laboratory suites in order to describe the process adequately. Students entering the building with one-week schedules (as opposed to the contemporary 36-week schedules), go to the outer part of the sanctuary and begin the day individually in special

63

carrels or in small groups as planned. Their special areas of concentration or study may reach through a broad spectrum from a study of live biological specimens in or about the stream (that flows through a portion of the building along the edge of the core) to a study of foreign languages in one of several centers set up throughout the area. The five study centers, each designed to accommodate a specific subject area, consist of bookshelves and study spaces arranged in changeable patterns. The remainder of the perception core is fitted with isolated study booths and shelves for general reading matter and instructional materials, including phonograph records and tape players with headphones; small slide projectors for viewing at a desk by one student; filmstrip projectors; microfilm, microcard and microprint readers; teaching machines; portable television receivers with headphones; small motion picture projectors for small groups; and portable radio receivers with headphones.

Such was the dream of someone. The realities of the perception core are these: first, the area is called the perception core. This term is used by staff and students alike. Second, the central locus of the area is the desk or checkout counter which is very similar to a library checkout counter in any public school or, more specifically, in any good children's library. Helen and her student assistants hang out here. Third, there have never been fish or biological specimens in the aquarium. This was not done in spite of the fact that a local store volunteered to stock the pond. I do not know why this was not accepted. For a time there was water in the pond, and for a time there were problems with children using it as a wishing well and throwing money into it. At this point I do not know why Jack never took the initiative to establish it as a major aquarium and wild life center. Fourth, the east end of the area over near the children's theatre was soon developed into an independent reading area for children from Basic Skills, especially team 4. It also has had wide usage by the Transition groups. In effect, it has become another instructional area for these very crowded division areas. By pulling some ten to thirty children out of the major instructional area and into this part of the perception core, the load is reduced in the other areas, and here the teachers move about reading with individual children as they, in turn, read from a variety of books at their ability and interest levels. I have very vivid images of Meg, especially, and Claire to some extent there; Jean, Sue, Wanda, Elaine, and Sarah (Elaine's replacement) heavily utilized this area. Although there have been differences between Wanda and Jean, for instance, in the relative accent on having common materials with a text basis, with Wanda arguing for more of this, and with Jean arguing for less, the reading program has been intensive and has involved all of the children in almost a maximal way. Except for the very real difficulty about the unavailability of primer materials, this program has moved hard and has moved in the best individualized or differentiated fashion.

A further dramatic image I have of the perception core concerns the extensive use of encyclopedias. Never in my experience in and out of elementary schools have I seen so many children utilizing encyclopedias on so many different topics on so many different occasions as I have at Kensington. The perception core has had a constant flow of kids looking up Egyptian and Chinese writing, a host of biological things concerning frogs, snakes, and worms, and a variety of other information from literally every aspect of the curriculum.

Also, in the perception core there is an image of a few kids who are perpetually wandering around. I recall one day when Kay and I were watching one of the boys in her class as he moved from table to desk to leaning on the lowboy to punching a kid to bothering somebody else as he hopped from one portion to another portion of the area.

Furthermore, there were times when individual teachers tried to utilize the space. Alec, for instance, tried to teach maths there; Jack tried to hold science discussions; and Joe held his Friday morning counseling sessions over the western corner. This just did not work well. Joe's group was too noisy and uncontrolled, and we have some fine quotes from Helen who tried to shush them once and found she was talking directly to Joe. . . .

A final image of the perception core, and one that is older and weaker now, is of the area as a hallway. During the middle of the winter when it was cold outside, the traffic through here was very great and a continuing problem. As far as I know, no plans have been made regarding it for next year. Throughout the middle part of the day from 11.00 am to 1.00 pm there would be kids with trays of food going back and forth. Also it is the only hallway across the way to the theatre, to the art room, to the P.E. shelter, and to the office. Each of these places has maximal usage a good part of the day. More recently with the weather being pleasant, the outside walkway has been used to a very high degree, and this problem is almost non-existent. This controversy is rich with comments and quotations about whether or not the weather was inclement, and comments and problems regarding the dogs who ate the children's food, and the pneumonia that the parents thought the children were catching. . . .

The learning laboratory suites

The profile sketch reads this way. 'The designation of class-room spaces as laboratory suites avoids the association with homeroom and baseroom procedures which are absent in this program.' This is patently not so at Kensington. The school has moved continuously toward more and more spaces designated as homerooms and baseroom areas. The *Sketch* states:

> These 20 spaces, equipped with overhead projectors and other electronic and mechanical aids to be described in the section on the 'nerve center', comprise the outer ring of the area and are divided only by movable, visual dividers; and each class space thus loosely defined is made more mutable by the further possibility of subdivision through complete movability of all furniture and equipment in these spaces.

This sentence is generally quite true; there are overhead projectors in most of the areas. However, these projectors are only occasionally used. The teachers have moved much more toward the use of blackboards. As I think about this, the major difference in the blackboard and in the overhead lies in the necessity of pre-prepared transparencies. Here again, we are involved in the same problem that has been indicated in our earlier discussion. The staff has had neither the time, the energy, nor the resources to prepare an accumulating file of transparencies. Perhaps the most widely used ones exist in materials that Eugene uses to talk to groups of people who visit in the program. A gradually developing accumulating file of them implies that there are organized bodies of material that one wants to teach about and that will on later occasions also be taught. Such a file, like notes for lectures or like folders of pictures for particular events, becomes a portion of every teachers' armamentarium. Here the problem is quite acute in that no one will admit to having this kind of a curriculum, which is prebuilt or prepared prior to some particular moment of need. Most of the need or use of these has been a sort where one writes on them for the moment and then erases them later This kind of use is more easily adaptable to a blackboard. . . .

'Tote trays further enhance the freedom of peripheral activity.' These are physical facilities that have not existed in the building and about which there has been almost no discussion. Racks of them might well have provided storage space which was a continuous problem in the gym and which helped precipitate having pupil stations that belonged to individual children. A tote tray or two would have prevented the necessity for assigning kids to individual desks. As I think about this, I am struck by the larger generalization that very minute items in the materials arrangement that have been neglected have had far-reaching effects on the program and the later structures that have been developed. For instance, if each person had had two of these trays in which he could keep his books and other materials, one for total storage and one to carry with him as he went from activity to activity, then the whole complexion of the program would have been different. They could have been built as low storage units, perhaps, six or eight tote trays high and maybe six or eight tote trays wide, which would have permitted two per person in each of the areas and which could have been back-to-back in the various sections of ISD. With them the kids could have rotated among teachers among instructional areas, bringing just what they needed for whatever purposes they might have. Then they would not have been caught with the problems of needing a desk to store things and the constant quarrels over somebody using my desk or getting into my materials or taking my pencils, and the like. . . .

The description of the learning laboratory suites continues:

> The natural flow of the program carries the student from perception core to the laboratory suite where he encounters special teachers and assistants. Where his studies developed along lines of breath in the core, they now begin to close in on the specifics in reaching for depth.

This is so far from reality, it's impossible to make an intelligent comment on it. There is so little formal instruction for the majority of the kids, except for perhaps Irma's section of ISD, that one finds very little evidence of depth in any kind of study. The major exception to this is the large amount of writing on rather brief papers growing out of work with the encyclopedias especially. . . .

The children's theatre

Herein lies the actualized heart of the vista envisioned. Dan, Chris, Elaine, and occasionally Wanda, Carla, and others have made the theatre into a reality. The profile reads as follows:

> The perception core is separated from the children's theatre by the life-science stream and a glass wall. The theatre itself is unique. It was designed for the children. A large, open space is surrounded by three simple acting areas, each of which may be used for simultaneous production and two of which are joined by a bridge that crosses the life-science pool, extending into the theatre a short distance. With the

'open stage' concept, drama presentations are to be staged utilizing portable flats designed and built by the students. Creative thought is stimulated in this flexible space, student interest expanded by the acting tower, including an enclosed spiral stairway leading up to a balcony which looks out over the theatre.

In part, the physical description is inadequate. The pool only comes a short way into the theatre. There is no bridge that crosses over it. The phrase 'for simultaneous production' is ambiguous. If it means that the areas can be used for different productions at the same time, then, obviously, it does not hold true. The noise and the carrying of voices makes any kind of independent usage impossible. If by this is meant having two areas that can serve as separate scenes for the same play, then this meaning of simultaneous is very true.

The centre of the theatre is depressed two steps below the basic floor level of the building, and this area, all of which is carpeted, can be used as a seating area for pupils without bringing chairs from the classrooms. This, too, is a reality. Not only do the kids sit here without chairs, they lounge, they lie, they flounder about on the floor.

The theatre has been, perhaps, the most successful and the most creative part of the school. Just yesterday, for instance, Irma's group of the least able pupils presented a 'patriotic program' for Memorial Day. Although the theatre was not used in any novel or original way, it provided a focus for this kind of a meeting. The kids sit comfortably on the carpeted steps, lounge occasionally, and generally relax and partake of the various offerings. . . .

As I continued to listen to the broad generalizations stated by the writers of the *Sketch*, I am struck even more, as I have been on occasion in the past, with the need to ask for specific procedures and practices and examples that fit the overall generalization. Specifically again, the notion of utilization for 'large group instruction' sounds nice, seems to fit the jargon of the times, and yet, when you think concretely of what kinds of things are going to be taught to large groups and how are these groups to be managed and how is the content to be integrated, sequenced, and scheduled, then one is up against a whole series of knotty problems. Without the specific, concrete example to think through, then one cannot proceed in any optimal way. It seemed to me that this was characteristic of the thinking and planning all year.

The physical education shelter

The shelter is described in glowing terms:

> Combining vast savings over gymnasium construction (which is usually poorly utilized in elementary schools) with the enhancement of proper acoustical form for a community amphitheater and for summer evening band concerts, this shelter is an inexpensive improvement on an old solution. The multi-use concept applied here was deliberately conceived and planned to offset the 'multi-useless' room frequently built into the elementary school. Sides of the open shelter are protected by banks of shrubbery which deflect the winds which are then carried up and over by the shape of the roof.
>
> The infra-red heating units are ideal for the shelter, because rather than heating the air, which would be intolerably wasteful, these units heat to a comfortable degree the children and the objects which stand or pass beneath them.

It's difficult to know where to begin to describe the illusion and the reality. I, personally, have no data on the degree of utilization of gymnasiums in elementary schools. I would doubt that they are as 'poorly utilized' as the ADI *Sketch* describes them. A very simple study could well be set up to determine the adequacy of and the kinds of utilization of gymnasiums. This should be carried out in the context of varying climates. The 'California design' of much of this equipment seems inappropriate for a community like Milford, which has intolerably warm summers and damp and sloshy winters. Since I have been in the school, I have heard no remarks regarding the use of the amphitheater for summer band concerts or other kinds of activities. To my knowledge no use of the outdoor facility for any kind of total school gathering has occurred.

The use of labels such as 'multi-useless', although frequent in August and in the fall, has almost disappeared recently. On many occasions the staff has had strong reason to wish for inside play and multiple-purpose use of space. John, particularly has been tremendously handicapped in the P.E. program. During the winter the shelter was almost useless for his purposes. The notes are full of many, many conversations, with his total concern and defeatism over this.

It's important to note also that it was intended that the shelter would be protected by 'banks of shrubbery which deflect the winds which are then carried up and over by the shape of the roof'. This may be another of those very simple aspects that for reasons of finance or reasons of forgetting, or for reasons of change in intention, have not been implemented and that may have carried a tremendous burden. There seems to be little question that the shelter area suffered materially during the winter because the wind would blow in the rain and the snow. A bank of densely planted shrubs undoubtedly would have helped this condition. More recently, the shrubs would have shielded the shelter from some of the dust that has blown in from the unpaved and unsodded earth surrounding the area.

The *Sketch*, in describing the heating units, speaks of 'intolerably wasteful' in regard to any other kind of heating in this area. While that is a pretty phrase, it is also an inaccurate one. The heating units have been totally inadequate. They are mounted too high, and there are too few of them. What this meant during the winter was that the children played in hats and coats, almost as though they were out on an open playground. Only when one stood directly underneath the unit was it warm enough to be without a coat. And there, typically, it was under the units on the stage rather than in the open play

71

area with its higher ceiling.

In summary, the P.E. shelter has been one of the most widely acknowledged inadequate features of the school building. The wind, as we have commented, has been severe. In the winter it was rain and snow, and in the spring it was dust. The shelter has been a gathering place for dirt and leaves in recent months. My guess is that in the early fall it will become a very serious problem as the leaves fall and blow in. Day after day we have cited in the notes the fact that the area was dusty and dirty and only occasionally were there resources to clean it. . . .

Visual, acoustical, and thermal treatments

The *Sketch* statement continues:

> Though there is little need to defend the use of carpeting and air conditioning on economic grounds, it is significant here that the savings effected by the physical education shelter, the satellite kitchen, the lack of corridors and walls and by the form of the building have more than paid for the initial installation of these items.

Economically, we are in no position to make a commentary on these facilities. Unquestionably, space that does not go to corridors might well go for something else. . . .

'Satellite kitchens' is a fancy name for the fact that there is a very small kitchen and dishwashing area in the school. This demands that hot food be brought in daily from other larger and more well-equipped kitchen areas in the district. The notes are replete with statements about the difficulty in orbiting this particular satellite. Ultimately, the kitchen was located in area 105 that the building inspectors had deemed would be a hall and an emergency exit. . . .

The other half of the situation, that part involving where the pupils would eat, never did reach the same degree of solution. A multi-purpose room with tables that fold out from the walls for the lunch hour and where many children can eat at the same time did not exist at Kensington and, in effect, each classroom or laboratory learning suite became a cafeteria. From approximately 11.30 until 1.00 or 1.30 there are children in one area or another who are eating. The original idea of having children drift off individually to have lunch did not work out. In effect, each division then was assigned roughly one half-hour intervals in which most of their eating would be concentrated. This was to prevent jam-ups at 11.30. Perhaps the most basic problem that this created was that it tied the teachers down quite dramatically to the supervision of children. . . .

A further complication was the fact that food was all over the building. Some of this naturally got spilled, dropped, and slopped over. This provoked all kinds of problems, one illustration being an anecdote, told by someone, which we have recorded in the notes, about kids carrying hamburgers in their pockets to keep them warm when they made the outside trip. Beyond this, there is one huge streak in the rug in the hallway of the administrative suite. A pupil had dripped a sloppy joe along the way and someone tried to clean it up by using the wrong technique. This streak has been there for several months, and apparently it will take a major cleaning in the summer to get it out. Litter and garbage cans have accumulated and have been about in many areas. I am reminded here of sitting in Transition just yesterday and noticing under one of the highboy cabinets dust and dirt, scraps of paper, and crayons that seem to have been lying there for weeks, if not months. The major point I would make is that, with the food dispersed all over, the cleaning and maintenance problem is much more acute than it would be if eating were localized.

Perhaps at this point it is appropriate to talk further about the carpeting. Again, I do not know whether ultimately it will be cheaper and more economical than tile. Aesthetically, the carpeting is beautiful and is comfortable to walk on and to view. From the children's point of view, almost uniformly, it seems to me, they have responded very well to the carpeting. They like to run about in their stocking feet or go barefoot on the carpeting, and particularly now, when it is permitted only in the theater, they enjoy playing their Huck Finn type roles. They enjoy lying and lounging on the carpeting, particularly again in the theatre where it is more permitted. Also, the scuffling, wrestling, horseplay, and roughhousing of the boys benefits maximally from the carpeting in that one can roll, bounce, and tug without skinning elbows or bruising oneself.

On the negative side, the most important consequence of the carpeting, it seems to me, has been in the parental reaction. Uniformly at a meeting where complaints are being voiced about the district or about the school, someone is bound to mention the issue of the carpeting. It has become a rallying cry for those who are against 'the monuments' in the district. . . .

The nerve center

> The nerve system, also not so obvious to the casual observer, lies below the teacher work area and the production center at the very heart of the building. In it is housed the instantaneous storage and retrieval system geared to receiving audio or visual information from a number of sources, storing of such information and immediately dispersing it by way of television, recordings or tape, upon command by the dial system, to any part of the building.

As this is stated, it evokes dreamlike images. As one observes, the nerve center reality is very different. Instead of instantaneous storage and retrieval systems, basically we have Arthur, Marjorie, and Tom. Arthur is very busy as a general assistant and aide for handling materials, supplies and equipment. Marjorie is working hard daily on cutting stencils and running the ditto machine. Tom sits at his desk smoking his pipe, paging through catalogs, or writing lengthy statements to commercial companies who might give the school materials of one kind or another.

Metaphorically, the nerve center houses its greatest stimulant in the coffeepot. Here, each day are brewed two urns of very good coffee. Before school the place hums. . . . During the course of the day, the staff is in and out particularly for coffee but also for occasional words of comment to the others. Finally, the nerve center is the gathering place of the semiprofessional staff; Arthur and Marjorie are frequently visited by Helen, Joan, and Inez. It is a very busy place and it is very social.

The major problem actually lies in the fact that the school does not have the financial resources to provide the necessary equipment. . . . There have been no major storage banks of tapes that can be played on call in an individual classroom setting. . . . The individual tape recorders are scattered throughout the building. There has been very little production of materials that have broad universal and cumulative possibilities. . . .

The administrative suite

The administrative complex is located near the main entrance. It is in immediate viewing range of the Physical Education shelter, satellite kitchen, and ten of the twenty room spaces. The suite is an open space, divided with storage elements to include general and specific areas for principal and secretarial offices, reception area, clinic and guidance or counseling facilities, work space and conference space for parent or other lay conferences.

Little, it seems, needs to be said about the administrative suite. It does not actually open on to ten of the twenty room spaces as the brochure claims, nor is it divided with storage elements to include general and specific areas. The most fundamental fact of the administrative suite lies in the lack of privacy permitted anyone. As it stands now, the principal's section is partially walled off with cabinets but is basically open, and conversations can be heard while one walks from the front door into the children's theatre or as one stops and picks up his mail in the boxes located in the administrative suite. Similarly, the secretary's desk sits right in the middle of the suite, and the phone rings and conversations can be heard all over the suite. One of the administrative assistants sits directly across from the principal and handles a variety of the routine duties of the school. The nurse and the speech teacher who use the small conference table cabinet walled area also have no privacy. The space has not been adequate for couseling. Because of this, Joe has had his small counseling groups in the perception core instead of in the office area; even in that spot he has had considerable difficulty.

The atmosphere

This structure was designed to stimulate creative thinking, to facilitate purposeful motion and to assist thereby the development and flow of critical thinking in the creation of an educational experience such as our best knowledge has long told us was necessary – yet which our children of the past have too seldom had. The structure provides an open-life place – warm, inviting, and profoundly significant.

The rhetoric of the first sentence speaks for itself. It produces no concrete images. . . .

The building was not ready in September, as originally planned and hoped. The temporary quarters were abandoned in early December . . . The physical structure of Kensington was imaginative and beautiful in the judgment of everyone. In anticipation before the building was built, the Architectural Design Institute *Sketch* described Kensington in great detail. In equally great detail we have taken issue with this anticipatory account. We have tried to discriminate the 'reality' from the 'dream' or, as we called it more formally, 'the facade', the view of Kensington that has been presented in many forms to many publics. . . .

Physical facilities in social theory
INTRODUCTION

Perhaps, if we had been trained as architects, some of our observations and interpretations on the innovative physical

76

facilities would have been less naïve and more fundamental. . . . Fundamentally, we believed that the physical facilities were important to a teacher, and that dimensional concepts of material props and physical facilities, are a needed aspect of educational theory.

OPENNESS, PRIVACY, FREEDOM: MAJOR DIMENSIONS

Openness

As was noted earlier, one of the main features of the Kensington building is physical openness; this is clearly illustrated by the learning suites, the perception core, and the administrative offices. In our view the minimization of physical barriers necessitates considering a number of social and behavioural variables that tend to be more stable in traditionally designed buildings. . . . Behavioural implications of open-space plans may be cited. Openness creates possibilities for variety and sets up probabilities for a number of interactive sequences that would never occur in a setting with permanent physical barriers. The number and kind of teacher–teacher, student–teacher, and student–student interactions are increased greatly in an open setting. The relationship between openness and opportunities for increased interaction occurs whether the form of instructional organization is a self-contained classroom in an open setting . . . or a number of teams operating in the same area. In one respect the openness of the school was parallel to much of the intrateam structure and the interteam relationships. As indicated earlier, no decision-making structure was specified within teams, and there was no formally designated hierarchy. The belief system indicated by both physical design and formal doctrine was the one of pupil freedom, minimal teacher control, teacher–teacher–principal egalitarianism, and minimal rules for the organization. Physical openness was to facilitate these aspects of the school's social structure.

Privacy: a conflicting value

In an important sense, privacy is a value, like openness. As such, its behavioural implementation on occasion may conflict with other values – for instance, openness. The issue of privacy as it related to building design was experienced by the faculty and staff in a number of ways.

The low degree of privacy was no more keenly experienced than in the administrative suite that was 'open'. Initially, students frequented the administrative area. Its being near the main entrance enhanced its chances of becoming a part of the main traffic way. Private conferences were difficult to achieve. Although the movement of students was distracting to other students and teachers, it was also highly visible to visitors. Administratively, it was difficult to specify what visitors would observe. The high visibility in the perception core and ISD made 'control' of what visitors would encounter difficult. In one sense, four or five classrooms open to observation simultaneously restricted both the privacy of the individual classroom and of the administration, which might wish to select only certain classes for visitors to observe. Eventually the team operating in the smallest, enclosed area was cited to guests as functioning most like the specifications of the model.

Lack of privacy also characterized the counseling activities. No rooms for private consultation were available, and groups of children were counseled in view of other children.

Finally, adults who have not lived for long periods of time in the company of large numbers of children seldom appreciate the immense gratification that accrues from meeting such simple needs as moments of privacy, conversation – passing the time of day – with another adult, or the leisure of a cigarette. This dimension of a building we referred to as 'responsiveness to adult needs'. Kensington was to have a small teacher's lounge in the nerve center. Funds were not available to complete this. The Curriculum Center provided a functionally equivalent alternative.

I would guess also that the curriculum lab on the mezzanine

78

will become a favorite hangout of the teachers because it is somewhat removed and is the only large and convenient lounge-type space. Ultimately, I would guess that the coffeepot will end up there instead of downstairs in the nerve center where it is supposed to be now. Eugene and Tom tried smoking there as I was leaving, and if that works out successfully, then most certainly it will become such a spot (written 7 December).

The curriculum center did become a place where members of the faculty could eat lunch, work, or plan together. It assured almost complete privacy from student activities.

Freedom

In general, openness and privacy are intermediary values. They are important as antecedents to personal freedom. In schools, the chain of reasoning should lead to learning. Among various kinds of learning, Kensington's emphasis was on intellectual skills and affective goals, such as self-awareness and positive self-evaluation. Our data are intermediary to these final outcomes. We have been struck by the too easy generalization that physical openness, that is, an absence of walls, leads immediately, directly, or simply to freedom in teaching and learning. A case can be made, we believe, that physical privacy provides some major contributions to freedom. These contributions tended to be minimized in the open space design of Kensington. . . .

At this point we hypothesize that a setting characterized by physical openness will be accompanied by a greater amount of role-making, negotiating, and bargaining among role occupants than is found in environments that are less open. If shared open spaces have as a concomitant the increased contractual arrangements in the form of teacher–teacher and teacher–student agreements, they, in turn, require additional time for formulation and enforcement. The coordination of activities both within team spaces and in public spaces is required. This, in turn, may alter the timing, the mode of

79

presentation, and the content of instructional material. This would seem to be particularly characteristic of a program that emphasizes the use of new materials and equipment that require sharing by various groups of students and teachers.

In the case of Kensington, the frequent negotiations that involved time and energy expenditures and the lack of uniformity in the acceptance of supposedly agreed-on teacher and pupil behaviour culminated in the request for temporary walls and the issuance of rules. As we have indicated, the rules were issued by the principal to regulate the patterns of movement and other behaviour specific to the building and were to be enforced by the teachers. For some, the rules violated tenets of the formal doctrine about pupil freedom and teacher–principal equality in the decision-making process. Consequently, the rules received varied degrees of acceptance and adherence. Although the rules attended primarily to the usage of public space, many of the problems, such as sharing, privacy, noise, and coordination of activities, continued.

4

Knowledge at Lubavitcher School

B. M. Bullivant

Teachers in their own classrooms are constrained by the syllabus or curriculum laid down for them. The more academic the institution's aims, and the older the pupils, the more constrained is the teacher's control over knowledge. In Bullivant's study of an Australian School for Orthodox Jewish boys the staff were doubly constrained: by the Australian State exam syllabuses and by the Jewish Orthodoxy. The general issue of classroom teachers being constrained by external knowledge codes is demonstrated particularly well by this unusual case. The material which follows is drawn from two chapters (6 and 8) of Bullivant's book (1978, *The Way of Tradition*. Victoria: Australian Council for Educational Research). Bullivant's argument here is that the school has both a secular and a religious function, and that a teacher's classroom life is constrained by two knowledge codes.

* * *

The formal organization of knowledge

Taking a commonsense view of education, one thinks of the formal curriculum in a school as the major source of knowledge gained by pupils. They act as relatively passive recipients of ready-made information communicated by the teachers.

The selection of culturally valued knowledge is part of the curriculum, which also includes other learning experiences available to pupils. Musgrave has suggested (1973, p. 7) that the stock of knowledge offered by most schools can be divided into two parts. 'There is, first, academic knowledge which is largely in written form and relates to learned disciplines.' The second part is 'behavioural knowledge, which includes knowledge of the behavioural norms of the society'. Lubavitcher School represents two 'societies', and it is doubtful whether a simple dichotomy of the type Musgrave proposes adequately accounts for the stock of knowledge it communicates to the boys. A similar reservation must be held about comparable religious or denominational schools, and suggests that at least one additional category is required.

Academic knowledge seems logically related to the 'secular' function of such schools, that is, the preparation of their clientele for future occupations in society. Musgrave notes (loc. cit.) that 'it is preserved and largely added to by educational institutions at the tertiary level, or research institutions of a similar status'. This is a characteristic which was noted about the development of the academic tradition in Australia, and is an additional justification for equating academic knowledge with the largely secular domain of the school.

There is, however, a body of knowledge that cannot be thought of as academic. This is the corpus of religious literature. Agreed, it is in written form, and is preserved. But in the case of Lubavitcher School, at least, the notion that it could be added to, let alone modified, by a tertiary institution would be heretical. It is transcendentally derived or divinely revealed knowledge, and is immutable, in contrast to the empirical derivation of the knowledge in the academic tradition. Although it plays an important part in determining the behavioural knowledge adopted by the school, the body of religious knowledge can be considered separately, from the point of view of its derivation, as *super-empirical knowledge*. It is logically related to the Great Tradition and the 'sacred' function of the school, that is, the production of Orthodox Jews.

Accordingly, three categories of knowledge are adopted for analytical purposes: academic knowledge, super-empirical knowledge, and behavioural knowledge....

ACADEMIC KNOWLEDGE

The selection of knowledge offered by the secondary school through the formal curriculum is narrow and non-vocational. Enrichment, non-academic subjects such as Music, Speech, and Drama, are not offered. Even Art is only offered in the first and second forms, but is dropped thereafter.

Subjects in the lower and middle school

Similar subjects are offered to first and second forms: Hebrew (3), English (6), Mathematics (6), Science (3), Art (2), History (3), French (2), Geography (3). The figures in brackets refer to the number of 40-minute periods allocated to each subject. English and Mathematics get twice as much time as any other academic subject. Art and French get least time, and are not considered by the boys or staff as 'real' subjects, but rather token bits of more liberal studies. The latter owes its existence as much to the personal enthusiasm of the teacher in charge as to the official policy of the school....

The organization of knowledge in the two senior forms of the school shows an even greater academic bias than in lower forms. Every endeavour is made to provide opportunities for boys to take either science or humanities groupings of subjects. Fifth form offers Hebrew, English, Mathematics 1, Mathematics 2, Physics, Chemistry, Economics, Social Studies, Geography, Modern History, Commercial Principles, Accounting. These are significantly reduced in sixth form, with a science bias quite apparent, to English Expression, Applied Mathematics, General Mathematics, Pure Mathematics, Physics, Chemistry, Australian History, Economics, Social Studies. All subjects in fifth form are allocated five periods, with six periods in sixth form.

The significant omission at the latter level is Hebrew. The standard attained by the boys is so high, due to constant contact with the subject in both secular and religious studies, that they are able to take the matriculation examination if desired on the basis of their work up to and including the fifth form.

THE ROLE OF EXAMINATIONS IN THE CURRICULUM

Internal examinations and tests

Examinations at all levels are the rule rather than the exception in the school. Time is allocated at the end of each term for the first four forms to sit internally set and marked examinations or tests. Some teachers augment these results by cumulative tests during the term. . . .

EXTERNAL EXAMINATIONS

At the fifth form level all academic work is oriented towards the School Leaving Certificate examination at the end of the year in late October and early November. This is taken externally, and constitutes a terminal qualification for those leaving school. More commonly, however, it is a necessary step towards proceeding to the sixth form year and Higher School Certificate (HSC), formerly the Matriculation Examination. To enter for this a pass in at least four subjects of the School Leaving examination is required. However, most candidates prepare for five or six subjects, as English must be passed as one of the four subjects needed to enter for the Higher School Certificate examination. It must also be passed at HSC level, along with three other subjects, for the candidate to qualify for consideration for a place at university.

The School Leaving examination thus assumes a much greater importance than the kinds of examinations in fourth form. It is firstly a desirable terminal qualification for employment when a student leaves school. A candidate must obtain four subjects arranged in specified groupings before proceeding to the Higher School Certificate year, and both certificates are needed as one of the pre-requisites for university selection. It presents a formidable hurdle for boys to take.

In the school, this pressure is compounded by the difficulty some boys have with English, when Yiddish or another language is spoken at home. The school also presents its candidates to the final examination externally at unfamiliar examination centres. . . .

The main School Leaving examination papers are set by panels of examiners appointed for every subject by the Victorian Universities and Schools Examinations Board, in collaboration with the various subject Standing Committees of the Board. The examination is taken at special centres throughout the State. These are in public halls, large schools with facilities which have been approved by the Board to act as centres, and, in the case of Melbourne, at the large Exhibition Buildings in the city itself.

Similar administrative conditions operate for the HSC examination, though for this both the preparation and supervision are much more stringent. The chairman of each examiners panel must be from a tertiary education organization, and not from a school which does not present for the external examination, as may be the case for the School Leaving. The HSC examination is used for university selection, and high merit grades may qualify for the award of a Commonwealth Tertiary Scholarship, which assists with university fees and cost of books, and provides towards maintenance of the recipient. The HSC is also a terminal qualification for the school leaver.

With such rewards at stake, competition for success in the HSC examination is intense. Pupils usually take at least four subjects – the minimum required for a pass at one sitting –

while many attempt five. For university selection purposes, results in the best three are counted, excluding English expression for which grades are not awarded, the subject being marked on a pass/fail basis. . . .

In contrast to the gradually increasing severity and external character of the assessment from fourth to sixth forms, that in the middle and lower school is far less rigorous. Whereas preparation for the examinations imparts direction and motivation to both teaching and learning, work at the lower levels has only the incentive of being preparation for transition upwards to the next level. There are no similar rewards to compete for as in the three senior forms. However, the dominance of the higher levels over the direction of the curriculum is very apparent, and confirms its pronounced academic orientation and adherence to the academic tradition.

SUPER-EMPIRICAL KNOWLEDGE[1]

The basis of the curriculum content

Three closely related and interdependent bodies of knowledge constitute the basis of the formal curriculum of the Great Tradition. They are the Bible (*TeNaCh*), the Talmud and *Schulchan Aruch*. *TeNaCh* – a contraction of three words – comprises the *Torah* ('Instruction', 'Law') *Nevi'im* ('Prophets'), and *Ketuvim* ('Writings' or 'Hagiographa'). The first is made up of the first five books of the Bible (*Chumash* or Pentateuch), the second comprises the Early Prophets (*Nevi'im Rishonim*) and Later Prophets (*Nevi'im Aharonim*), the third is a collection of miscellaneous books of historical, devotional, poetic, dramatic and narrative literature. This comprises Psalms, Proverbs, and the Book of Job, together with the Five Scrolls (*Megilloth*), the most important of which is the Scroll of Esther read at *Purim*.

Torah is the foundation of religious and ethical instruction. For centuries it has furnished the principal curriculum of Jewish education in which the child begins his schooling, and returns to again and again. To the Orthodox Jew it is the supreme and unquestioned authority in religious life. Together with *Nevi'im* and *Ketuvim* it furnishes the spiritual roots of the Talmud. This embraces both the Mishnah and *Gemara*, the former being stressed in the curriculum at the school. The Mishnah can be thought of as a textbook rather than a code, and gives the essence of the Oral Law and ancient tradition as it was known to the sages during the period culminating in the compilation of the final authorized version *c.* 220 C.E. The Talmud is, in effect, a body of jurisprudence fulfilling the injunction of the Men of the Great Assembly to 'make a fence around the *Torah*' (*Avot* 1.1).[2] Not surprisingly every page of the Talmud is filled with citations from *Chumash*.

The *Schulchan Aruch* or Joseph Caro first published in 1565 is a convenient codification of Jewish law and practice derived from the Talmud. It is divided into four parts. *Orach Chayyim* deals with the ritual obligations of daily life from waking to sundown. *Yoreh Deah* deals mainly with dietary and ritual laws including mourning, vows, respect to parents, charity, etc. *Even ha-Ezer* deals with personal status, marriage, divorce, etc., and *Choshen Mishpat* embraces the entire body of Jewish civil law as far as it is applicable under Diaspora conditions. Subsequent writers further condensed this codification, and the *Kitzur Schulchan Aruch* is also a basis for the curriculum, especially for the boys in junior forms.

Organization of religious instruction

Boys start the Talmud (Mishnah) in Grade 5 by tradition at *Baba Metziah* (Aramaic – 'The Middle Gate'), dealing with small portions of the easier tractates concerning responsibility for property, and accepting liability for damage. At this level, possibly no more than one or two pages are considered during the entire year. Study of the Mishnah continues in greater depth, and deals with more content, as a boy proceeds up the school. He tackles sections from different tractates in higher forms, such as those dealing with marriage, divorce, prohibitions on *Shabbos*. In senior forms, for instance, modern technological developments such as having to turn on a light switch are explored in relation to the traditional prohibition of work on *Shabbos*. By sixth form, boys may be tackling some 20 pages of the Talmud during the year at much deeper levels of interpretation and sophistication. Starting at *Baba Metziah*, seven or eight tractates are dealt with in all, and the progress of the boys is geared to those tractates studied in much greater depth at the *Yeshivah Gedolah* so that the boys can receive coaching and personal help after school from the rabbinical students.

The study of *Chumash* with commentary by Rashi starts in Grades 1 and 2 with Genesis, and proceeds systematically through the subsequent books grade by grade until all Five Books have been completed, and study begins afresh from the beginning but at greater depth. Some consideration is given to other sections of *TeNaCh*, especially *Nevi'im*, but is necessarily restricted due to lack of time. However, by the end of their schooling the boys will have covered the majority of *TeNaCh*.

Study of the *Kitzur Schulchan Aruch* in lower grades and the unabridged version in higher forms takes place mainly before each Festival. Considerable time is devoted to studying its ritual laws and ceremonial observances. However the *Schulchan Aruch* is studied on other occasions though, in comparison with *TeNaCh* and the Talmud, less time is devoted to it.

A feature of the curriculum for the secondary forms is the gradual introduction of Chassidic philosophy in conjunction with studies of *Chumash*. In Forms 1 and 2 teachers might explain Chassidic interpretations of the weekly portion of *Torah* once or twice a week. Instruction would be given orally with pupils taking notes. No formal textbook of *Chassidus* is used. However, by Form 5, pupils are able to start tackling the main philosophy in some depth, and are introduced to some parts of *Tanya* which is the basis of the Lubavitcher (*Chabad*) philosophy. Once again, lack of time limits what can be tackled.

How traditional are these elements of the curriculum? In

origin they are very ancient, dating back to biblical times and the post-biblical period during which the Oral Law was gradually compiled and finally approved in its authorized form. We can gain some insight into Lubavitcher notions of what traditional Orthodox Jewish education should be from an account of the controversy between Rabbi Menachem Mendel, the 'Tzemach Tzedek' of the line of *Chabad*-Chassidic tradition, and proponents of the *Haskalah* movement during the five-year period after 1845.[3]

In reply to the Russian Bureau of Religions' unacceptable proposals for the curriculum of Hebrew schools, the Tzemach Tzedek made a number of cogent *responsa* in a lengthy pamphlet. Among his many points were the following, in which we can detect the essential roots of the religious program of the school (Schneersohn, 1962, pp. 71 ff.):

> The words of the Torah are eternal, true, and just. This must be impressed upon the minds and hearts of the pupils at the outset. (*Yoreh Deah* 245, 6: 'One is obliged to teach his son the Written Torah in its entirety . . .').
>
> Even the curriculum recently issued for Government schools for Jews explicitly states that first grade children are to study the first books of the Pentateuch and the *Mishnayos* of the Tractate *Shabbos*. In the second grade they are to complete the Pentateuch, Joshua, Judges, Samuel, Kings, Isaiah, Jeremiah, Psalms, Proberbs, Esther, *Mishnayos Brachos* and the Orders of Festivals, Civil Law, and Sacrifice, Talmud Tractates *Be'a*, *Succah*, *Pesachim*, and *Shabbos*, and many sections of the *Schulchan Aruch* (as planned in 1843 by the Commission). The curriculum stipulates all the books of the Bible, Mishnah, and Talmud, with no mention of omissions.

In view of the types of religious teaching staff employed at the school and particularly the developments which have taken place since my study, the organization of most Chassidic communities under the Tzemach Tzedek's direction is also of interest. Their religious staff consisted of

Rabbis, *schochtim*, teachers (who were also charged by the Rabbi with organizing public study group for Mishna, Talmud, *halacha*, *agada*, and Chassidus), and a *mashpi'ya*. The *mashpi'ya* was a Chassid chosen by the Rabbi to be responsible for Chassidic training, especially of young men and boys (*ibid.*, p. 60).[4]

Some comments on methods of instruction

Several features differentiate the formal curriculum of the Great Tradition from that of the academic tradition. Firstly, a hierarchical arrangement of subjects grade by grade is absent. Progress in the study of *Chumash*, the Mishnah and *Schulchan Aruch* is highly individualistic, and depends on the capabilities of the students and interests of the teachers. Thus it is not possible to specify exactly what is studied grade by grade. There is a close parallel with Eastern European tradition. 'The general principle of the yeshiva is independence and self-reliance. The program of study allows for infinite variation' (Zborowski and Herzog, 1952, pp. 97–8). Secondly, tradition has had to defer to the demands of secular work and the inroads this makes into pupils' time, energy, and capacity for sustained Jewish studies. For instance, it used to be customary in the traditional *cheder* or elementary school for the study of *Chumash* to commence at Leviticus. This is now skipped and left for older classes, while the younger boys start with Genesis. However, even this is not an invariable procedure and depends on the ability of pupils and the teacher's preferences.

Thirdly, several important pedagogical techniques are employed for all studies. Particularly in higher forms, boys work individually at the Talmud in small groups which rarely exceed four. They also work at their own pace. It is also clear that a form of 'spiral curriculum' operates. A boy may tackle a part of *Chumash* in a junior grade, progress to other parts as he proceeds through the school, but in senior forms return to the part he first studied but tackle it at greater depth and rigour.

This applies particularly to *Chumash*. In the Talmud, on the other hand, though some spiral tendency is apparent, study is a matter of progressing from topic to topic (tractate to tractate) of increasing depth and complexity. Fourthly, a great deal of the curriculum emphasizes the acquisition of knowledge (the cognitive domain) and certain skills such as those necessary to sustain a discussion on a passage from the Talmud in higher forms.

BEHAVIOURAL KNOWLEDGE

Behavioural norms and values of the Great Tradition

Solomon's description of traditional Jewish education (1973, p. 174) indicates clearly how closely the school has modelled its program of religious instruction on traditional practice. It is also the source of the 'ideal' behavioural norms and values that the boys should follow.

> The traditional curriculum of Jewish studies was textbook- and subject-centred, divided into stages based on the study of the Pentateuch, the Mishna, and the Talmud. Whereas intellectual knowledge was the basis of the curriculum, the goals of education included both cognitive and affective objectives, meaning knowledge, behaviour, the acquisition of values, and the training of character.

The assumption is made at the school that learning knowledge of *Torah* will lead to the adoption of the correct behaviours set out therein as the 613 Precepts (Heb. *taryag mitzvot*), or commandments of the Law of Moses. These are subdivided into 248 positive and 365 negative precepts. The concept of *Torah* connotes 'guidance' and 'direction', and implies that knowledge of *Torah* provides an individual with a program of norms and values to guide both his most private actions and his relationships with the community. Chassidism is, in essence, an ethical and aesthetic interpretation of the divine ideals embodied in the 613 Precepts of Judaism. The

91

elements of Lubavitcher philosophy, to which the boys are exposed, thus have the effect of reinforcing the values and norms learned in their more formal studies of *Torah*. . . .

It is a basic affirmation of Judaism that man is a creature who makes free ethical choices and decisions for which he alone is responsible. A boy at Lubavitcher School may have the Precepts held up before him as models of behaviour: it is up to him whether to make them part of his 'recipe knowledge', and the basis of forming the typifications of others, which guide his interpersonal relationships.

Behavioural knowledge gained from studying divine Precepts is reinforced by knowledge derived from a variety of animate and inanimate sources in the school. These range from homiletic injunctions given at the various types of ceremonies . . . through comments of lay and religious teaching staff during periods of religious instruction, to precepts contained in literature from the Lubavitcher Rebbe, which is pinned to notice boards and doors in the *shul* and its adjoining rooms. . . .

Homiletic injunctions in publications about the school stress a number of themes, which relate to the value of *Yiddishkeit*. This is made even more explicit by the distinction, which speakers or writers make between 'general education knowledge' and Jewish knowledge. The former has only one purpose, namely to acquire skill, but not to acquire character. The latter 'shows us how to live properly in Jewish life'. The objective of the school is to develop *Yiddishkeit*: teaching an aim and direction in life, through Jewish morals and ethics which kindle children's minds. In this way it is hoped that the school will turn out knowledgeable and responsible Jews. Through the high standards of *Yiddishkeit* at the school the boys gain a deep awareness of their religion. The school is a 'banner of *Yiddishkeit*': its intense Yiddish atmosphere is bolstered by harmony between teachers and pupils. The study of *Torah* and Jewish education has always been an ideal of the Jewish people. It is necessary for moral living: no one can be pious without knowledge. . . .

Folk of Jewish ethnic customs are also an important

component of *Yiddishkeit*. 'The term has a warm ring for the *Ashkenazi* Jew, denoting the positive aspects of Jewish habits, often of folk origin' (Werblowsky and Wigoder, 1965, p. 410). Most of the congregation associated with the school originated from Eastern Europe, and their customs feature during Festivals such as *Purim, Simchas Torah* and *Chanukah*. Some date back to medieval times and earlier. Masquerades, fancy dress, and a carnival atmosphere with games (Yidd. *Purim spiel*) occupy boys' attention during *Purim*. Spinning the top (Yidd. *dreidl*) becomes a playground game when *Chanukah* occurs. The Festival of *Lag Ba-Omer*, which occurs between *Pesach* and *Shavuot*, is the occasion for outdoor field games and activities in the parks close to the school. The limited extra-curricular activities include a school choir, which is formed in the months prior to Speech Night, and has a repertoire of Israeli and Jewish folk songs. These are a feature of the relatively rare school assemblies in the dining hall.

Cultic-ceremonial knowledge

A further type of behavioural knowledge relating to the Great Tradition is cultic-ceremonial knowledge concerning the meaning and correct performance of the rituals and *mitzvot*. It is explicitly taught in religious studies through studying *Torah*, the Talmud, and *Schulchan Aruch*. When each Festival approaches, some attention is given in class to rehearsing the meaning of its associated rituals, even to the extent of demonstrating the use of the cultic-ceremonial objects involved. Thus, at *Rosh Hashanah* the use of the *shophar* or ram's horn is shown. At *Succos*, the *lulav* and *esrog* feature in lessons. Boys are able to handle these objects, and practise the correct methods of using them.

In addition to these explicit, didactic teaching methods, the school complex as a whole is a source of countless instances of cultic-ceremonial knowledge being learned from the example of others. Ritual behaviour is involved in the frequent ablutions or washing of the hands before meals and prayers.

The boys in primary grades are taken to wash-troughs as a matter of course, and their ablutions are supervised by the teacher. The school secretary tries to ensure that boys wash their hands in the dining hall during lunchtime. The saying of the Blessing and Grace is similarly prescribed. . . .

Behavioural norms and values of the academic tradition

Fundamental to the academic tradition, as we have seen, is the concept of educating the 'whole man': the building of moral character and the production of leadership qualities through prefect and house systems. Aesthetic qualities are learned through such non-academic subjects as Drama, Art, and Music. Other norms and values commonly associated with the academic tradition involve such vague ideas as 'playing the game', 'good sportsmanship', 'clean living', and the like, which are all held to contribute to the concept of the whole man.

The school follows the academic tradition to the letter by having a prefect and house system. The senior master had introduced the former some years prior to my research in a bid to improve the status and image of the school in the eyes of the Jewish community by giving it something of a 'public school' character. The latter had been formed, also some years earlier, by a non-Jewish master who had had experience of a house system in his previous independent school. Both were thus 'imported' traditions. . . .

Aesthetic pursuits are almost completely absent. No music is taught. Drama is not a permanent feature of the curriculum, although a small group was intensively coached towards the end of the year in preparation for Speech Night. Art is limited to junior forms. By third form it is dropped. There are no clubs run on an after-school basis to encourage boys to take an interest in creative pursuits.

Sport occupies an anomalous position in the school, which reflects the low value placed upon it in the Great Tradition. Part of the lack of interest must be attributed to the poor handling of sport by two part-time masters, who were replaced

94

in the middle of the year by the full-time sports master. This produced some revival of interest and greatly improved standards of teaching and supervision especially for the more enthusiastic junior forms.

However, the arrangement of the campus and facilities affects the participation of the boys. Restrictions of space and equipment curtail what can be done. A variety of elementary gymnastics mainly using tumbling mats or 'Swedish drill', cricket, basketball and volleyball are the main activities. Boys are also taken to the nearby Jewish sports centre for swimming during the summer, and a nearby park on occasions. Informal sporting activities by the boys also include some Australian Rules football in winter, though usually only the ubiquitous high kicking from one end of the playground to the other that can be seen in most schools during the football season. Soccer is also played intermittently. . . .

In general, sport is not taken seriously nor thought to be an important part of the curriculum. As boys get older it loses a great deal of attraction. In view of other demands on their time, and irregularities in their study periods, senior boys do not have compulsory sport or a set time for physical education. The sports master tried to arrange opportunities for boys in Forms 5 and 6 to have some sport, but, apart from a few enthusiasts, attendance fell away, especially towards the end of the year and approaching examinations.

Less formal sources of behavioural knowledge are members of the secular teaching staff. During lessons and at other times when they are supervising boys, teachers place most emphasis on procedural values: punctuality, orderliness, tidiness, quiet behaviour, respect and good manners, and similar *desiderata* to ensure effective teaching and learning. There is very little, if any, concern for encouraging 'pastoral' behavioural values, as these are the province of the rabbis.

THE EIDOS OF LUBAVITCHER SCHOOL

The organization of knowledge in the school makes itself

obvious in an all-pervasive atmosphere of learning which can be seen in what Bateson (1958, p. 118) has termed the 'eidos' of a social group. This is the 'standardization of the cognitive aspects of the personality of the individuals' whom the group comprises. Evidence for it can be seen on all sides, and is one of the several abiding impressions that the observer gets over a protracted period. Learning is obviously valued, as in most other schools, but the style of learning encouraged in Lubavitcher School makes it quite unique on the Australian educational scene.

The outstanding aspect of the eidos of the school is the way the social organization of two traditions stimulates boys, rabbinical students, and rabbis to an intense form of intellectual activity. Great emphasis is placed on accumulating purely cognitive information, feats of memory, rote learning, and the ability to reason and argue dialectically in the pilpulistic tradition, drawing upon stocks of biblical, Talmudic, and to a lesser extent, secular academic knowledge. Examples of boys reciting long passages of Scripture or the Talmud from memory are not uncommon.

The method of dialectical argument and reasoning derives from Eastern European rabbinical scholarship, and illustrates the influence of tradition in the eidos of the school. However, it can lead to extremes of casuistic hair-splitting, which are condemned by the rabbis, but often occur in secular lessons. On such occasions one can be entrapped in virtually endless argument. Each of one's points is met by a counter argument, often prefaced by 'yes but'. The pilpulistic approach is most developed in the *Yeshivah Gedolah* and, as the Torah Evening demonstrates, is still appreciated by members of the congregation. Their close involvement accords with traditional practice.

Debating style is forceful, noisy and often disorderly. As many as possible want to put their points as quickly as possible. Verbal 'attack' is emphasized by the kinesthetic technique of 'holding' a debating point between the finger and thumb, and proffering it to the listener. Other points are emphasized by a downward jab of the finger, or an upward motion of the clenched fist. If a book comes into the argument, a page will be opened dramatically, and thrust under one's nose.

Learning is also highly physical. In strict rabbinical tradition, learning new knowledge is achieved by vocalizing aloud.

> A person should take care to pronounce with his lips and make audible to his ears, whatever he studies, and he should concentrate his mind upon it, for it is written (Joshua 1:8): 'This Torah shall not depart from thy mouth, and thou shalt meditate upon it,' etc. (*Kitzur Schulchan Aruch*, 27, p. 5)

The strong kinesthetic component in learning is evident in the ubiquitous body swaying that accompanies reading, whether aloud or silently. Even if a person reads silently, his lips move, and he sways in time with the rhythm of the words.

The similarity to the Eastern European tradition of learning in the *yeshivah* and the *shtetl* is striking (Zborowski and Herzog, 1952, pp. 92–3).

> Swaying as one reads, and chanting the words in a fixed melody, *nign*, are considered necessary for successful study.... The swaying and the chanting become automatic. Later, the students will acquire also the appropriate gestures with the index finger and the thumb, sweeping the thumb through an upward arc of inquiry and nailing down the point of the answer with a thrust of the index finger. Study is not passive but active, involving constant motor and vocal activity.

Erudition and biblical, Talmudic scholarship are revered. The Principal introduced the *shochet* to me as 'a scribe *and* a scholar', with an inflexion on the 'and' which clearly indicated the esteem in which he is held in the community. During the year one of the fourth form boys won second prize in a local biblical knowledge competition organized by *B'nai B'rith*, thereby gaining the chance of competing in the national finals.[5] This was an event of some note, and brought credit both on the boy and the school. The Principal made a special point of visiting the classroom and publicly announcing the honour to the rest of the boys. They were visibly impressed, despite the inevitable 'ribbing' they handed out to the young scholar after the Principal had left the room. For weeks thereafter the boy was the focus of both spoken and non-verbalized admiration from his peers. His knowledge of *Torah* almost became proverbial. It was noted above that similar esteem is given to the specially selected class of primary school children whose knowledge of the Talmud was also discussed respectfully by far older boys. . . .

The intellectual hub of the school is the *Yeshivah Gedolah* in the *bet midrash* located just off the *shul*. Its atmosphere of almost supercharged learning is a striking example of the dynamics pervading the eidos of the school. The room is dimly lit, lined with books, and furnished with large tables and a few reading stands cluttered with large tomes of Talmud. Students study individually rocking backwards and forwards in their seats, with lips moving in the accepted rote learning style. Others argue passionately in small groups, emphasizing their points with sharp, pointed fingers or by an emphatic slap of the hand on the table. One student, bearded, coatless, wearing a *yarmelkeh*, and with *tzitzit* swinging at his waist, reads aloud in Hebrew from a large folio on the stand with a vigorous intensity amounting to passion. He punctuates each phrase with an emphatic forward sway and stamp of the foot, as if pounding the information into his mind with a rhythm that matches the cadence of what he is reading.

All these activities go on simultaneously in what appears to be bedlam to the external observer, but amid it all a white-bearded rabbi strolls unconcernedly from group to group, elucidating a point here, discussing a question there. He smokes a cigarette most of the time, and is obviously quite at home and relaxed in the highly charged atmosphere, despite the burning intensity of his students. This is the accepted, traditional style of Talmudic study. The whole scene is almost medieval, and immediately brings to mind what one has read of the great *yeshivot* of Eastern Europe. As Steinberg has commented (1959, p. 101): 'As an institution of learning, the Yeshivah was a masterpiece of disorganization'.

The countervailing curriculum

The problematical nature of learning is most apparent in what can be termed the countervailing curriculum. This comprises those unplanned experiences and the informal knowledge which convey conflicting messages and meanings to boys wherever they meet as groups in interaction settings. Each of these contains stimuli in the form of other boys or people who may be present, together with artifacts and a range of written or pictorial media. All of these can convey meanings that are at odds with, and often contradict, those intended in the formal curriculum. Their overall effect is to cast doubt on the certainty of the knowledge available through planned and intentional learning experiences.

The operation of the countervailing curriculum occurs in several ways. Knowledge can be directly challenged in a quite overt manner. Customary behaviour, attitudes and feelings are similarly challenged. However, there is also the constant covert influence of the countervailing curriculum present at all times and in nearly all interaction settings. Its effect is less easy to establish with certainty as nothing is done or said in this case, which might suggest that an alternative experience and its meaning are being transmitted to those present. Despite this, it is clear from boys' reactions that a countervailing influence is at work, even though the evidence is nearly always impressionistic and based on often fleeting evidence gathered while one goes about his routine work.

OVERT CHALLENGES TO KNOWLEDGE

The emphasis both traditions place on mastering a great deal of purely factual or cognitive information, which forms much of the content of their respective curricula, inevitably leads to situations where established knowledge and beliefs come under direct challenge. Some boys are alert to this possibility and seldom fail to question the validity of what is being taught in a lesson. With some twenty other boys present in a class, there is always an attentive and appreciative audience. The most dramatic challenge occurs during lessons dealing with topics and phenomena for which there are two potentially contradictory explanations – those available from scientific thought in the academic tradition in opposition to those from religious thought in the Great Tradition.

The creation of the world is one such topic. Orthodox Judaism, as we have seen, dates its calendar from the moment of Creation in 3760 B.C.E. On several occasions with my fifth form a geography lesson would touch on an aspect of geology and the age of rocks. 'The Silurian rocks in this region were laid down some 400 million years ago,' I would state, only to have one or the other of the most Orthodox boys challenge the statement. 'This cannot be. In *Chumash* it says that the world was created 5729 years ago.' For the young Chassid it became something of an obsession to correct me each time. 'We know the truth,' he would say emphatically, 'because Moses has given it to us. Yours is only a theory, and like all theories can easily be proved wrong. We have the truth.' Form 5 was not alone in challenging scientific knowledge. Periodically during the year similar occasions would arise with other forms, and my statements would be greeted with scepticism and even outright rejection by boys in Forms 3 and 4 whenever what I taught ran counter to biblical teaching.

The strength of such conviction is well illustrated by the following incident with my sixth form social studies group. During discussion about aspects of Chinese civilization, I mentioned Toynbee's concept of historical cycles, and asked the boys whether it could be applied to events in Jewish history by way of illustration. Five thousand, seven hundred and twenty-nine years have elapsed since Moses I was told; the

100

Messiah would come by the year six thousand or earlier. The Lubavitcher Rebbe had once prophesied that the Millennium was imminent; and had affirmed his prophesy on several subsequent occasions. I risked a few questions.

'Doesn't it worry you when I put forward different ideas such as these historical cycles?'

'No, those are only theories. We know. We don't even have to worry about it.'

'But doesn't it get you upset?'

'Why should it? We are quite certain. It's something we do not even worry about; it's not a question of belief but part of us.'

'But false prophets have arisen before – look at Shabbetai Tzevi, the seventeenth century pseudo-messiah, and what followed when he renounced Judaism.'

'Yes, we know, we know. There will always be false messiahs; this we accept, but when the true one comes we will know.'

Such conviction is all the more surprising in view of the many developments of the twentieth century, one of which was imminent at the time. This was man's first landing on the moon, but even it could be coped with. After some hesitation and much consultation with staff, the Principal permitted a large television set to be set up in the assembly hall. Classes were grudgingly allowed to come in for short periods to watch the moon landing preparations and final landing. The time for *Minchah* came and boys were being called to prayer, yet still a group lingered around the set. One of the rabbis bustled in obviously annoyed. 'Come, *daven Minchah*, it's time. Leave that, it is not important. *Minchah* is more important, come.' There could be no compromise with Orthodoxy.

Challenges to scientific knowledge could occur over such apparently trivial matters as getting Sabin oral vaccines against poliomyelitis. Teams of doctors travel around the schools in the State, administering the vaccine almost as a routine measure. The day is known beforehand, parents sign a form giving their consent, classes assemble *en masse* and, despite interruption to classwork, the whole business is over and done with relatively quickly.

Not so for some boys in my own form. Just prior to trooping over to the hall to get their doses, two boys protested in all apparent sincerity that the vaccine was *tref*, and could not be taken without breaking the *kasruth* laws.[6] Would I give an opinion please? My hesitant reply did not satisfy some boys, who promptly went to seek the rabbi's advice, before going to get their vaccine.

Kasruth prohibitions cropped up several times during the year. The most obvious occurred during a stop at a small country shop to get a snack on an extended geography excursion with my own form. The available food was inspected carefully, its *kosher* quality discussed at length, and then rejected in favour of soft drinks and potato crisps. Several boys appeared to go hungry rather than risk buying something they were uncertain about. . . .

Religious ritual behaviour becomes problematical when boys go on an excursion. One of the first questions they ask concerns the availability of water to wash their hands before a meal, and a place in which they can pray *Minchah*. The latter is not always vital if the group can get back to school, and pray in the *shul* before the time for this prayer expires. However, washing the hands and saying the Blessing and Grace are of vital importance for the more Orthodox boys.

Their solution is to take with them an aluminium pitcher to pour the water, a towel to dry the hands, and small prayer books for as many as want them. The visit of third and fourth forms to the Royal Melbourne Show saw one of the most Orthodox boys getting off the bus with a pile of prayer books, and a pitcher wrapped up in the towel. Apparently he knew of a tap in an unfrequented corner of the Showgrounds. One of my geography excursions had to be planned so that the lunch stop would occur at a place where the boys could wash their hands. This some 50 per cent did, at a tap on the reserve, before taking over one of the picnic rotundas in which to eat

102

their lunch. As usual this was accompanied by Blessings and Grace.

In mid-year, the visit to a neighbouring high school by my own form to sit for the CSSE posed fewer problems. A classroom had been set aside in which the boys could eat lunch, after washing their hands in the cloakrooms. I brought food, and we ate lunch together. Afterwards the boys said the *Minchah* prayer, one of them leading the rest. He stood facing a wall and recited most of the prayers off by heart. Another boy stood at his elbow to act as prompter when he faltered. As he told me afterwards the Lubavitcher order of prayer differs from that used in his own *shul*, and he found it difficult to follow. . . .

After *Minchah* the boys went to the playground, where the majority played basketball, keeping themselves segregated in one court. Here they were quite conspicuous and obviously different from the other, more casually dressed students, by virtue of their *yarmelkehs*, caps, and school suits. My hat completed our group identification. Several jeers came from other students, and on two occasions a stone was lobbed in our direction.

This was not uncommon, several of my boys informed me. More often than not, most provocation and even physical assault comes from non-observant Jewish boys rather than from *goyim*. In the previous year, the boys had been disturbed and attacked during their lunch and prayers by others, and a fracas had developed. From first-hand experience I was able to share in the feeling of being persecuted and the apprehension of both my boys and the Principal, which had resulted in his request that I should stay with the boys during their lunch time.

In this instance, the effects of the countervailing curriculum were mostly indirect results of the requirements of the Great Tradition obtruding into what was essentially a keystone in the academic tradition, i.e. its examination system. Similar tensions were generated for boys from the fifth and sixth forms, when they sat for their final School Leaving and Matriculation examinations held at the Exhibition Buildings in the city. The problems of prayers, lunch, washing hands were all present at a time when maximum concentration was needed on academic matters. . . .

THE COVERT OPERATION OF THE COUNTERVAILING CURRICULUM

Whereas the overt effects of the countervailing curriculum are manifest in the verbal interactions of those within interaction settings, its covert effects are less easy to reconstruct. They arise from other components in the total 'environment of objects' to which each individual will attach meanings. Thus we should take into account such aspects as spatial arrangements, artifacts, inanimate symbolic communication – signs, notices, display material – together with the 'inarticulate experience' derived from the actions of others. Their meanings for those individuals who are present can be assumed to complement those already obtained through the overt countervailing curriculum.

Artifacts in the environment

The classroom contains a medley of artifacts relating to both traditions. Boys' phylacteries in their bright, velvet bags can be seen in desks, on cupboard tops, even on a window sill if it is conveniently situated near a boy's place in class. Religious books may be neatly arranged in cupboards, though quite often, especially following a period of religious instruction, they are left in apparent disorder on top of the teacher's table. A *mezuzah* is attached to the jamb of the doorway. Those artifacts one customarily associates with classrooms are also littered around, or kept neatly in their appointed places according to the tidiness of the teacher and boys. These are blackboard dusters, chalk, rulers, board compasses and other geometrical equipment, models used for demonstrating scientific principles, textbooks of all descriptions. A duality is at once apparent in the two types of artifacts, as there is in virtually every component in the school. . . .

Symbolic media of communication in the environment

Most interaction settings within the school complex have material on display which relates to both traditions. In the fifth-form room, a large chart occupied part of the pin-board on the rear wall. Published by the Lubavitcher Movement, it lists in Hebrew and English the thirty-nine labours forbidden on *Shabbos*. At the beginning of the Jewish year the Lubavitcher students drew up a chart in Hebrew showing the exact dates and times for daily prayers, the lighting of *Shabbos* candles and putting on *tephillin*, and added this to the board display. A diagram and detailed instructions showing the correct way to attach phylacteries also appeared. This was part of a *tephillin* campaign which was advertised in *The Australian Jewish News*, and supported by a 'pastoral' letter from the Lubavitcher Rebbe displayed prominently on a notice board in the foyer of the *shul*. Both pieces of advertising leave no doubt as to the directness of the message and the logic to which it adheres. . . .

In stark contrast to these display materials, are those relating to the academic tradition and curriculum. They vary according to the lesson topic, but in due season are pinned up on the display board next to material of the Great Tradition. Tangible evidence of two logics and meanings are thus juxtaposed for all who care to look at it. . . .

Dualism of languages in symbolic media

An important feature of the great majority of religious material is the two languages in which the whole or parts are printed. English and Hebrew commonly appear on the same sheet. In the case of the Lubavitcher Rebbe's letters English, Hebrew and Yiddish versions are available. Such juxtaposition of languages emphasizes in a quite fundamental way the duality of the learning experiences available to the boys. The development of logics and thought are determined by language, i.e. by the linguistic tools of thought, and by the symbolically-mediated socio-cultural experience of the child. Language is crucial in the construction of knowledge as Berger and Luckmann note (1971, pp. 85–6):

> Language objectivates the shared experiences and makes them available to all within the linguistic community, thus becoming both the basis and the instrument of the collective stock of knowledge. Furthermore, language provides the means for objectifying new experiences, allowing their incorporation into the already existing stock of knowledge, and it is the most important means by which the objectivated and objectified sedimentations are transmitted in the tradition of the collectivity in question.

We need only extend this view, by considering the plural languages present in interaction settings at the school, to appreciate that two sets of experiences are being objectivated (i.e. created as a reality common to members of a group), two stocks of knowledge augmented, and 'sedimentations' transmitted in two traditions. Indeed, two cultures are being mediated to the boys. . . .

Notes

1 I am indebted to the Director of Religious Instruction at the school for the information on which this section is based, though the comments and interpretation under the sub-heading *Some comments on methods of instruction* are entirely mine.
2 Men of the Great Assembly: a spiritual and legislative assembly of the post-prophetic era (*c.* 200 B.C.E.) consisting of between 85 and 120 sages.
3 *Haskalah* (Heb.: 'Enlightenment'). The movement among Jews of Eastern Europe in the late eighteenth to nineteenth centuries to acquire modern European culture and secular knowledge.
4 The Director of Religious Studies at Lubavitcher School would be the equivalent of the *mashpi'ya*.
5 *B'nai B'rith* is an Independent Order founded in 1843 with the object of uniting Jews for social, cultural and philanthropic purposes.
6 *Tref* (Heb.: lit. 'torn'). Meat unfit for consumption. By extension applied to any ritually impure food. Its opposite is *kosher*.

Part three
Teachers' worlds

This part of the reader corresponds to Chapter 3 of *Interaction in the Classroom*. The paper by Warren Peterson is a classic of symbolic interactionism, and deals with how teachers of different ages relate both to their colleagues and their pupils. The development of the teacher's career over a thirty-year period is sensitively analysed, in a paper that is unjustifiably neglected in the literature on teachers. Martyn Denscombe's paper looks at how the noise emanating from classrooms provides a teacher's colleagues with 'clues' about her competence. Finally, Anne Swidler's analysis of teacher-pupil relationships in two 'free' schools where no official rules govern their interaction throws into relief such relationships in more conventional institutions. The contrast between the schools in Denscombe's and Peterson's work and those studied by Swidler are clear cut and dramatic. Taken together the three papers show the features of privacy, immediacy and autonomy highlighted in *Interaction in the Classroom*.

5

Age, teacher's role and the institutional setting

Warren A. Peterson

Originally published in B. Biddle and W. Ellena (eds) (1964) *Contemporary Research on Teacher Effectiveness*, pp. 264–77, 288–301. New York: Holt, Rinehart & Winston.

* * *

From a study of the ways that teachers adjust to age and generational differences and to one another, some important facts about effectiveness have emerged. The teacher's role changes as she grows older; morale, and perhaps teaching competence, may be affected by age and generational conflict; and, most fundamentally, career teachers want recognition as they grow older – recognition for having dedicated their lives to other people's children.

The research reported here was based on comprehensive interviews with a relatively small sample of public high school teachers in a city of medium size and mid-western location. The analysis techniques were those of comprehensive interviews with emphasis on the development of insights. Techniques were qualitative rather than quantitative and concerned social patterns and processes rather than prevalence or reliability. The validity

109

of the data rested on the honesty and competence of teachers as observers of their own role in a social system. The objectivity of the results depended upon the responsibility and degree of insight possessed by the interpreter. . . .

Sampling and interviewing

The present research differs from previous occupational studies of teachers in several respects. Although most of the analytical problems are not new, the range of inquiry was broadened to include the full work career with special emphasis on age and career changes. Thus the intent was to deal with a broad range of analytical problems – but a relatively small and homogeneous group of subjects.

The sample (confined to white, female, high school teachers thirty to seventy years of age) was drawn, at random, from an annual directory of personnel in an urban school system. In 1953, when the sample was drawn, less than 12 per cent of the teachers in the system were under forty years of age and less than 7 per cent were married. Sampling ratio categories for age and marital status were devised, and the sample was stratified accordingly. From an original sample of seventy-two teachers, fifty-six respondents completed the interview. The final sample closely approximated the original sample in distribution among high school units and among high school subject fields. Approximately two-thirds of the teachers interviewed were single, and approximately two-thirds were reared in small towns and rural areas.

The principle data-gathering technique was an informal, conversational interview. Sessions were structured partially by topics but were largely unstructured in the wording and the order of questions. Interviews were conducted in the respondents' homes and averaged two hours in length. Unless the respondent objected, interviews were recorded on tape. . . .

Career research

The problem in career research is that of discovering and

110

explaining the role and status sequences that characterize members of an occupation during the span of life at work. Aging is a basic element in movement through life – it is a common denominator. If aging is related to the varied conditions of modern industrial organization, it should also serve as a point of departure for generalizations about the metabolism of the occupational career. For example, among established middle-class occupations, there tend to be four distinct phases: (1) a learning-oriented exploration phase in young adulthood accompanied by apprenticeship status and involving progressive acceptance or rejection by older, established members; (2) a secondary membership phase marked by high productivity in relation to the functions of the organization but lacking full recognition or responsibility; (3) a full membership phase that, in the middle class, seems to occur in middle or late-middle age and involves maximum formal and informal prestige, authority, and responsibility within the organization; (4) a period of membership decline characterized by deference rather than by prestige and by honorary, rather than functional positions.

The development and validation of generalizations like the above are likely to occur through comparative research on several occupational careers. Although a general model has been employed as a guide in the analysis, there are more modest objectives in this paper. The careers of a specific group of teachers are described and explained in terms of the structure of school systems, the character of student-teacher interaction, the pressures of woman-role expectations, and the effects of social class and rural-urban mobility. In addition to its implications in the direction of understanding common occupational career processes, this study helps to explain the special function of the teaching occupation in society and in the institutional system with which it is associated.

The teacher in the school system

The teacher in the urban public school works in a social milieu that provides regular contact with pupils, other teachers, and principals. Less frequent contacts are made also with staff specialists from the central administrative office, with parents of pupils, and with service and clerical workers. Inducing socially valued changes in students appears to be central in the teacher's occupational purpose, her sense of mission, and her rationale for occupational commitment. Within the administrative organization the teacher holds a staff-terminal position; but, because of professional status and the separation of classrooms, the teacher's role includes more autonomy and less direct supervision than that of many other staff-terminal workers. Terminal in the authority system, exposed to public opinion, subject to stereotyping, and set apart from many other occupations by the specialized occupational role (and by the predominantly female composition of its membership), teaching is characterized by intensive colleagueship and a pervasive occupational identity. . . .

As with most occupations in which women predominate, teaching is an 'early plateau' occupation characterized by relatively minor changes after the beginning phases of training and apprenticeship. However, institutional arrangements are such that teaching offices are standardized from one unit of a city system to another and from that system to others that are politically and geographically separate from it. Occupational mobility among teachers, thus, takes several forms – movement from one grade level to another (most typically from grade school to high school teaching), movement to school systems of greater size and prestige with increases in salary and security, and movement from one unit of a city system to another. . . .

Career changes in the teacher's relationships with others of importance in the work setting have not been subject to any degree of empirical investigation. There are some indications that young adulthood is the most effective age for a teacher. The Chicago studies, however, suggest that older teachers are more likely than young adults to be accepted into the colleague group, have greater power and authority in the school, and develop a greater interest in maintaining established procedures (Becker, 1953).

Relating to students as young teachers

It seems important, in approaching the matter of relating to students, to point out the special age structure of the teacher-student group. This group is vastly different from the parent-child model, and the difference results from the application of the full adult, life-work career to teachers and the fragmentation of students into narrow age grades. A teacher begins teaching children when her age position to them is like that of an older sister; in mid-career she is about the age of their parents; and if she continues teaching to the age of retirement (age seventy in the urban system studied) she may be older than their grandparents.

Except on occasions when they encountered students beneath them in class or ethnically strange (in mining, industrial, or cotton-belt communities) teachers interviewed gave a warm and glowing account of their feelings for students in early career. Although some of the 'pleasant experience' feelings may have been due to the fact that some teachers were closer to their native surroundings than they were later in the city (or to the substantial recognition that teachers receive in small towns), many teachers attributed such feelings to age. In general, when asked about the best teaching period, either for themselves or for a teacher in general, they recognized a short orientation period, a 'best teaching period', while still young and vigorous. Later, a decline was indicated.

> I: What do you think is the best period for a teacher?[1]
> 19s: Probably after one has had a year or two of experience, then while you are still young you have the most fun with the kids. Then later on – forty or so – it becomes more burdensome, after you get up in years.

In the small town the orientation period seems to be relatively short. For example, in discussing her first teaching experience, 16s moved rather rapidly from being terrified 'the first hour' and insecure about her knowledge 'the first year', to feeling that 'it was a lot of fun'.

> 16s: I know the first hour I was scared to death because I had students from a rural area – this was a small town – I had students almost as old as I was; big as I was, that's for sure. And I taught geometry and advanced algebra. The first year I was afraid they'd think I didn't know as much as they did about it. But it was a lot of fun, I really enjoyed it. I can't remember any particular problems.

In discussing early career experiences, teachers repeatedly stressed the idea that they were not much older than the pupils; this is an important aspect of 'having a wonderful time'. In 31w's case, discipline problems were approached with a sense of challenge.

> 31w: The first teaching job I had was in a small town. I had a wonderful time. Another girl and I went out there together. The pupils were just about as old as we were. We dated and had a wonderful time. It was supposed to be a difficult school. They had run out [sic] other teachers. But we gave them a run for it. We out-smarted them. I never had such a good time. I have friends there that I've had all these years. My partner married one of the boys. I had a good time with them; got more work out of them than we could possibly have gotten otherwise. It was an interesting town, hidebound in many ways. But, as I say, we gave them a run for it.

The young teacher in the small school usually applied herself with vigour and enthusiasm. In retrospect, there was bewilderment about how she was able to undertake so much. The close relationship with students was supplemented with warm relationships among young teachers, with joint activities with students, and with joint dating activities. There was, as 52m

114

reported 'no distance between students and teachers'.

> 52m: I taught English and did all sorts of other things. I
> sponsored a page on the schools in the local paper,
> sponsored the senior class, produced plays – I was the
> dramatics department, such as it was. And I started
> the pep club. I was quite busy.
>
> I lived there with three other teachers who had
> rented a house. The other three had been there the
> year before, but they were young. The oldest one was
> 35, but she was very youthful and sort of the follower
> type. The others were just slighly older than I. It was
> very friendly, and we had a wonderful time. The kids
> would drop in all the time, whenever they felt like it. I
> think it was partly because they could get away with
> some things in our house that they couldn't at home.
> There was no distance between students and teachers.
> I have kept in contact with some of the students. . . .

Age changes in relating to students

Students are blamed for making the job more difficult as
teachers grow older. One might say that students actively
engage in age-grading teachers. When a teacher becomes
informal with students, they are apt to question her about her
age. Very significantly, this is associated with questions about
why she hasn't married. A fifty-year-old unmarried teacher
commented:

> 40s: They are intensely interested in their teacher's age. If
> they could ask me one question and find out the facts,
> I suppose the first question that they would ask me is
> why I haven't married, and the second question would
> be, 'How old are you?' Those are the two questions in
> which they are the most interested. They would not
> ask me anything about history; they would not ask
> whether I could cook or sew or if I make my own
> clothes or anything else, but 'How old are you?' and

115

'Why haven't you married?' I know because they ask me all the time.

In this instance, the teacher showed concern because students asked about the least presentable aspects of her personal identity – the old-maid features.

Student interest in the age of teachers is, apparently, one of the important factors in teacher sensitivity about age. This sensitivity was evident throughout the interviewing – as well as at the point when the interviewer attempted to secure the teacher's age. In the following quotation, a married teacher, in her early thirties, explicitly attributed this sensitivity to student interest.

I: Why are teachers so sensitive about their ages?
52m: I don't know exactly, but they certainly are. I think it is partly because the kids are concerned about it. I have begun to notice it about myself, being sensitive that is. I have forced myself to tell them my age when they ask. I catch myself dodging and then grit my teeth and tell them. I have often wondered how they look on me. I think they consider me ages older than they are. I never had that feeling when I was teaching before, but I do now. I don't know how they show it, partly in the distance they keep and partly in other ways. I was bothered about this when I first went to that school, because I thought I was losing the intimate friendly relations I had had with students before.

This quotation rather neatly packages and illustrates a number of features of the student role in age-grading teachers. It is noteworthy that all teachers, married or unmarried, are aware of a change in their relationship to students. It is not merely a matter of students regarding the teacher as an 'old maid' – it is more general than this. It is a matter of loss by the teacher of some kind of intimate, friendly contact with students, a matter of increased distance and formality. Stu-

116

dents seem to age-grade teacher by age-distancing teachers away from them.

Teachers in their thirties were, among respondents, the most self-conscious and concerned about age-propelled changes in their relationships with students. At thirty-six years of age, 13s seemed to be reflecting intensely on this problem.

> 13s: I always start my youngsters out in the fall by saying they can call me anything they want as long as I don't hear it. I sometimes wonder how youngsters, how they actually picture me.
>
> I do wonder about that, if I seem old to them, or just how they feel about my age. Every once in a while they ask me how old I am.

The change in student-teacher relations is not necessarily a one-way process. Another teacher in her thirties, 38s, expressed concern about becoming mechanical and 'routinized' in her work.

> 38s: I look back when I first started teaching. I think maybe that was the happiest, because it was a new experience and I just went into it with everything. I think sometimes as we grow older we get careless and do things sort of mechanical. I think it makes your entire outlook different, and I would say maybe it happens around thirty-five years of age.

Teachers in the late forties and fifties also showed concern about aging but placed less emphasis on the loss of intimate, informal contacts with students and more emphasis on declining physical vigor.

> 4s: I said to one of the other teachers just the other day – we both try very hard to push our shorthand students just as fast as they will be pushed and to do that we have to work awful hard – so I told her the other day I wondered if ten years from now we could do this. She said she wondered too.

On the whole, middle-aged teachers – in comparison with teachers in their thirties – seemed more secure and relaxed, less worried about their teaching, and considerably more subject to routinism. Apparently, in the course of becoming a parent-like authority figure, many teachers found that discipline problems decreased.

> I: How do you think your life has changed in the last ten years?
>
> 17s: Well, I don't worry like I did. I'm more bored than I used to be. I don't worry as much. I used to come home and teach all night. One of the happiest things that has happened is that I can come home and forget my work. But I don't have the enthusiasm that I used to have, and I don't have the disciplining problems. I am about as peaceful now as I ever was.

There were some indications that this feeling of increased security and relaxation also included greater autonomy relative to the administration. While young teachers were dependent on and sensitive about principals because of desire for acceptance in the system, and most elderly teachers seem to cling to principals because of fear of change, some middle-aged teachers felt that they had become more indifferent and less vulnerable.

> I: You said you thought you had gotten over some things. What do you think you have gotten over?
>
> 20s: Well, I think I am less inclined to worry about other people's opinions of me than I was then. I remember when I began teaching, I had a fear of the principal and what he thought of me. Now I don't particularly care what he thinks. I would rather he liked me, but if he doesn't like me we can still carry on because it doesn't bother me a bit. Then, if I did something, I would wonder, 'Now what is he going to think about that?' Now it is, 'What am I going to think about it?' I think that I am very much less sensitive to other people than I used to be. Sometimes I am kind of sorry

118

I do this in my work because sometimes it doesn't turn out. I mean I get a little indifferent and easy-going.

. . .

In general, there was among teachers in the late forties and fifties considerable concern about the long stretch ahead, the possibility of the burden becoming heavier, of interests declining, and of the distance between teacher and student increasing. Respondent 40s, fifty years of age, drew a distinction between being the age of the students' parents and being the age of their grandparents.

40s: I have a theory about this matter of teaching that I probably shouldn't state. I think that teachers retire too late in life. I think we should have voluntary retirement at fifty-five, put it on the basis of thirty years of experience if you wish, but I think fifty-five is the time to retire with compulsory at sixty. I feel that as long as I am the age of the students' parents, I should be their teacher, but when I am the age of their grandparents, I should step aside.

I: Do you think that the student himself reacts differently to an older teacher?

40s: I think that a young teacher may lack in scholarship, but she has enthusiasm, and young people respond to youth. If a teacher is young and pretty, they like her, and it is easier for them to learn. . . . I think that our high school students assume that we are much older than we are. Being with young people does not make one young. There are times when being with them makes a greater gulf in ages really come true.

Similar views were expressed by a sixty-year-old teacher who advocated a retirement age at fifty-five although she was herself past that age.

35m: I don't think that I have the kind of influence that some teachers have. Part of it may be because I'm growing older. I think there is no doubt about it; it is

119

difficult for a teacher to do effective teaching as she grows older.

. . .

Most mature teachers did not explicitly spell out the possibility – so threatening to self-esteem – that they might not get the same response from students that younger teachers get. Yet, they seemed to be saying the same thing implicitly. When asked about the best teaching period, either for themselves or for teachers in general, they generally agreed that the early years were better, complained about the cumulative burden of teaching, and wished for earlier and better retirement arrangements. . . .

The mature teacher's refrain – very general among those interviewed for this study – was one of frustration and helplessness, which alluded to administrative policies and the public attitude toward teachers, but which tended to be focused on students 'getting worse every year'. Teachers were not certain if this was due to their own aging or if it was involved with broad changes among students. . . .

31w, a widow with grown children of her own, is an example of a teacher who concentrated on the second theme, placing blame on the times, the pace, and direction of civilization, on mothers for working and not looking after their children, and, to some extent, on the school system for lowering standards.

> 31w: The discipline problems are getting worse every year. That is true all over the country – not just here. I have a friend out in California who wrote me that she is so anxious for vacation this year because the discipline problems have been so bad.
>
> I: Why is this?
>
> 31w: Why? Because we are in an age of moral decadence. It is just part of the pattern everywhere in this country, in every line of work. It is a matter of getting by with what you can. It has permeated the whole country from top to bottom. The parents don't have the control over the children that they used to have. It is

just our kind of civilization. The mothers aren't in the home much; they work or go out.

I remember when my children were young; they had a good time, but they didn't have to have a car of their own. They didn't do all the frantic rushing around and getting into trouble. . . . I don't know what anyone wants to be a teacher for. Not unless you feel the urge very strongly and wouldn't be happy doing anything else. I certainly wouldn't advise it for the money. And, I think, teaching is harder than it used to be.

I really wouldn't want to give advice to a young teacher. In my own field they have lowered the standards to such an extent. We just hit the high places. The whole trend has been to cater to those of lower abilities. We cheat young people who are superior. I often wonder if any of them are going into teaching. If they are, then are we giving them the right foundations?

I always try to have them read some Shakespeare. We used to give them *As You Like It* or some other light comedy when they were freshmen and then *Julius Caesar* when they were sophomores or juniors. Now, with my sophomores and juniors, I still have them read *Julius Caesar*. Most of them, a lot of them, have never heard of Shakespeare before. It is just amazing how little they know. And their grammar when they are sophomores and juniors!

It should be noted that this statement from 31w contrasts markedly with her statement on experiences as a young teacher in a small-town school: 'I had a wonderful time. . . . The pupils were just about as old as we were. We dated and had a wonderful time.' It is reasonable to suppose that her bitterness about the current generation of children derives at least as much from lack of student interest in a woman of sixty-five as it does from lack of interest in the subject matter. . . .

Middle-aged teachers generally viewed themselves as the strong, stable backbone of the teaching staff. This is partially generational in the sense that they view themselves as the 'hard knock' generation, the group that fought a difficult mobility route in an era when teachers were in surplus and requirements were raised higher and higher. To some degree, it is also age graded in the pure sense: middle-aged teachers feel they bear the heaviest load because young teachers are inexperienced, and more important, uncommitted; old teachers tend to withdraw from auxiliary responsibilities.

5s: Well, I think we're more serious about our work, maybe more concerned about doing a good job and we've been doing it so long that we know what it is that we're going to finish. So many of the young people stay in only two or three years before they get married, and I don't think they are quite as interested in the work outside the classroom as the teachers who have been doing it a good while and plan to finish out their career in teaching. The middle-aged group, I believe, is the one that has the biggest burden of the load. The older ones are given fewer and fewer extra responsibilities and the younger ones necessarily, because of lack of experience, are given a much lighter load – that's why I believe the main burden rests with the middle-aged group.

Age and generational differences in extra-curricular activities

Middle-aged persons seem to carry the largest proportion of the load in most work organizations and voluntary organizations in our society. In schools, the central function of teaching is divided among all teachers, but the auxiliary functions, such as extra-curricular school activities and the affairs of professional associations, seem to fall heavily on the middle-aged. This can be viewed as resulting from processes occurring on two levels – the organizational setting and the personal career. The middle-aged teacher is thought to be most available. In the schools, as in most organizations, this is a result of many acquaintances and greater familiarity with program. With time, it comes to be assumed that the teacher is satisfactorily performing the central teaching function, that she is generally reliable, that she can afford the time for and can be trusted with other functions.

In addition to organizational factors, critical early changes in the teacher's career seem to have the effect of making middle-aged teachers susceptible and responsive to auxiliary responsibilities. As contacts with students become more formal and less intimate, and as spinsterhood comes to be accepted, the teacher becomes more deeply committed to the teaching career, more professional, more thoroughly colleague-oriented. In interteacher relationships, this tends to separate members and creates a strong tendency to reject young teachers as not committed, not legitimate full members.

This lack of acceptance is seen in several areas, among them the professional association. Teachers' organizations in the city studied can be divided into two types. There are (1) professional associations organized within the 'cooperative council' or affiliated with the state education association and the NEA; and (2) two unionlike interest-group organizations from which administrators are excluded. The NEA affiliate (often called the 'company union' by teacher members) offers membership to any teacher in the school system. However, judging from the age of sample teachers who are now active, and from comments about others who are active, it appears that members who hold the most responsibilities are middle-aged, and those who hold offices tend toward being late middle-aged.

In the case of the two interest-group organizations, the middle-aged also carry the main burden of responsibility. These, however, make an important addition to the age-grading pattern. Although neither organization has succeeded in recruiting more than a minority of teachers, and although they compete with one another for membership and with the NEA affiliate for loyalties of members, they do not consider young teachers to be desirable additions.

4s: A lot of young people that come into the system have no idea of feelings. They don't care whether you have retirement or whether you have a pension, or what is going to happen ten or fifteen years from now; they are just interested in what's right now and that's all. For that individual, the union, you see, is of no value to them. With your young people you get a lot of them with that feeling.

In the AFT, we prefer to hold back a bit to see what they are going to be and then ask them. We invite them to join and then they are voted in. In the other organizations, all they have to do is just pay a fee and then go in. While we want new members, we prefer to see what they are going to be like before we take them in.

I: You said that you wanted to wait and see what kind of people they were. What kind are you looking for?

4s: We are interested in two things in particular, I would say, and one is that we want someone that is interested in teaching and in making teaching a profession and the teaching career a better career and is also interested in having a better school and better situation for the students, instead of just for themselves.

Respondent 4s, forty-eight years of age, is active in a number of commerce-teacher activities as well as being a leader in the American Federation of Teachers. While such functions may be viewed as auxiliary to classroom teaching, they seem to be vital to the collective solidarity of the colleague group and perhaps also vital in providing career-committed middle-aged teachers with leadership opportunities to compensate, in part, for other career ceilings. The fact that the younger generation of teachers is not turning out to be led seems to be responsible for some of the resentment of middle-aged teachers toward them.

16s: They're not dedicated to their work at all. They're not going to do anything extra – activities or professional organizations or anything else. When the bell rings, they check out – school's out. Now, we were brought up to feel that we were getting a lot out of it because we were putting a lot into it. I don't think they feel that way at all. It's just a job to them. I feel that they don't have the same devotion to the teaching profession that we have.

Like the middle-aged, older teachers are concerned about young teachers' lack of commitment and dedication, but they also are greatly concerned about the younger generation's preparation for teaching and methods of teaching. Many older teachers, because they hold firmly to traditional education, feel bitter and abandoned. Young teachers, along with students and society at large, have moved away from the cherished, and now somewhat sanctified, values of their youth.

I: How do you think your generation of teachers compares with the younger generation of teachers?

48s: There is a great deal of difference. . . . I hate to sit in judgment on others, but I don't think they have been held to the standards themselves, these teachers who have been coming out of the schools now, not the standards that we were held to. I have teachers coming from the teachers' college to do practice teaching. I can see that they haven't been held to do things just so, or maybe they are products of the war too. They aren't good spellers; they can't go to the board and write out a sentence for the youngsters and spell correctly. And some of the colleges are saying, 'What if they can't spell, some of the smartest people can't spell'. Well, I say that if they can't, they had better learn, and things like that, you know – being held to correctness. I just thank teachers who did so much to wake me up. I don't know whether we will ever get back to that standard or not. I don't know.

All of this reflects the identification that old teachers have made, through the years, with the field of education and with the teaching profession. These are people who have long been committed and who, by virtue of this and of energy expended,

125

have a large investment in the profession. In the course of time, sacred qualities are attached to the conditions and procedures of the school, the forms of organization and interaction in the work setting, and the model of teacher and teacher career. . . .

For the old unmarried teacher, the recent acceptance of marriage as a part of the teacher's career line is the most radical change of all. Perhaps, because of an awareness (threatening to self-esteem) that devotion to the teaching profession has had the effect of closing out full womanhood experiences, the young teacher's interest in marriage receives special attention. In the interviewing, it appeared that the greater the affective pitch of the criticism of young teachers, the more likely it was to include reference to the young unmarried teacher's interests in dating or to the young married teacher's interests in husband and family.

> 9s: Our experience in the past has been unmarried girls come into the profession, and now we have the married girls coming in. It has just been since World War II. Before that, you forfeited your position. I think that it isn't probably a question of preparation or ability or anything like that we feel differently, but you know yourself that your interest is divided if you have a home, a husband, and teach. If you aren't married, you are perfectly free to go to all the meetings and attend them and join the different school organizations. There is that difference in the girls with the home and husband to think about and her having to curtail things she does outside of the schoolroom because of that and the teacher who is free to do and go and take part. The married girl is not so apt to take part and belong to the organizations, those professional things that go along with teaching.

The advent of young married teachers threatens to reverse the process of professionalism that represents the teacher's identification with the occupational group. The acceptance of

126

married women as teachers has the effect of diminishing the worth of the old unmarried teacher's more complete commitment and of calling into question the wisdom of her earlier decisions.

The interview with 9s is unusually revealing. Having voiced such extreme objections to married teachers, later in the interview she gives an unusually blunt statement of her own regrets about not having married.

> I: If you had your life to live over, is there anything you would have done differently?
>
> 9s: I probably would have gotten married.
>
> . . .

Among the teachers in the sample, one had married for the first time at the age of fifty-five. Even in this case (although she did marry and although she was excited about and apparently gained prestige and self-esteem through marriage), the description of preparing for marriage suggests that teaching remained primary in her life.

> 35m: You see, I've only been married five years. I wasn't young when I got married. Before I got married, I consulted Mr —— he's in charge of personnel downtown – and I consulted my minister and doctor. Mr —— said, 'There'll be a position for you as long as you want to teach'. He said that the trouble with so many older teachers is that they have no outside interests. He said that it was nice to know that I would have outside interests and that I would be a better teacher for it.

The fact that marriage should be defined as an outside interest, by both teacher and personnel director, may be viewed as symbolic of the marriagelike quality of the mature teacher's commitment to the occupation – a commitment that sets her apart from young teachers and that sets the tone of inter-teacher relationships along an age-generation axis.

127

Sponsorship, intergenerational conflict, and age-graded cliques

In portions of the interviews dealing with career experiences, old teachers loomed important, and often forbidding, in young teachers' experiences in the city system. Mature colleagues seem to have been the most influential of all agents in the incoming teacher's world. In some cases this was in the form of guidance and sponsorship, but in most cases it involved ignoring, hazing, or blocking the newcomer.

These forms of interage relationships among teachers are not confined to the young teacher's first year. In a system staffed with large numbers of mature single women, teachers may be considered young for some time – until they reach the late thirties or early forties. It appears that a young teacher is most likely to continue to be viewed as young and in need of help if she accepts initial guidance and sponsorship from mature teachers.

I: How did you feel the first year you were there?

37s: I wouldn't be a very good example of that in general reactions because one of the teachers out there had known me since I was six. . . . Of course, she gave me a wonderful send-off with the principal, and they all sort of hovered around me as if I were about ready to fall apart. They didn't think I was quite bright I guess. And they still act that way. It is kind of hard for them to realize that I am grown up and quite capable, so I just listen to them and then go my own way.

Respondent 37s is now thirty-six years of age and has been teaching at the school for six years. When she entered the school, at the age of thirty, she would not have been considered young in most adult circles. Her view of herself as not a 'good example' seems to imply that being ignored by mature teachers or having conflicts with them is normal in the high school. At the conclusion of the passage she intimates that if she did not accept this relationship, she might be faced with alienation.

128

Elsewhere in the interview, she indicates that she is the youngest teacher in the school.

It happens that one of 37s's motherly colleagues is 35m, an older teacher who was also interviewed in the study.

> 35m: When she (37s) first came here – we are in the same department – she wanted to know about things, and I told her I would be glad to help her. She said she was concerned about taking too much of my time, but I told her that I was just passing on what was passed on to me. She wanted the children to have confidence in her, and she thought it would help if they were on the same pages I was.

In her approach to young colleagues, as in her approach to students, 35m functions as a mother counselor. In this, she is drawing from her own experience – her career being the most sponsor-laden among those of teachers interviewed. A high school principal influenced her to enter teaching, a small-town banker financed her education, a state teachers college superintendent intervened to get her a job and, in the city system, she developed a close mother-daughter relationship with an older teacher.

> 35m: She was a teacher when I was there and became principal after I left – has remained a very dear friend of mine all these years. She died this year, died in April. She was eighty years old. That was just after they had had a surprise party on her eightieth birthday. You may have read about it in the paper.
>
> She inspired so many people! I had good training there under her when I first came here to teach. She was teaching the seventh grade then.
>
> I: How did she help you?
>
> 35m: Well, that is pretty hard to say. She was just very fine and sincere, well-liked. She was a very good friend of mine. I knew she was a very good friend of mine.

She was quiet, unassuming, real, scholarly, just about everything that a teacher should be. Four years after I came here my mother died. She stepped right in then. She was a lot like my mother. She served as auntie and mother to me.

. . .

Perhaps because of a need on the part of old people to maintain contact with the growing-developing younger generation, unmarried old teachers seek to extend their services as mothers or aunts to young teachers. Young teachers seem to reject such offers unless unusually immature or lonely. The cumulative wounds of such rejections may result in rigid antagonism among old teachers and a collective intergenerational hostility.

In any case, among teachers as a whole, intragenerational ties seem much stronger than intergenerational ties. In most descriptions of early experiences in the city system, there were accounts of uncomfortable situations with mature teachers. These extended all the way from concern about being ignored, or 'cold shouldered', to open conflict. It seems to be partly because of such difficulties that young teachers form into generational cliques.

Most of the cases of conflict reported in the interviews involved an older and a young teacher in a situation carrying implications that, in standing up for her rights, the young teacher was fighting a cause for her set – while the old teacher was a leader of 'old guardism' in the school.

42s: Well, the school was very crowded the first year I was there. Since I was new I had to change rooms and sort of fit in where no one else was using space. There was one older teacher who was quite a character. She was the one who gave us the most trouble. There were about eight of us who were the same age as I was. She used to call us 'the brats'. Let's see, I was twenty-three then. But we were young enough so that the janitor would stop us to prevent us from going places where the students weren't supposed to go. Anyway, I never really got along there until one time I stood up to this older teacher and after that she had respect for me.

One of the rooms I had was next to the physics lab and it just wasn't large enough for my class. Finally I found out that the reason I had the small inconvenient room was because the older teacher was using one down the hall, and had insisted on having it. And that it was purely for her personal convenience; in fact, the room was vacant sometimes and I wasn't assigned to it.

So finally I went to the vice-principal and he supported the older teacher. He said that this was being done out of respect for the older teacher. I told him that I thought things might be arranged in such a way as to suit the needs of the students for space.

So finally this had gone so far and so many people were buzzing around about it and everything that I went to the superintendent and he backed me up. I had risked offending two persons – the vice-principal and the older teacher. But after that the older teachers were quite nice to me and I never had any more trouble. Apparently it was necessary to do something like that in order to gain their respect.

A mathematics teacher, 42s, now fifty-three years of age, is a spunky, individualistic person who led one of the union-type teachers associations in a successful drive for salary increases. It appears that such a person, while still young, may gain a position of relative equality with mature teachers. Young teachers who accept motherly guidance are treated as young and immature for some time. . . .

The most serious intergenerational conflict was reported by a young married journalism teacher who, apparently without being aware of it, committed an act that old teachers in the school interpreted as evidence of great disrespect for the life investment of mature teachers.

52m: But something did happen this year. This year a teacher who had retired died. She had been quite friendly to me. I didn't know her well; I didn't know any of them well. But we put a brief obituary in the paper about her death. We might have done more with it but the students who were writing it didn't know her. It was a regular obituary item.

Well, at lunch one of the older teachers, the so-called head of the English department, landed on me. She was just simply furious about this. She was very overwrought about the whole thing.

And the thing that seemed to bother her most was that we had printed her age. This teacher that died was seventy-one, respectable age to die, really. I didn't know whether they thought that her age should not have been disclosed because she was too young to die or too old to have just been retired or what. The kids had gotten her age from an obituary in the local newspaper. . . . Well that started things off. There was an undercurrent all through the school. I'm sure that each of these older teachers read this as her own obituary. They thought, 'When I am dead and gone, after serving all these years, is this all the recognition I will get?' . . .

There is a group of older teachers out there that we call the twenty-seven year club. They are always talking about their twenty-seven years of service to the high school. Most of them, of course, lined up with this older teacher who had started it. Some of them mentioned their indignation in their classes. I know that one in particular did it.

And the principal is halfway scared of her. Eventually he showed up with an editorial she had written in praise of this teacher that had died. He asked me to print it. I just told him that this had gone too far, and all over nothing; that I would quit before I printed it. And I really would have. I would have been glad to have printed it if she had come around quietly after seeing the obituary and said that she wanted to write an editorial for the next issue. . . .

Well, this thing over the obituary just dragged on and on. My lunch hour was the same as this older teacher that caused all the trouble, or started it. I would go down to lunch and grit my teeth and eat at the same table with her. Neither of us were going to back down on that. But it was kind of nerve-racking. And not very good on the digestion. We never spoke to each other but we always ate at the same table. It was all so silly. In the first place, we print the paper more for the kids than for the faculty. And the kids didn't demand a long, flowery editorial.

This story is an extreme example of intergenerational conflict. It is an incident that involves a threat to the service and sacrifice-based recognition claims of old teachers and one that demonstrates their manner of reacting toward those who threaten such claims.

Note

1 In the quotations given, 'I' stands for the interviewer; respondents are identified with a number and letter indicating marital status – 's' refers to single teachers, 'm' to married, 'w' to widowed.

6

'Keeping 'em quiet': the significance of noise for the practical activity of teaching

Martyn Denscombe

Originally published in P. Woods (ed.) (1980) *Teacher Strategies*, pp. 61–83. London: Croom Helm.

*   *   *

Teachers do not regard themselves as free agents in the classroom. They experience a number of constraints on their activity which influence their aims and ambitions and, as Leacock (1969, p. 202) has observed:

> Teachers cannot simply interact with the children in their classrooms according to their desires and personal style. Instead their behaviour often takes on characteristics beyond their immediate aims or intents. They must adapt their style, not only to the children but to the institution, to the principal's requirements, to the other teachers' attitudes, and to the standards according to which they will be evaluated.

Research in two London comprehensive schools[1] served to affirm the point. The staff clearly distinguished between those things they would like to do and those which the real situation

134

permitted, and regularly juxtaposed the 'real' with the 'ideal' circumstances of the classroom. They argued that the circumstances in which they operated were far from ideal and that, since the chances of changing the situation were remote, they were obliged to adopt approaches which, though not regarded as desirable under ideal circumstances, reflected what was possible in 'reality'. As the head of music at one of the schools put it:

> Perhaps if I found myself in ideal conditions – which one never expects – I mean, you'd be living in cuckoo-land . . . you'd never get anything done. So, I tend to get round to doing what I *can* do with what I've got, as it were.

The notion of ideal circumstances had little relevance for the practice of teaching because teachers neither expected it nor used it as a cornerstone for their approach to teaching. More significant for teaching were the uncherished realities of classroom life which guided and limited what they regarded as the appropriate forms of activity. Noise was one such limitation. It constituted a practical constraint on teacher activity which, whilst acknowledged by teachers, has remained largely neglected by sociologists.[2]

To argue that noise is a problem for classroom teachers is hardly to propose a novel or controversial point. Quite the contrary, for the vast majority of teachers it will be received more as a truism than any astounding insight into the nature of teaching. Competent teachers already know that noise poses a problem for their routine activity and adopt courses of action designed to keep noise within what they regard as acceptable limits.[3]

In observing this state of affairs, however, we are drawn to the question of why noise should be regarded in such an adverse light and why efforts to 'keep 'em quiet' should be so central to the routine activity of teachers. The answer might seem simple. Noise interferes with instruction by teachers and concentration by pupils and therefore hinders the learning process. This explanation certainly offers an account of the problem with which most teachers would concur, and owes something to the belief that quiet orderliness in the classroom is a prerequisite for learning and that a fundamental feature of the teachers' routine task is to provide the appropriate conditions for learning. It is, however, a partial account of the problem of noise and does not provide the whole answer. Careful examination of the situation of teaching reveals that 'keeping 'em quiet' is a strategy which derives not only from pedagogic assumptions about a learning context, but also arises as a method of protecting teachers from the connotations which accompany noise in classrooms. Working within a community of teaching colleagues, there are shared assumptions about the meaning of noise in classrooms which can foster a concern to 'keep 'em quiet' for reasons analytically distinct from the pedagogic preferences of individual teachers. In particular, noise emanating from classrooms carries with it connotations of a lack of control in the classroom and a certain lack of competence on the part of the teacher in charge, and this informally shared meaning of noise, it will be argued, underlies the strategy of 'keeping 'em quiet' as a means for protecting and promoting the impression of competence within a community of teachers; it obviates the possibility that noise emanating from the classroom be treated as evidence of lack of control in the classroom.

This potential connotation of noise is predicated by the existence of a close classroom organization in the school, and special attention is given in the analysis to closed classrooms as 'settings' (Goffman, 1971) which teachers need to take into account when contemplating action.[4] Because this analysis is concerned with secondary education, and because closed classrooms are the prevalent form of organization at this level, closed classrooms constitute a 'normal' setting within which teaching occurs, even though significant alternatives exist at other levels (e.g. open-plan primary classrooms) and, to a lesser extent, within the secondary level itself (e.g. games lessons).

Closed classroom organization provides a formally established environment which fosters the concern for 'keeping 'em quiet'. With its assumptions of 'privacy' and the individual responsibility of the subject teacher for control of the classroom, it has an inherent tendency to separate teachers from one another and severely restrict each teacher's knowledge about what is going on behind the closed doors of their colleagues' rooms. It means they have to rely on meagre and informal sources of information in order to deduce the nature of events in other classrooms. The noise is one such source of 'publicly available information'. One aspect of the *social* significance of noise therefore, rests in its status as 'evidence' about a state of affairs in closed classrooms – specifically the ability of the teacher to achieve control of the class and the consequent implications of this for their competence as teachers. 'Keeping 'em quiet', as a strategy, aims to protect the teacher from the accusations of incompetence which potentially accompany noise emanating from the classroom.

By offering a brief analysis of noise as a social rather than eductional problem, we may contribute to the emerging data on the reality of the classroom situation as *experienced by teachers* and thus facilitate the kind of critical examination which is necessary both for constructive teaching training programmes and for the successful implementation of educational innovations. Teachers, after all, stand at the interface between educational theory and the pupils' learning experience and an understanding of the teachers' experience of the situation is vital for the prospects of successful educational innovation.

The problem of noise

Jackson, in his perceptive account of the social organization of classrooms (1968, p. 105), has observed that 'Classrooms, by and large, are relatively quiet places and it is part of the teacher's job to keep them that way.' It follows that, in a general sense, where noise occurs it confronts the teacher as an aberration of proper classroom circumstances and provides the teacher with a problem to be dealt with and remedied.

There are, in fact, a number of ways in which noise poses a problem for teachers, each having a particular significance and warranting attention in its own right. Teachers might attempt to minimize levels of noise in the classroom, for instance, simply because they find noise unpleasant. In a society where noise is easily associated with aggression, we should not be surprised if quiet classrooms are valued in their own right – as a pleasant setting for teaching rather than a necessary prerequisite for the learning process.[5] And attempts to control noise might also stem from the desire to avoid the fatiguing effect of working with constant high levels of noise. Teachers, after all, are employees who suffer the same ill-effects of being subject to noise over a period of time as those in other industries, and by actively seeking a quiet environment they can reduce one of the many tiring aspects of their job.

Such considerations significantly affect the attitude of teachers toward noise in the classroom and provide a predisposition to control noise which stems from the personal preferences of the teacher and/or cultural factors beyond the realm of the school. Treated in this manner, however, attention is drawn to noise as a problem in its own right with analysis subsequently being directed to either the psycho-physiological effects of noise or the wider cultural genesis of the significance of noise. In either case, teacher activity designed to control noise is seen to stem from a teacher understanding of the situation in which the problem *is* noise, rather than what noise *implies* in the social situation of the school. If teachers are concerned to control noise for these reasons, it is because they have a basic preference for quiet settings and thus treat the control of noise as an end in itself rather than as a strategy to avert any wider implications which accompany noise in classrooms.

One crucial feature of the problem of noise, however, is precisely that it has implications within a community of teachers (and generated within the school situation) which provide an analytically distinct source of teacher predisposition to control noise in the classroom. Quite apart from individual levels of tolerance or personal feelings about noise, teachers' attitudes toward noise in the classroom are influenced by their existence in the social situation of the school and the social pressures brought to bear as a direct result of working in the school environment.

At Ashton, the music staff were acutely aware of the issues involved. As the Head of Music indicated during an interview, music was particularly susceptible to problems of noise because, to a greater extent than other subjects, its instruction relied on listening and practical work. The intricacies of sound involved in the subject increased its sensitivity to interference by noise and on occasion caused severe difficulties. As she went on to say:

> We haven't any real music facilities here, you know, architecturally-wise.
>
> Two of us, you know, including myself, are working in a canteen . . .
>
> And it's the same at the lower school where the teacher there also works in a canteen. And it's even worse there because the canteen's smaller, therefore you've got all the noise of the dining room staff clanking and clinking. And you have P.E. and drama lessons in the hall which adjoins the canteens – so the noise problem is phenomenal.
>
> If you're trying to do music – which is essentially aural . . . even if you're playing an instrument you're listening all the time to what you're playing and seeing if you're in tune, is it making some sort of sense . . . and it's very difficult under those sort of conditions. So much so that that's why I've got a member of staff now leaving after one term's work. She can't stand it. She can't cope with the situation. And we've had six music teachers since I came here in three years in that building, and it's for that reason . . . because the conditions are so bad that the teachers have found that . . . that it's an impossible situation.

Though such subjects were specially prone to interference by noise impinging from external sources, other subjects were not immune. The Head of Music went on to recall, with some irony, how a move away from the canteen had proved impractical because the noise *generated* in music lessons interfered with lessons in adjacent classrooms.

We had a mobile hut built in the grounds, very close to the main building. And, everyone pointed out that the mobile hut ... it'd be a good idea to put it right away, far away from the building, so if music was going on it wouldn't disturb five classrooms – three lower and two upstairs – with the noise of instruments and singing and pianos and record players. But the Brent Borough refused because that meant the expense of building a concrete path leading to the hut, whereas if they placed it at the side of the main building the path was already there.

And in the summer, because there's so much glass and everybody wants to open the windows, I mean, the situation's impossible. They begged me not to teach music as such ... could I just talk to them. I mean this was the approach. I mean it is very, very difficult. And then the noise was so much there that then we were taken out of the hut and put back in the canteen. For a while, you see, we had a respite, you see, from the canteen, but we've been put back again because one music class was hitting five classrooms the way it was positioned ... as I say, three there and two upstairs. So it's really hell.

Interference by noise from adjacent classrooms, indeed, appeared to be a general problem experienced by teachers and one which existed, in this sense, irrespective of the type of noise or its causes. Problems could arise as much from Mozart as 'messers', as a languages teacher at Beechgrove indicated when arguing that he 'suffered' from the audio-visual aids employed in an adjacent room:

I'm not saying (the other teacher) is wrong to use tapes and so on ... er, in fact they're good, I think. But it doesn't help me. Sometimes you can't hear yourself think and ... er, it's

140

very difficult to teach the kids when everyone can hear what's going on next door.

Noise from outside the classroom was seen to hinder the learning process and interfere with the progress of instruction by interrupting pupils' concentration on work, and thus it constituted an aspect of the problem of noise which was specific to the situation of teaching, rather than a product of personal preference or predisposition. Yet, as the situation of music at Ashton served to illustrate, such a concern with the effects of noise on instruction was double-sided. Operating in settings which were not soundproofed, teachers were aware that their classes were far from isolated in terms of noise and that, as the Head of Music had noted, noise created within their own classroom would be audible to colleagues and could interfere with colleagues' lessons. The problem of noise, consequently, was not just one of interference from outside, but also entailed a concern by teachers to prevent noise in their own class from affecting adjacent rooms. Acknowledging that they occasionally suffered the adverse effects of noise created in colleagues' classrooms, it appeared that teachers sought to prevent the possibility that they would be responsible for a similar misdemeanour.

During research at Ashton and Beechgrove this practical concern became evident in teachers' accounts of their arrangement of desks in the classroom.[6] In effect, teachers demonstrated an awareness that shrewd manipulation of seating arrangements could have advantages in terms of both learning and control:

> I had a class and they were hell ... couldn't do anything with them. They were real sods ... girls, all girls ... and they really hated my guts. And there was no way I could try and get them to stop talking, and somebody worked out ... worked out this brilliant idea.
>
> And it was a needlework room I took them in, and set all the chairs ... only about 20 or them ... all the chairs in a line. It was a rotten thing to do. And each chair slightly separate from the next, but in a line. And do you know, it

worked! . . . 'Cos they were cut off from each other, you
know.   (English Teacher: Beechgrove)

Whether or not they took advantage of the possibility to
rearrange desks, however, depended not only on the perceived
pedagogic advantages but also on the practical implications of
any such move.[7] The time involved in rearranging desks, for
instance, proved largely prohibitive for those staff who did not
operate in their own classroom and who needed to alter the
setting at the start of the lesson and revert to the original
arrangement at the finish, and noise generated by such
manoeuvres simply served to exacerbate the problem and
provide a formidable deterrent to such classroom innovations.
The classroom furniture at Ashton and Beechgrove was heavy
and wooden and, with no carpeting on the floors, the prospect
of desk rearrangement unaccompanied by high levels of noise
was remote. Given the proximity of classrooms and the lack of
soundproofing between them, teachers recognized that desk
rearrangement would almost certainly entail levels of noise
which would impinge on, and interfere with, lessons going on
in adjacent rooms and had to weigh this effect against the
anticipated benefits for their own classroom situation.

For practical purposes, that is, teachers did not regard
themselves free to operate according to their personal preference *despite the setting of the closed classroom*. Although they had
individual responsibility for the classroom they were not
entirely freed from the influence of external agencies and, in
their conduct of the lesson, they exhibited a concern to prevent
noise emanating from their classroom. This concern subsequently influenced their approach to classroom teaching by
inhibiting methods that generated noise. And, although the
autonomy afforded by closed classrooms meant that teachers
were ostensibly free to experiment and innovate according to
their individual wishes, it was evident that they took into
consideration the level of noise that would accompany any such
innovation and that where they anticipated high levels of noise
they were reticent to use the approach even where they
recognized potential pedagogic advantages.

142

Now, to indicate that noise is a problem for teachers because it interferes with the progress of lessons and that teachers generally make efforts to prevent noise in their classrooms from disturbing other lessons may appear to be banal. It tells teachers nothing they do not already know. It does, however, present the problem of noise as an educational issue and, when considering the problem of noise for the practical activity of teaching, it is worthy of note that the teachers' concern with noise was significantly affected by their appraisal of the impact of noise on the ability of pupils to concentrate on work. The analysis which follows is not intended to denigrate or deny this aspect of the problem but to offer an analytically distinct source of the problem of noise and a separate, if complementary, reason for 'keeping 'em quiet'.

It should also be noted that one common source of interference by noise was adjacent classrooms and that the 'educationist' problem of noise, as presented so far, serves to draw attention to the commonplace physical and organizational environment from which the problem arose – that of the 'closed classroom'. In their accounts of the problem, it was taken for granted by the staff that teaching generally occurred in such situations.

The closed classroom

The closed classroom is characteristic of conventional secondary schooling. It is the physical setting in which the vast majority of school teaching occurs and typically entails self-contained units, rectangular in shape, separated from others by walls and corridors, and containing one teacher with a number of pupils. It is a setting with which most teachers and pupils are familiar.

Familiarity, however, can dull the senses to the particular effects of such arrangements and the setting can become so taken for granted and commonplace that it comes to be regarded as a natural and inevitable feature of the organization of schooling. Though such a belief may be reasonable for the

143

staff and pupils who operate in them, for whom the prospects of changing the situation are remote, it should be recognized that closed classrooms have not always been the norm, and that they entail specific socially approved assumptions about curricular and pedagogic arrangements (Bernstein, 1971; Young, 1971). They reflect and reinforce assumptions about subject boundaries and the responsibility of individual teachers.[8]

The extent to which closed classrooms reflect and reinforce the individual responsibility of the teacher has been the subject of considerable research. Specifically, closed classrooms have been seen as a 'sanctuary' against the interference of administrators, parents and colleagues in matters concerning the classroom (e.g. Anderson, 1968; Lortie, 1964, 1969) and as a 'structural looseness' (Bidwell, 1965) in the bureaucratic organization of the school which enhances teacher aspirations to professional autonomy. The closed classroom, in this vision, protects the teacher against incursions on his/her autonomy and provides a greater degree of freedom than might otherwise occur – it allows more scope for choice and professional discretion within the process of teaching.

Closed classrooms have also been studied as settings which foster a particular social context containing its own set of pressures on the participants – a setting which facilitates a *socially* as well as architecturally discrete unit with a social order that is fragile and subject to constant negotiation (Delamont, 1976b; Jackson, 1968; Waller, 1961). In this view, the expectations and demands placed on teachers have their genesis within the social situation of the closed classroom and constitute a 'hidden curriculum' to be coped with by the participants (Jackson, 1968; Snyder, 1971; Woods, 1977, 1978).

Both approaches to the impact of closed classrooms on the practice of teaching emphasize (i) the social nature of the phenomenon and (ii) its degree of isolation from the environment. The picture thus portrayed is one in which the closed classroom has the effect of minimizing the teacher's accountability to those beyond the bounds of the classroom whilst, at

144

the same time, generating a specific set of pressures to be confronted by teacher and pupils.

However, because the 'discrete' and 'social' nature of the setting has been emphasized by these approaches, there is the prospect of accepting closed classrooms as units that are entirely separated from their environment and freed from external pressure. Such an oversimplification needs to be avoided. Whilst they certainly provide some protection from the demands of external bodies, they do not provide complete insularity: pressures from parents, the community, administrators and colleagues do filter into the 'sanctuary' (Warren, 1973).

The manner in which external pressures impinge on the closed classroom are of two varieties. The first concerns the expectations of members of the classroom, the other concerns the sources of information which transcend the isolation of the setting. In the first instance, it is clear that, though social situations entail their own sets of practices, assumptions and expectations, the participants also bring to the situation their own expectations derived from their personal biography. So, whilst the closed classroom is a social unit entailing particular expectations about behaviour, it is not entirely isolated from the social circumstances in which it is situated because participants are influenced in their attitudes to classroom order by their experiences in other spheres of social life (Leacock, 1969; Sharp and Green, 1975; Willis, 1977). Because members of the social situation do not entirely separate their classroom experience from all other influences on their lives, closed classrooms cannot be, in this sense, completely discrete social systems.

In the latter case, the 'discrete' nature of closed classrooms is challenged by factors which provide information, however inferential or vague, about what is going on in the classroom to those not immediately engaged in the proceedings. Such sources of 'publicly available information' exist despite the visual insularity of events in the classroom and are not based on direct observation. They are indirect sources of information –

clues which allow outsiders to infer what is happening behind the closed doors of colleagues' classrooms. Examination successes, staffroom gossip, feedback from pupils and use of the house system are examples of such publicly available information, but noise emanating from the classroom constitutes the most immediate and, under certain circumstances, the most significant source of information.

Noise is a medium through which teachers become aware of events in other classes despite the fact that they cannot (visually) observe the proceedings and it is specifically because noise transcends the isolation of the closed classroom that it becomes a highly significant factor for the practical activity of teaching.

Noise and control

It has been argued so far that the practical activity of teaching is influenced by considerations of noise and that this results, in the first instance, from its interference with learning and instruction. In this case the *level* of noise appeared to be a more salient issue for teachers than the particular type of noise or its cause since any noise which impinged on the lesson constituted a potential hazard to the progress of the lesson and thus posed a problem for the teacher.

Teachers were more discerning about the source of noise, however, when treating it as a clue to what was happening behind the closed doors of a colleague's classroom. Where noise was used as publicly available information about events in closed classrooms it was a particular source of noise which was regarded as significant – *pupil initiated noise*, noise created by pupils (and/or their teacher's response) and noise generally stemming from non-curricular activity. It was noise created by pupils, rather than by music or audio-visual aids, which constituted significant clues because, in the closed classroom situation, it could be taken to *be indicative of a lack of control in the classroom.*[9]

146

The importance of pupil-initiated noise emanating from the classroom, when treated as indicative of a lack of classroom control, will depend, of course, on the centrality of control for the activity of teaching. Available evidence suggests that, for the practical activity of teaching, control is crucial. The staff at Ashton and Beechgrove considered it essential to competent teaching and a basic requirement for successful teaching. It was a common complaint that teachers straight from colleges of education or post-graduate training failed to appreciate the necessity of gaining control prior to any attempt to inculcate knowledge, and the training establishments were frequently indicted for their overemphasis on establishing personal relationships at the expense of stressing the centrality of classroom control to the practical activity of teaching.

Recognition that control was the vital precondition for a teaching/learning context appeared to be something which new teachers learnt as part of their rites of passage from trainee to competent membership of the teaching community – learning first the need for control, then the criteria of control and finally the strategies for gaining and maintaining control in the classroom. Yet, as the teachers at Ashton and Beechgrove generally acknowledged, it was not something which was taught in the colleges nor was it necessarily something which could be directly demonstrated to new teachers in the classroom situation.

Where schools adopted a closed classroom organization the extent to which colleagues could demonstrate the requirements of control would be tempered by the individuality and isolation inherent in the closed classroom setting. As Edgar (1974, p. 246) has argued:

> Teaching differs from the professions in the relatively small amount of colleague interaction it affords newcomers. Isolated in individual classrooms, experienced colleagues have little time to 'socialize' the new teacher into the 'teacher subculture' other than in terms of broad 'general acceptability'.

147

Teachers operating behind closed doors do not generally see more experienced teachers in action, nor are they watched or advised in any detailed manner. Teachers are rarely subject to observation by colleagues even during the probationary year (and certainly less after that) and formally instituted channels for evaluation and feedback are negligible.

In the absence of such formal communication, therefore, the manner in which teachers come to learn the rudiments of control depends on the existence of informal social pressures which operate despite the insularity of closed classrooms and which allow the assimilation of recruits to the reality of teaching. An example of such subtle methods is given by McPherson (1972, p. 32) recalling her experience at 'Adams':

> In the effort to let others observe that which was ordinarily hidden, the Adams teachers developed an 'open door' policy, a non-verbal series of clues that were never discussed but were tacitly understood by all. A teacher kept her classroom door open during the teaching day to show her control over her class. A good disciplinarian's door stood open; a poor one's door was frequently shut. Unless a teacher ... was going to have art (an allowably noisy subject) or do dramatics ... her closed door meant that her class was too noisy and she was afraid of being overheard.

McPherson's description is interesting in particular because it explicitly relates noise with questions of control. Noise and control are presented as mutually exclusive features of the classroom situation, with quiet orderliness in the classroom being seen as a desirable and necessary prerequisite for learning. As she goes on to point out (p. 33):

> Justifying order and discipline as good in themselves, the teachers ritualistically assumed that without them learning did not result. The Adams teacher believed that where teachers failed to achieve discipline, that where confusion, noise and rudeness abounded, no learning occurred.

Noise emanating from the classroom, then, was seen to

148

indicate the absence of both a learning context and, by implication, control of the classroom. As a corollary, where quiet orderliness existed in the classroom it became associated with a controlled learning situation. Both assumptions, it should be noted, are predicated by the closed classroom situation which precludes direct observation of other classrooms and which consequently fosters a reliance on 'publicly available information' such as noise emanating from the classroom in order to know anything of what transpires in colleagues' classrooms.

Noise, or the absence of noise, thus provides a social link between the isolated classroom units – a link used both in the socialization of neophyte teachers and as a means for gauging the presence or otherwise of control in the classroom. Teachers face social pressures to conform with the expectations of colleagues and, as Leacock (1969, p. 87) has observed on the basis of her research in four schools in the United States,

> A new teacher soon learns that it is her success in maintaining classroom quiet and order, in the narrow sense, which is first noted and which is apt to be the school administrator's first measure of her performance.

So, new teachers, it seems, need to adjust their approach to teaching to meet the social, as well as educational, exigencies of the situation and need to recognize two complementary aspects of their practical everyday task; first, that control of the classroom is elemental, and second, that control (or the lack of it) can be inferred by the amount of pupil-initiated noise generated in the classroom and/or emanating from it.

From this it follows that their practical concern is unlikely to be with literal 'states of control' so much as with the 'appearance of control' as signified by levels of pupil-initiated noise in the classroom. Teachers in closed classrooms, indeed, are encouraged to become oriented toward the means for inferring control rather than the actual (real) existence of a state of control because, *in the absence of direct observation, noise provides an 'evidential strategy' for the recognition of (a lack of)*

149

teacher control in the classroom.[10] Classroom control, that is, from the view of the practising teacher, can be more usefully understood as a *socially organized phenomenon* – as a product of inference, appearance and interpretation, by both the classroom teacher and colleagues outside the bounds of the closed classroom, guided in large part by issues of noise – rather than a condition existing within the classroom at any given point in time.

Noise created by pupils consequently has serious connotations because it implies a lack of control and thus a failure to comply with the essential prerequisite of teaching: it implies incompetence. Because control is regarded as so vital for the success of teaching, any evidence that there is a lack of control becomes a major concern of the staff. Recognizing this point, staff at Ashton and Beechgrove argued that they experienced practical pressures for 'keeping 'em quiet' which existed quite distinct from personal pedagogic evaluations of the necessity to maintain quiet orderliness. Whether or not quiet orderliness was seen as a prerequisite for learning and whether or not quiet orderliness was seen as reflecting a state of classroom control, in the closed classroom situation, the actual task activity of teaching was oriented to achieving quiet orderliness because alternatives which entailed (pupil-initiated) noise ran the risk of identifying the teacher as one who failed to implement classroom control and whose competence was thus in question.[11]

An important caveat is warranted at this point. The research on which this argument has been based centred on two London comprehensive schools in which there was an under-representation of high-ability pupils and a declining intake ability. They drew on predominantly working-class catchment areas and received markedly higher than average proportions of 'immigrant' pupils. As argued elsewhere (Denscombe, 1977), these factors contributed to a 'low achievement orientation' in the schools – a situation where staff held modest expectations about the achievement potential of the pupils, and pupils exhibited limited aspirations in terms of academic careers.

Under these circumstances, the teachers' ability to gain classroom control became a particularly salient factor for the attribution of competence. Where there was a high achievement orientation, however, the attribution of competence to a teacher might owe more to his/her ability to inculcate knowledge, with the ability to gain classroom control being less problematic and receiving less credit as a teaching skill. Situations of 'high achievement orientation' would still entail a practical concern to minimize the level of noise emanating from the (closed) classroom but as a feature of routine concern it would be less fundamental whilst the poignancy of such noise would be greater where there was a low achievement orientation and where the control element of teaching took on added significance.

It should be recognized, also, that acceptable levels of noise may differ from school to school and that the problem of noise in this instance does not depend on absolute levels of noise or quiet either within particular classrooms or absolute decibel levels to be associated with particular schools. What is in question is the level of a particular type of noise emanating from a classroom relative to the norm for the school and the way in which this significantly contributes to *impressions* of classroom control where closed classroom organization precludes direct observation.

The disruptive pupil

The implications of noise for teacher competence mean that noise is a feature of the classroom to which staff are particularly sensitive. It provides a 'cue' for intervention by the teachers and identifies those kinds of (pupil) activity which warrant urgent attention. Pupils who are noisy are 'disruptive' because, not only do they interfere with the establishment of a learning context,[12] they also pose immediate threats to the *appearance* of control in the classroom.

Disruption, treated in this manner, highlights the way in which teachers come to identify species of pupil activity as disruptive, and contrasts with those analyses which have tended to assume that what constitutes 'disruption' is self-evident and which focus attention on the causes of that kind of behaviour – causes such as psychological disturbance (Blackham, 1967; White and Charry, 1966), social background (Linton, 1966; Sugarman, 1967), organizational career (Cicourel and Kitsuse, 1963, 1968; Hargreaves, 1967; Lacey, 1970), the inadequacy of teachers (Cox and Boyson, 1975) and techniques of classroom management (Kounin, 1970). Such analyses attempt to specify the causes of disruptive behaviour at the expense of considering how that behaviour comes to be regarded as disruptive by teachers in the practical classroom situation.

Those studies which *have* focused on the teacher's attribution of such labels have either employed the notion of a psychological 'set' (e.g. 'disorderly behaviour set', Stebbins, 1971) or the transcendence of classroom rules (Hargreaves *et al.*, 1975), both of which have a tendency to treat the teacher's assessment of 'disruption' in isolation from their membership of a community of teachers operating in a formally organized setting. Though they do consider the teacher's understanding of disruptive behaviour, they treat this understanding as a phenomenon of the individual teacher rather than a product of the social organization of teaching, and do not consider the practical pressures on teachers operating within a community of teachers to identify certain modes of pupil conduct as disruptive.

The social significance of noise for teachers in classrooms provides one such source of pressure and Kounin (1970), for instance, has found that noise and talking are the major criteria used by teachers for identifying the kind of pupil behaviour which they regard as problematic. Such behaviour provides 'cues' for intervention by the teacher[13] and alerts the teacher to events that warrant his/her attention. New or sudden noise in particular implies that something significant is happening in the room – it provides a cue for the teacher to attend to some form of pupil activity (usually deemed deviant) and draws attention to its source as a cause for investigation by the teacher.

Pupils, for their part, can use noise as part of a repertoire of strategies of resistance to teacher control of the situation. By generating noises which the teacher cannot locate or which the teacher cannot treat as intentionally contravening agreed conventions,[14] pupils can signify resistance to a teacher imposed requirement for quietness in the classroom and generally 'play-up' the teacher. The twang of rulers that ghosts around the room, the exaggerated cough whose contagious powers seem powerful and immediate, the shuffling of feet and a host of other noises can be used by pupils to annoy teachers simply because of the general attempt by teachers to control noise in classrooms.

There is also strong evidence to suggest that where pupil behaviour is not noisy it provides little immediate problem for the teacher even where it is not behaviour appropriate to the learning situation. 'Not paying attention' or 'being away', for instance, 'although subverting his teaching aims, is a more palatable form of disorderly behaviour for the teacher than almost any other' (Stebbins, 1971, p. 229). Similarly, Hargreaves *et al.* (1975, p. 37) quote from the notes of one of their fieldworkers: 'It seems obvious that anything the pupils do that does not make a noise is acceptable. Three or four pupils are obviously not paying attention to the reading but because they are quiet, their conduct is acceptable.'

Quiet non-learners, then, do not pose *immediate* practical problems for the teacher.[15] In fact, the quiescence of pupils could possibly be misconstrued by teachers as a sign of academic involvement. Dumont and Wax (1969) have noted such an instance at a Cherokee reservation school in northeastern Oklahoma. Though the pupils appeared as ideal and diligent to the 'outsider' teacher there was little progress in terms of the inculcation of curricular knowledge. The researchers indicate the reasons for this to be not a lack of ability, but a resistance on the part of the pupils to particular types of teacher control. Their resistance, however, constituted a quiet and orderly recalcitrance. The pupils' reaction and recalcitrance was not of the overt kind to which the 'culture-bound' teachers were accustomed, but existed nonetheless in a form which was recognizable primarily between the pupils, and evident only to the skilled eyes of the ethnographic researcher. With sophisticated and subtle forms of reaction the pupils were able to demonstrate to each other that they did not accept the teacher control of the situation. Because the behaviour did not threaten the quiet orderliness of the classroom, however, the teacher was unable to recognize the behaviour as intentionally disruptive of a learning context.

At Beechgrove the situation was illustrated in a fourth-year social studies group where the teacher's attention was constantly focused on four boys who were 'cheeky', walked round the room, called to each other in loud voices and exhibited a penchant for slamming desk lids. Three girls who sat at the back of the class reading magazines or quietly talking to each other about their social lives received far less attention and were cajoled to get on with their work only on occasions when the four boys were settled. Although the behaviour of neither group was conducive to a (curriculum) learning situation, it was invariably the boys who were attended to first. It was the noisiness of their non-learning behaviour which gave it overriding importance for the classroom teacher.

In sum, for practical purposes disruptive behaviour was identified by its noisiness. Although other kinds of non-learning behaviour are of concern to teachers, they will generally receive attention only after the noisy behaviour has been seen to. In the context of the present argument, this primary orientation to noisy behaviour can be understood not just in its implications for pupil learning, but also because of the significance of noise for the *appearance of control* when operating in the closed classroom situation.

Summary and conclusion

The significance of noise for the practical activity of teaching,

154

it has been argued, stems in part from the fact that noise provides

(a) a channel of communication between the ostensibly (physically and socially) discrete closed classroom units which characterize secondary schooling – channels which
(b) provide a means for socializing new teachers and
(c) provide practical pressure on teachers to operate in a way which they might not regard as appropriate under ideal circumstances – despite the teacher's apparent autonomy and isolation in the closed classroom situation. In particular, in the absence of direct observation, noise emanating from the classroom
(d) provides publicly available information about classroom events and an 'evidential strategy' for inferring classroom control such that
(e) noisy classrooms could serve to impugn the competence of the teacher in charge.

Where notions of classroom control are central to the competence of teachers, and where such control is inferred rather than observed, efforts to minimize the level of noise emanating from the classroom may become a major feature of the 'practical task activity' of teaching, and one for which the newcomer may be ill-prepared. As Swift (1971, p. 190) has noted:

Many scholarly men and women were totally unprepared for the harsh realities found in schools where 'keeping 'em quiet' required more than a masters degree in history.

Indeed a concern with 'keeping 'em quiet' may be particularly prevalent where schools exhibit a 'low achievement orientation', and the significance of this for the practical activity of teaching is demonstrated by teachers' special sensitivity to noisy behaviour in classrooms rather than to quiet non-learning which, though it may be just as negative in terms of the inculcation of curricular knowledge, poses far less immediate problems for the classroom teacher.

155

Three main conclusions can be drawn from these observations:

First, that control in closed classrooms can be usefully regarded as a socially-organized phenomenon rather than a literal state of affairs in the classroom. Because control is hardly ever 'observed' or 'taught' by colleagues, what constitutes a state of control is merely *inferred* on the basis of criteria which transcend the isolation of the closed classroom – criteria such as pupil-initiated noise emanating from the setting. The intricate relationship between noise in the classroom and teacher perceptions of classroom control is fostered by closed classroom arrangements.

Second, that where teachers operate in closed classrooms they appear to experience a social pressure to minimize noise and may, in practice, exhibit a fundamental preoccupation with maintaining quiet orderliness in the classroom irrespective of the pedagogic implications. Such pressure is structured by the closed classroom organization and the sense of social structure appropriate to competent teaching.

Finally, that educational innovations which involve the likelihood of increased amounts of noise – whether generated by audio-visual aids or increased pupil contact/movement – pose particular problems in practice because their implementation potentially jeopardizes the appearance of control in the classroom. So long as 'keeping 'em quiet' remains a teacher strategy geared to obviating the appearance of a lack of control in the classroom, such innovations are unlikely to be adopted, not through any inherent pedagogic fault, but because of the practical circumstances within which teachers operate. If noise is to become less significant as a deterrent to educational innovation, it would seem that alternatives to the closed classroom warrant serious consideration. Team teaching in open-plan classrooms, for instance, though it may exacerbate certain educational aspects of the problem, might so fundamentally affect the *social* significance of noise as to provide an overall transformation in noise as a practical problem for teachers and thus facilitate pedagogic methods which have proved unacceptable within the conventional framework of the closed classroom.

Notes

1 The research from which this argument stems was conducted over a period of four years at two comprehensive schools in London, one in Camden (Beechgrove) and one in Brent (Ashton). Extensive classroom observation complemented by both formal and informal interviews were used in the process of understanding significant features of the sense of social structure appropriate to competent teaching in the schools and the features of school organization which promoted this teachers'-understanding-of-the-situation (see Denscombe, 1977). I am indebted to David Hargreaves and Peter Woods whose observations on an earlier draft have influenced this version of the work.

2 Though see some of the work associated with the deschooling movement, e.g. Jules Henry and Herbert Kohl (ed.).

3 Such strategies can be inferred from studies of teaching undertaken by Hargreaves *et al.* (1975), Kounin (1970) and Woods (1977) amongst others.

4 It should not be inferred that such settings have a determining effect on classroom activity because essentially it is only the *meaning* of those settings for the teachers which can influence their activity (Stebbins, 1973). Closed classrooms, however, do have a particular significance for the way in which teachers interpret events and it is in this sense that they are influential on behaviour.

5 Such a preference for low levels of noise would reflect membership of a wider culture rather than membership of a specific occupational culture but would, nonetheless, significantly affect teachers' attitudes toward noise in the classroom situation. This association of teacher views with everyday 'commonsense views' is examined more fully in Mardle and Walker (1980).

6 The impact of seating arrangements on interaction in classrooms has been well documented. See, for instance, Adams and Biddle (1970), Breed and Colaiuta (1974), Sommer (1967), Walberg (1968).

7 Contrary to traditional modes of teaching which attempt to limit inter-pupil contact and to channel communication through the teacher, progressive modes of teaching are concerned to facilitate such contact to enhance the learning process (Gross *et al.*, 1971; Lawton, 1973). Teachers concerned to rearrange desks in this

manner regarded the move as innovative and in the vein of progressive education.

8 Alternatives to individual teacher responsibility have been evident in team teaching experiments dating back to 1957 in the USA (Shaplin and Olds, 1964; Chamberlin, 1969; Davis, 1966). They remain, however, both in Britain and the USA, aberrations of the closed classroom norm for secondary schooling with its inherent individualized responsibility.

9 Teachers' sensitivity to noise emanating from classrooms fosters a particular adeptness at distinguishing between *types* of noise which become audible, even the types of noise generated by pupils. The discerning ear could impute different causes to different types of noise, but the present purpose is to explore the structural genesis of noise as a problem rather than examine the finer constitutive elements of the problem.

10 The notion of 'evidential strategies' is derived from Hargreaves *et al.* (1975).

11 There are two aspects to the notion of competence as used here. Firstly, there is the teacher's ability to recognize a situation as of a particular type and as warranting a course of action deemed appropriate amongst the community of teachers, i.e. competent *interpretation*. Secondly, there is the ability to implement the appropriate course of action, i.e. competent behaviour. For present purposes it is the former which is more significant for the argument, but failure at either level which results in unacceptably high levels of pupil-initiated noise runs the risk of being regarded by colleagues as indicative of a lack of control.

12 'Disruptive' behaviour has been consistently associated with interference with the establishment of a learning context with, for instance, Baily (1970) seeing it as 'any event which significantly interrupts the education of students', and a recent NAS 'Report on Violence in Schools, (Lowenstein, 1975) regarding it as any behaviour short of physical violence which interfered with the teaching process and/or upset the normal running of the school.

13 As Stebbins (1971) has indicated, however, teachers might be aware of such behaviour yet choose not to intervene if they envisage a greater disruption occurring from the intervention itself. There may be, in Stebbins's words, the 'avoidance of provocation'. Hargreaves *et al.* (1975) similarly note that teachers have an 'intervention threshold' beneath which they are reluctant to intervene because more disturbance will be created by the process of intervention than is warranted by the amended behaviour of the pupil(s).

14 The strength of such strategies lies essentially in their 'sub-reactional' status (cf. Hargreaves *et al.*, 1975). Though recognized by the staff as intentionally contravening accepted (teacher definition) rules, the teacher may feel constrained not to intervene either because he/she cannot identify any particular culpable rogue(s) and may not wish to 'take-on' the whole class (cf. Stebbins, 1971 'avoidance of provocation') or because the activity itself cannot be labelled unequivocally 'deviant'. The pupils' skill resides squarely in retaining the status of the activity as open to equivocation.

15 It should not be inferred that such non-learning posed no problem at all; in terms of its salience for the control of the classroom, however, noise was of far greater practical significance.

7

Pressures for intimacy

Ann Swidler

Extracts from Ann Swidler (1979) *Organization Without Authority*, pp. 57–71. Cambridge, Mass.: Harvard University Press, Copyright © 1979 by the President and Fellows of Harvard College.

* * *

Everything about life in free schools tends to drive teachers, metaphorically and sometimes literally, into the arms of their students. As I have already noted, the informal atmosphere of Group High and Ethnic High facilitated the formation of close personal ties between teachers and students. School life continually spilled over into personal life, so that students and teachers learned a good deal about one another as individuals. Teachers felt free to express the attractive, charming, funny sides of their personalities; they allowed themselves to appear vulnerable, in need of comfort or reassurance. Similarly, teachers could come to appreciate students for their sense of humor, good judgment, or sensitivity in a variety of informal situations where teachers and students found themselves interdependent in ways that traditional schools seldom allow.

For some teachers, involvement with students fulfilled

personal needs. Some unmarried teachers, for example, turned to students for companionship. At Ethnic High Gloria, recently divorced, became close friends with Lisa, a student; at Group High Alice, also divorced, spent considerable time outside of class with students. She occasionally went to a movie with students on a weeknight, and she once had the women's studies class to her house for a weekend slumber party. Some male teachers at Ethnic High went to student parties and joined students on weekends smoking dope, attending political rallies, or just riding around.

But student-teacher intimacy was more than a solution for occasional loneliness. Even teachers who had full personal lives or other absorbing interests were continually pressured to come to school meetings, attend parties, and go on school outings. For both students and teachers school life continually encroached on personal life – absorbing family, friends, evenings, and weekends. Teachers found themselves inviting students into their homes, sharing more and more of their time and their personal histories, and becoming increasingly involved with students' private lives. Even teachers who valued their time and their privacy sacrificed both to make their teaching work.

There were strategic as well as personal reasons for cultivating friendships with students. Free school students had significant power over their teachers. Although it is true that teachers in general are more effective if students like them, their destinies are usually controlled by colleagues, principals, and school boards, not by students. But at Group High and Ethnic High, some teachers' jobs depended directly on enrollment, and popularity with students was often the most important determinant of a teacher's eventual fate. Because the schools' budgets were based on enrollments, a teacher who attracted numerous student admirers won security and status with other teachers. In addition, pressure from the Office of Education and the school district to ensure that the schools were racially balanced placed a special premium on attracting students from particular ethnic or racial groups. A teacher with

161

a following of minority students had great bargaining power. When Ethnic High's Asian teacher left, most of her students left with her; Group High lost almost all of its black students when a popular black teacher left the school. Attracting students was a necessity for all teachers, and a loyal student following could be a source of security, status, and power.

Teachers also needed access to the student peer group and to information about students' personal lives in order to do their jobs. For instance, when Denise, the Ethnic High codirector, noticed that a group of students had stopped coming to school, she stopped Cisco, one of her student friends, in the hall to ask him what was wrong. Janet, despite her weaknesses as a teacher, was well liked by students and could be counted on to know what students were thinking and what was troubling them. She could find out why they had turned sullen and unresponsive in a class, or what was behind a wave of vandalism in the art room. When a student couple broke up and Ethnic High's leading clique was in an uproar, Janet was the first to be told, and she was given a detailed description of the reconciliation. She also learned about personal crises that affected students' school participation: one student was pregnant and ashamed to come to school; another student, also pregnant, was being pressured by her boyfriend to get an abortion; a third student became hostile and aggressive because he was having trouble at home.

Understanding students' personal lives was central to the teachers' conception of their proper role. Like most free school proponents, they had a fundamentally 'therapeutic' model of the educational process, which says that since children learn spontaneously unless their capacity for learning has been stunted or inhibited, the role of the teacher is to penetrate students' emotional and social worlds and open them to the experience of learning. For example, George Dennison (1969, p. 45) at the First Street School reported that he sought to break down the emotional barriers that prevented students from learning. When Maxine, a bright but difficult student, became so aggressive she was unable to learn or to get along

162

with other students, Dennison used his knowledge of her family situation to deal with the problem. He helped her act out her feelings about the birth of a new sibling, releasing the unconscious anger that was interfering with her school performance. In a similar way, teachers at Group High and Ethnic High felt they had to understand students' private lives to teach them effectively. At Group High teachers' goals included making students more independent of their parents, helping them handle sexual anxieties, and freeing them from excessive reliance on the opinions of friends and authority figures. At Ethnic High teachers frequently discussed students' difficulties and their progress in terms of their family problems, drug usage, or the ups and downs of their romantic lives. This approach to teaching required that teachers maintain extensive friendly contacts in the student world.

Intimacy between students and teachers had other advantages as well. Teachers could involve students in class discussion by asking them to share personal experiences or relate the class material to their own lives. Some classes, like the women's studies class at Group High, consisted largely of personal exchange. Alice, the teacher, described dilemmas in her love life, her own attitude toward marriage and children, and her feelings about being a woman. Students in turn discussed many personal, sometimes painful, experiences: virginity and fears about sex, conflicts with parents, and problems in love relationships. In such a class, Alice's willingness to share her own life was in some sense the precondition for openness and commitment on the part of students. The class was suspicious of anyone who wanted to participate without becoming personally involved. Such shared intimacy made the class engrossing for students, while it gave Alice the satisfying feeling that she was reaching students and helping them deal with important issues in their lives. Even in classes with a less explicitly personal focus, personal discussion could be used to fill time, to reach students, and to win student favor. Raymond, a teacher at Ethnic High, usually organized each class by asking students for personal experiences related to the day's topic. He also reminisced freely about his own life, sharing his experiences with students in an effort to win their understanding and affection. Intimacy was both useful and necessary for teachers at Group High and Ethnic High; it provided the informal context and much of the content of their day-to-day teaching.

An incident in Janet's class at Ethnic High illustrates how personal ties with students could create a reserve of good will, protecting a teacher against student dissatisfaction or rebellion. During a student-run course evaluation, the students in Janet's class, meeting without her, agreed that the class was disorganized and that they were learning very little. Some students then pointed out that Janet was young and new to teaching and that the students themselves were at fault: they were lazy and sabotaged the class by talking too much or teasing Janet. One student said, 'Hey, you know her husband? He's that Williams, the brother of Bobby Williams. He's good looking!' Other students chimed in to discuss Janet's baby and other aspects of her private life. The students then muted their criticism, reporting to Janet only that she should give them a little more to do.

The Monday following the evaluation, Janet was a bit worried about student dissatisfaction with the class. She reacted by trying to deepen the personal bonds between herself and the students, by sharing herself with them even more fully. When her suggestion for a class assignment was met with the complaint that it was Monday and students were too tired to work, she said, 'Okay, I'll give you guys a break. But tomorrow we're going to practice note-taking.' Then, sitting on the edge of the desk, she said, 'I'll have to tell you guys how I got into teaching.' Janet confessed that she had not initially wanted to be a teacher. She had started out substituting because it was the only job available. However, she happened to find that her personality was suited to teaching and she liked it. 'I'm naturally easy-going, and I think I get along well with people, so that's my teaching style.' She said, 'I think you guys have just accepted me, you feel comfortable with me and

164

accept me the way I am.' Jerome, one of the students, interjected in a friendly tone, 'Of course. What can you do? You can't change a person.' Janet then concluded, 'I'm pretty nice and I can communicate with students pretty well. Maybe my one fault is that I'm not tough enough.' This friendly talk filled up the time without straining Janet's resources as a teacher or the students' willingness to work. But increased intimacy was also Janet's way of warding off the implicit criticism of her teaching, while she made explicit her notion that being a good teacher meant being friendly and getting along well with students.

The uses of personal appeals

Teachers were particularly likely to invoke intimacy when they needed student cooperation. A personal appeal or an admission of vulnerability compensated for the attempt to assert control. For example, when a Group High art teacher wanted to make his class more organized, he put the issue in personal terms. He announced that from now on the class was going to be more structured and he was going to exercise more authority. He explained that his psychiatrist had said that unstructured situations made him anxious. Fred's announcement was made half humorously, but the admission that he was seeing a psychiatrist was clearly meant to blunt the effect of his demand for more structure.

George Dennison, in *The Lives of Children* (1969, pp. 112–13), emphasized that personal involvement was essential for his influence on students (in this case José, a difficult but rewarding thirteen-year-old): 'My own demands, then, were an important part of José's experience. They were not simply the demands of a teacher, nor of an adult, but belonged to my own way of caring about José. He sensed this. There was something he prized in the fact that I made demands on him.'

Personal appeals, and corresponding admissions of vulnerability, were the major ways in which teachers at Group High and Ethnic High tried to influence students. A dramatic

165

example was Carol's response when, as director of Group High, she found herself faced with a serious violation of school rules. She has taken a large group of students on an overnight camping trip. Although students had been told that regular Berkeley High rules would apply, they smuggled in wine and some hallucinogenic drugs. Two of the students had 'bad trips', and Carol had to take them to the hospital. Although the school did not get caught for this incident, Carol was shaken. At the meeting which was called, her whole collective was to deal with the issue. Carol made the opening statement. She said, 'I felt personally, emotionally abused by what happened this weekend.' She then went on to say that students claimed equality and yet they still expected her to take responsibility when something went wrong. Some students replied that that was 'your hang-up' – that they didn't expect her to take responsibility. Others pointed out that Carol's job was at stake and the students had been unfair to her. In a situation in which a traditional teacher would certainly have reasserted authority, or at least have appealed to school loyalty, Carol chose entirely personal terms in which to lay her case before students.

In both Group High and Ethnic High, teacher defeats were often followed by a personal revelation. Whether these self-revelations, pleas, and reminiscences were designed to gain sympathy by exposing the teacher's vulnerability, or were a way of acknowledging student victory by renegotiating the relative statuses in the relationship, I do not know. However, the pattern was quite regular: each defeat or difficulty stimulated increased intimacy.

Erving Goffman (1961) points out that breaking role is often a way of dealing with a stressful situation. During a particularly tense operation, a surgeon will forego the deference he normally receives from nurses and interns: he will joke with his subordinates and allow them to joke with him. As Goffman describes it, this informality is 'a kind of bargaining or bribery whereby the surgeon receives a guarantee of equability from his team in return for being "a nice guy" – someone who does not press his rightful claims too far' (p. 122).[1]

Since teachers at Group High and Ethnic High did not have many rightful claims to dignity or deference, it is surprising that they so often tried letting down further barriers to intimacy when they were in a tight spot. Yet over and over, when teachers made one of their rare attempts to assert control they became even more personal, less teacherly than usual. When Janet made an uncharacteristic attempt to bring some order into her classroom, she turned to the unruly students and shifted dramatically into black, saying, 'I'm getting tired of you. You better behave or I'm going to hit you across the mouth.' Raising her hand in mock anger, she said, 'I'm going to slap you in your teeth.' The effectiveness of these threats depended on Janet's abandoning teacherly style for an in-group persona she seldom employed in school.

But personal appeals did not always succeed. Indeed, many of the most dramatic moments at Group High and Ethnic High occurred when teachers threw themselves on students' mercy and were rebuffed. Yet despite repeated failures, teachers persisted in making personal appeals when they wanted to influence students.

Raymond began one of the first school meetings at Ethnic High by saying that since all members were part of a community and had to live right on top of one another, they were very interdependent. He said, 'I am sorry I have to start this way, but I want to take care of this at the beginning. During the summer there has been some stealing. I personally have lost some of my most valuable possessions. Gloria's purse has been stolen.' Raymond turned to Gloria and asked her how much money she lost. She said thirty-five dollars. Raymond said this really hurt him. 'I don't know if they [the thefts] were directed at me personally or if they were somebody's idea of a way to get back at the system. If I catch anyone I will let the school as a whole deal with them, and if the school doesn't want to do anything about it, then maybe I have come to the wrong place. Maybe I will have to reconsider my commitment to the school.' This combination of threat, appeal, and admission of personal vulnerability received a cool response from students at the meeting; and when similar incidents occurred during the year, students made it clear that they were not particularly moved by either remorse or compassion for Raymond. Indeed, in the following incident, students re- ponded to a personal appeal by explicitly distancing themselves – saying, in effect, 'That's your problem, not ours.'

Raymond began another meeting by saying that he was sorry to start the meeting this way, but he had almost decided not to come at all because he was so angry. But he wanted the school to deal with this problem. 'We had printed up a whole lot of information about [Ethnic High] and we were getting it ready to mail out to the parents. Yesterday, a hundred stamps were taken from the office. . . . We got no full-time secretary now, and I'm trying to run the school, teach, and run the office all by myself. It's almost more than one person can do.' Students sat through this speech without responding. Later in the meeting, Gloria raised a problem and also appealed for personal sympathy. She said: 'I also have been having a problem of kids coming in class and disrupting the class. Also, when Fernando [her three-year-old son] is here in the hall he gets what I would call abused. Also, he learns patterns of behavior I don't like. I can't afford to pay a sitter. It would take most of my salary.' Rather than sympathizing with this appeal, the students turned on Gloria. Bernette, one of the leading women students, said: 'Now, I don't want to insult you, but that kid's a monster.' (Laughs.) 'I can't have that kid come around here, cussing, calling me names. He call me names, I'm going to slap him around. You got to control that kid.' Gloria answered that you could not 'control' a three-year-old child. The students were outraged. Manuel said, 'My father controlled three of us boys. He hit us till we couldn't sit down.' Danny chimed in, 'You got to slap his butt!' to which there was a chorus of assent. Gloria, by bringing her personal life into the discussion, had opened herself to an attack which became almost bloodthirsty. Tony said, referring to Gloria's son, 'If he come up and spit on my slacks, I'll knock his teeth down his throat. I pay a lot of money for my clothes, and I'm

168

not going to put up with that.' Yvette burst out, as if pushed beyond endurance: 'He's going to go around some day and he's going to call some big person a name, and they not going to be here [sarcastic], oh no. And they going to work your kid over. They're not going to just hit him, they going to really work him over.'

The limits of personal appeals

What accounts for the relative ineffectiveness of personal appeals? And why did teachers persist in this way of handling their difficulties? In approaching these questions, the differences between Group High and Ethnic High must be taken into account. Personal bonds between teachers and students were important at both schools, but only at Group High, with its largely middle-class, counterculture students, were personal appeals legitimated by ideology. The students at Group High believed in equality with teachers, particularly in matters of personal style. And the interpersonal norms of the counterculture, with its emphasis on openness and self-actualization, made personal appeals a way to prove one was honest, straightforward, and willing to share oneself with others. Because students embraced this ideology of openness and mutual honesty, the success of personal appeals was not dependent solely on students' liking a particular teacher. When Carol said she felt 'emotionally abused' by student misbehavior on the campout, she was making the kind of appeal students believed they ought to respect.

The working-class minority students at Ethnic High had a very different attitude toward teachers' use of intimacy as a source of influence. As Janet's case illustrates, warm personal ties could lead students to protect a teacher in a tight situation, to 'help her out', but student ideology concerning intimacy was more ambivalent. Although students liked the freedom and respect they felt at Ethnic High, they themselves often had a relatively traditional conception of the proper role of a teacher. Indeed, if we re-examine Gloria's interchange with students

169

over the problem of controlling her three-year-old son, we may see in it the students defending their conception of authority: rather than acclaiming freedom, openness, and self-expression, the students wanted Gloria to control her son, to hit him if he failed to obey, and to force him to show respect. However little they themselves obeyed rules or respect their teachers, they believed in the principle of respect. Toward the end of the debate about Gloria's son, the students gave what they felt was the clinching argument: 'Then he going to call you a name, his mother! You going to put up with it? You can't put up with that!' Gloria, half-shocked, half-amused, muttered softly, 'Call me names! He does much worse than that.' Cassie, a woman student, said, 'If I cussed at my mother, she'd beat me 'til I couldn't stand up straight.' Manuel said, 'You got to hit him', and Bernette, laughing, summed up the students' view: 'That kid going to get lynched.'

The students advised Gloria to demand respect from her son as their parents had done and as they did with their own children (some of the students were themselves parents). However, the discussion also bore on the relations between students and teachers at Ethnic High. Gloria made the connection explicit early in the debate. She said, 'My philosophy is that I won't punish Fernando for what he *says*. When he actually *does* something bad, I spank him. But I don't believe he should be punished for just talking. In my class I don't punish students for what they say.' Gloria's attempt to link her leniency toward students with her philosophy of child-rearing was what precipitated Yvette's angry outburst about how someone was going to 'work your kid over'. The students seemed to be saying that they should be disciplined by the teachers, made to show respect for their elders.[2] An appeal for personal sympathy, to the ties of friendship between teachers and students, did not seem to the students an appropriate basis on which to resolve a school problem.

A direct rejection of shared responsibility for school problems occurred later in the same meeting. Gloria was again the teacher-protagonist. Raymond announced that the school had to deal with a very serious situation, and Gloria then described a complex prank in which a group of students had tried to hot-wire her car. She concluded her account by trying to see the humor in the situation: 'Now when I got there, I gave the situation a kindly interpretation. After all, if they wanted to steal a car, they wouldn't steal mine which I had just left them in. In addition, they know I have a violent nature. What I saw there was a group of four-year-olds.' Raymond asked what the students were going to do. Bernette again took the lead, saying, 'This is between those two [Gloria and the students involved].' Raymond said, 'But aren't we a community?' Bernette retorted with great emphasis, 'We ain't in a community with no guys down there hot-wirin' no car! You can just call the police.' Students were not impressed by having teachers' troubles laid out before them. These teachers, at least, would have to take care of their problems themselves. And such failures of personal appeals were made more likely by Ethnic High's more traditional ideology of authority, although teachers at both Group High and Ethnic High found the effectiveness of personal appeals limited.

The second point to be made about the limits of personal appeals is that, apart from differences between Group High and Ethnic High in ideologies about student-teacher relationships, in both schools intimacy was likely to be most effective for teachers whom students liked or admired. When students were hostile or indifferent, increased intimacy was of little value, and personal appeals inspired little empathy or concern. Janet, whom students liked, was able to use intimacy to protect her position and to compensate for indifferent teaching. Gloria, who had fewer close ties with students, found them unsympathetic when she turned to them for help. Raymond (who, in his forties, was considerably older than the students and the other teachers) frequently appealed for sympathy and support, but it was seldom forthcoming. He often talked to students about his own feelings, about his childhood, and about his philosophy of life. But they found his reminiscences, like his problems, boring and irrelevant to their own lives. Intimacy, then, did not work for all teachers. The effective use of personal appeals was dependent on friendship, admiration, or attraction, which only some teachers were able to generate. (At Ethnic High, the question of personal compatibility between teachers and students was often confounded with that of ethnic and racial identification: teachers had the best chance of establishing personal ties and a basis for identification with students from their own ethnic group – particularly if they also shared with students a common cultural style.)

Another weakness of personal appeals is that they are so easily overdone: intimacy is most valuable when it is sparingly bestowed. Because teachers have adult status, students may at first find it interesting, or a privilege, to see into their private lives. But when students are already on familiar terms with teachers, when teachers are not distant, intriguing figures, students may not set great store on friendship with them. At Group High, for example, Andrew had become an object of friendly condescension for his students. When he wanted students in his room to turn down a transistor radio, he yelled, 'Turn that off or turn it damn low.' A student mimicked him, 'Damn low,' and said, 'Andrew, you're so crabby.' Andrew occasionally tried to turn a conversation to titillating allusions to his own broad sexual experience, but students found even this unimpressive. Revelations of his private life no longer held much luster. Familiarity could easily breed contempt.

Even a teacher who is liked by students may overuse intimacy. Alice, who taught the women's studies class at Group High, was so friendly with students that she worried at times whether they were tired of her, whether they still enjoyed her companionship. they sometimes talked about her like a younger sibling: 'I'm worried about Alice. She seems to be unhappy this semester.' Teachers who want to use intimacy successfully have to work to retain some glamor. They must exploit the adolescent crush and develop the subtle art of seeming friendly and egalitarian while preserving some mystery about themselves. A teacher who would use intimacy to

172

gain influence must, like Salome, worry about what to do when the last veil is removed.

It is also possible to make a different, more psychological argument about the limits of intimacy. To the extent that students see teachers as parent figures, they may wish to be closer and more equal to them and at the same time want the teachers to retain their distance and superiority. This ambivalence would then be expected to show itself in scenes like that described above between Gloria and the students at Ethnic High. The students were angry at Gloria for failing to be a competent, authoritative parent, both to her own child and to the students. Students in free schools sometimes complain that freedom is really just an excuse for the indifference and laziness of adults. Whatever the underlying motives – whether intimacy is a resource that may become devalued or whether there are more complex issues involved – the teacher's problem is much the same. Teachers in free schools are dependent on warm, intimate relationships with students, yet they must also try to maintain a sense of distance and mystery.

A question remains as to why teachers so frequently turned to personal appeals even though these often failed. I do not have a complete answer to this question. Intimacy may be less a resource for influence than a way of reequilibrating status when the stock of one part has slipped. Perhaps when students won a battle, the teacher had to be slightly humbled, intimacy serving symbolically as a status equalizer. The other possible explanation for the teachers' continuing reliance on intimacy is simply that they had no alternative. When they were in trouble, the traditional options – to get angry, make threats, and reassert control – were closed off. Personal appeals were the only strategy teachers had for coping with the alternative school setting. The effect of this strategy was to put a tremendous premium on a teacher's ability to make himself charming, interesting, or glamorous enough so that intimacy would be an enticing reward.

The public use of private lives

Free school teachers cannot rely on their status as teachers for authority over students, but alternative sources of influence such as intimacy or friendship are easily depleted or devalued unless backed up by outside resources. Teachers in free schools find that their private selves, what they are as adults in the larger culture, is essential to their effectiveness as teachers. They are then driven to self-dramatization – and to self-exploitation – as they ransack their private lives for material that will make them interesting to students. The demands of teaching fall on the whole personality of the teacher, with the frequent consequence that even the best free school teachers are drained and exhausted by their work.

George Dennison (1969, p. 113) explains that his success as a free school teacher depended on his having an eventful, interesting private life:

> It was important to José that I was not just a teacher, but a writer as well, that I was interested in painting and had friends who were artists, that I took part in civil rights demonstrations. To the extent that he sensed my life stretching out beyond him into (for him) the unknown, my meaning as an adult was enhanced, and the things I already knew and might teach him gained the luster they really possess in life. This is true for every teacher, every student. The life meaning which joins them is the *sine qua non* for the process of education, yet precisely this is destroyed in the public schools.

For teachers at Group High and Ethnic High, the lack of separation between their roles in school and their 'real' selves created enormous pressure to have independent interests outside the school – ideally, a second career – to provide teaching material and a source of personal prestige. The two art teachers at Group High, for instance, were both practicing artists who continued to produce and show their work while they taught. This activity both glamorized the teachers,

174

enhancing their status and personal influence with students, and directly contributed to making their classes work. For example, students were excited by photography field trips, partly because these trips exposed them to new ways of thinking about visual images and partly because, on these trips, their teachers took photographs that were later shown in galleries and museums. Students on occasion could see their own faces on a museum wall.

At Ethnic High the celebrity of a published poet hired to teach creative writing inspired an enthusiasm the regular teachers were unable to elicit. Two other popular and effective Ethnic High teachers were a professional jazz musician (with a locally successful band) who taught jazz and an intermittently employed actor who taught drama. The latter's prestige among students soared when he used his media contacts to have a student production of a play he had written filmed for a local television station. Other teachers with distinctive talents drew on them for both inspiration and status. Steve, who taught psychology and physical education at Group High, was skilled in judo, Tai Chi, gestalt psychology, backpacking, and other countercultural specialities. (To these were added a wife and baby, hippy van, and an earthy, rugged style.) Carol's involvement in civil-rights activity and union politics lent her an aura of moral authority and political commitment. Alice, when she became interested in the women's movement, started a course on women's studies.

But even possession of a second career provided no guarantee of respect from students. A worldly Group High student reported that in an argument with Fred, her art teacher, she said, 'If you were a real artist, you'd be in New York, not hanging around here teaching high school.' And what about teachers who were 'just teachers' – for whom teaching was their only career? The most telling evidence of the peculiar pressures created by alternative schools is that teachers who were not artists, actors, or activists, who did not have a second career with which to nourish their teaching and buttress their status, felt the strain and with striking regularity tried to develop outside resources to shore up their position within the school.

Alice, for example, was a good and experienced teacher with a master's degree in English and a genuine commitment to alternative education. Though popular with students, she complained that the school had swallowed up her whole life, that she didn't 'have any friends my own age any more.' She felt exhausted and drained by her job. Diagnosing her teaching troubles as stemming from her uneventful private life, Alice enrolled in an evening course in gestalt psychology. The class gave her something to talk about in her own classes, led to a romantic involvement which made her personal life more exciting (and more interesting to discuss), and taught her group process techniques she could use in teaching.

Raymond, during his first year as director of Ethnic High, developed a passionate interest in film. He bought video equipment for the school and tried to induce students to use it. Very often, instead of chairing school meetings or even participating in them, he videotaped them. Although his success in involving students in film was only partial, videotaping or showing a film gave him something to do if a school meeting went badly or he ran out of things to discuss in class. Raymond's interest in film was at least partly an escape from teaching, but most other teachers also drew on their outside activities for their teaching. Gloria began attending an extension class in psychological symbolism and claimed that the class inspired her teaching. Marion, an expert seamstress, began a sewing class for students and another class in how to work in a fabric store. As a partner in an interracial marriage, she also drew on her personal life as a resource for teaching. Paula was involved in civil-rights activity and developed a class whose subject was how to work for political change. In contrast, neither Luis, who taught ethnic studies, nor Mark, who taught folk music and American literature, had an exciting personal style or was involved in outside activities that particularly interested students. Without these supplemental sources of attraction, both teachers eventually lost their jobs.

Successful teaching depended on the ability to generate, and communicate, an interesting private life.

To the degree that free school teachers are made personally vulnerable by the ethic of openness, they need alternative sources of self-esteem and emotional sustenance. To the degree that their personal experiences are the major ingredients of their teaching, they need a life outside the school to provide raw material. If teachers rely on personal attachment to influence students, they must try to be people who have exciting or glamorous enough personal lives to be worthy of student interest. Herbert Kohl (1967, pp. 158–63) says that his students were interested in the fact that he had recently fallen in love and that they learned from his recent exposure to graduate school, to Harvard, to life. Despite his already sophisticated background, Kohl 'did a lot of probing and research, tracing Greek myths to earlier African and Asiatic sources, discovering the wonders of Sumer and Ak-kad. . . .Other teachers thought there was something ludicrous in researching to teach at an elementary level' (p. 54). But for less outstanding individuals, who perhaps have not just fallen in love or who may not have engrossing outside interests, free school teaching can make demands they are unable to meet.

There is evidence in other reports on free schools that these problems are not unique to the schools I studied. Joel Meister (1972, p. 172) describes the unique pressures on teachers at a small, extremely open free school:

> We saw the teacher as a craftsman, the student as an apprentice. The student's recognition of the teacher's superior competence would legitimate his authority; and, we hoped, a change in role-defined relationships would result in more extensive and intensive personal contact through which a student could also learn from the manifold experiences of his teacher . . . The resulting pressures on the teachers were considerable. In effect we offered ourselves as models of adulthood; at the most, embodiments of maturity, creativity and wisdom.

Teacher exhaustion

The requirement that free school teachers be personally involved with students and that they sustain an interesting life outside school leads to another phenomenon typical of free schools: teacher exhaustion. Free school teachers tend not to last very long in their jobs. In the published accounts, except that of Summerhill, teachers last only a year or two. They may not lose faith in open education – indeed, they often move from school to school or found new schools – but they feel a need to start afresh.

At Group High the teachers found that the school, although successful, was consuming their whole lives. Alice left Group High at the end of the year and returned to school to study humanistic psychology. Carol, the director, left to take an administrative post. Fred, saying he was tired of teaching, went on half-time leave the next year and on full leave the year after that. Although he eventually came back to teaching in a free school, he swore at the time he left that he would never teach in a free school again because it was so demanding. Steve, the psychology teacher, left to complete graduate school; and Andrew, who had been elected the new director, stayed another year, during which he was deposed, and then left. The three teachers who were still teaching by the beginning of the second year after my study were Phil, the math teacher, who had never taken up the school's intense interpersonal style, Joe, an English teacher, who went on to become director of another alternative school, and Ricardo, an art teacher, who was not rehired by Group High, but went on to teach art elsewhere.

At Ethnic High, which was a more discouraging place to teach than Group High, the two codirectors, who were new the year I studied the school, were by the middle of the year both talking longingly about going on leave. They had each limited their commitment to the school to two years and both planned to leave after that time. Denise said she just wanted some time to herself. Raymond talked about expanding his interest in film into a career, and when I once talked to him about a college to which students might apply, he asked whether he might be able to get a job there. Gloria left the school at the end of the year, while both Luis and Mark were let go before the year was out. Marion and Paula both planned to stay only one more year. Only Janet seemed unaffected by the school's peculiar pressures. She stayed on, friendly and relaxed with students, without trying too hard either to challenge or to impress them.

The relatively pessimistic evaluations of free schools that have appeared in recent years give evidence of that exhaustion, that sense of having invested too much, that plagued teachers at Group High and Ethnic High. Herbert Kohl (1973, p. 48), in an article on open education, says, 'We placed the school at the center of our lives and then began to realize that school was only a small part of the children's lives and that we were using them as a means for our own re-education.' The themes of teacher exhaustion and frustration are heard again and again. In a disenchanted look at Bensalem, an experimental college, its former director writes, 'We come full of enthusiasm, yet as quickly leave, often with bitterness. In the three years of its existence, Bensalem's faculty turnover has been well over 100 per cent' (Freeman, 1973, p. 31). Faculty, he notes, have difficulty living entirely in a student-dominated environment where they lose the advantage their superior knowledge might give them. They have little time to prepare material and no forum in which to present what they know. Inevitably, they fail to meet the demands students make on them. 'The demand is to become involved in a loving, supportive relationship with students. It is frequently more important that the professor be "one of the boys" on recreational trips than that he has some learning to impart. In indirect ways the students seek in the lives of faculty members the embodiment of the ideals of the experiment. It is something like a small town where the citizens forbid the pastor to smoke but smoke themselves' (p. 35).

John Holt, in *Freedom and Beyond* (172, pp. 73–4), analyzed the problem of teacher exhaustion after reporting his conversa-

179

tion with a friend at an open alternative high school in Norway: 'Anyway, she was telling me about some of the teachers who had been in the school when I first visited it. So-and-so has left; he was just exhausted. What about So-and-so? She is leaving too; she has to take a rest. And So-and-so? Oh, he has been there three years; he is completely exhausted.' Holt asked why free school teachers who had 'taught for years in conventional schools without getting exhausted, saying all the time how they hated the narrowness, the rigidity, the petty discipline' were now so worn out. His answer was that teachers, like a waiter desperately trying to satisfy a rich customer who found fault with every dish, were frantically trying to please children who no longer had to accept what teachers offered. Holt concluded, 'It is not a proper task or a right relationship. It is not a fit position for an adult to be in. We have no more business being entertainers than being cops. Both positions are ignoble. In both we lose our rightful adult authority' (p. 75). His solution for this dilemma was that teachers should teach what they themselves were interested in, not something prepared especially for children: 'What we really need are schools or learning resource centers that are not just for kids, but where adults come of their own free will to learn what they are interested in, and in which children are free to learn with and among them. How can children be expected to take school learning seriously when no one except children has to do it or does it?' (p. 76). But this solution – that adults should teach out of their own adult interests, should feed their teaching with their private lives – creates precisely the kinds of exhaustion that occurred in Group High and Ethnic High.

Teachers are not fatigued only by failing at alternative education. Quite the contrary: in Group High and Ethnic High, the most successful, enthusiastic, and lively teachers paid the heaviest toll. Wearing out teachers is part of the way free schools work: because teachers have responsibility without authority, they must fuel their teaching with their private lives. This process is exhausting, and the more successful teachers are at it, the more worn out they become.[3]

'That an adult, with a life of his own, was willing to teach [them]' was, says George Dennison (1969, p. 113), the modest demand children at the First Street School made upon their teachers. But many free school teachers find that being such an adult, creating an independent life in addition to the life of a teacher, and being in intimate contact with students having one's personality, charm, and interests as one's only resources, is too wearing to sustain for very long.

Notes

1 Peter Blau (1963, p. 312) has noted that such informal bargains are basic to all authority. Full compliance with authority – 'willingness to work hard or to exercise initiative' – cannot be ensured solely by the formal powers of bureaucratic superiors: because there is an imbalance between the formal powers of management and the kinds of cooperation it seeks from workers, the bureaucratic official must win his subordinates' good will by relinquishing some of his formal power to sanction. By this process of negotiation 'coercive power is transformed into personal influence'. Personal influence is then transformed into 'legitimate authority' when subordinates feel 'collectively obligated' and 'group norms enforce compliance' (p. 313). Similar informal negotiations – in which superiors demand less formal compliance than they might in order to procure fuller voluntary compliance – can be observed in all 'people-changing organizations' where clients cannot be transformed without their willing cooperation. It has been noted, for example, in a treatment-oriented institution for delinquent boys (Street, Vintner, and Perrow, 1966, pp. 168–80) and in junior high schools where 'developmentally oriented' teachers exchanged relaxed classroom discipline for greater academic effort on the part of students (Metz, 1978, p. 114).

2 Mary Metz (1978) reports very similar attitudes among lower-track (largely poor and black) students in the junior high schools she studied. Students tried to get away with as much as they could, yet in response to an interviewer's questions about examples of nonconformity in the classroom, 'these students were the fastest to recommend that the teachers turn to punishment and they gave the most severe punishments' (p. 82).

3 Joyce Rothschild-Whitt (1976), studying several alternative organizations in the same community, discovered that although 'burning

out' was a problem in each of them, staff who left one free school or free clinic often turned up later as committed members of a food collective or an alternative newspaper. This finding is compatible with my own, reported above, that while some free school teachers left teaching altogether, others solved the problem of exhaustion by changing schools. Thus, perhaps, it is not the teachers as persons who wear out but their reserves of fresh revelations, insights, and idiosyncrasies. In my terms, teachers use up their supplies of intimacy and can restore the mystery and interest of their own personae only by moving to a new context.

This section corresponds to Chapter 4 of *Interaction in the Classroom* and deals with two different aspects of pupil culture. Leila Sussman discusses how peer groups operate in 'progressive' classrooms in the USA, with an emphasis on their sexist and racist aspects. John Furlong uses a clique of British West Indian boys in a comprehensive school to illuminate the dilemmas facing the liberal comprehensive. These are, in a mild form, the echo of the dilemmas discussed by Swidler in Part three.

8

Innovation at Coolidge:
open classrooms

Leila Sussman

Extracts from Leila Sussman (1977) *Tales Out of School*, pp. 180–92.
Philadelphia: Temple University Press.

*   *   *

The innovational input

The Sundale school district was very receptive to innovation.
For more than twenty years, it had been in the avant-garde of
educational change. Here is a description of those years from
an interview with an assistant superintendent:

> I think I can go back to the early 1950s. I think Sundale was
> a rather comfortable place in which to teach. There wasn't
> the pressure there is now. Then, with Sputnik, we shifted
> into new math, the new sciences, and so forth. As a matter
> of fact, we designed a new social studies program, too. As I
> look back on it, we were sort of caught up in the various
> academic disciplines in this period. But Sundale was very
> much involved in the new – everything. That went on for
> about seven or eight years. There was a real start of a

movement toward open classrooms beginning in the mid 1960s, then a real jump into affective education, then a sloughing off of the cognitive, I think, really frankly, in the late 1960s; and all through this tumultuous period, when we proliferated the student choices, we were more concerned about how humane the atmosphere of the school was. And now we're in another phase. I don't think any of us know what is really happening. I think we're beginning to turn back to a little more concern with what kids are actually learning and what they should be learning, and maybe moving off from the romantic push we were in.

The initiative for open education in Sundale came at first from teachers, who began opening up their classrooms on their own. The district was quick to respond to the teachers' new interests. As an administrator in Program Development described it:

> It really came from the teachers. Teachers began doing things in their classrooms or listening or reading or getting involved in studies outside the system, taking workshops or what not. Some of the new teachers were coming out of school with open education training or at least some exposure. Then we started offering workshops ourselves because of the teachers' concern for this kind of classroom.

From the first, open education was a highly charged issue in Sundale:

> Open education really came into the foreground about three or four years ago. People began to talk about it a lot. Some people became excited about it. Some people became very frightened.

Because the Sundale district never required its faculty to teach in any particular way, the personnel director said she was just about certain that no teacher was conducting an open classroom who didn't genuinely want to. However, even under these circumstances, an element of perceived, if not real, coercion might creep in:

Teachers are not pressured into having open classrooms, but you might find them *feeling*that they are. About half the primary rooms are now open. There's a lot of it going on, and when something spreads to such a point, teachers seem to get the feeling that they're under pressure from the district or their principal to do it.

Introduction of open classrooms into Coolidge

Open education was introduced into the Coolidge School in the way typical for the district. One primary teacher became interested in it at the school where she took her Master of Arts in Teaching. She first tried to implement what she had learned on her own:

> The first year I was here, there were three classes in this room (formerly the auditorium), but for the first half of the year, each of us ran her own traditional classroom. It turned out that two of us were very much interested in open education, but the third girl was not at all. By February the two of us changed the room around in such a way that we shared the space and began to set up learning centers on a very limited basis. We had a little money, which we spent on things we felt were vital, like sand and water. We made a lot of our own materials and all our games. When we went into individualized reading, we bought the books with our own money, because the money we were given was not enough.

Later, she got help from the Sundale workshops:

> That spring Sundale put on its own workshop in open education. They gave it for fifty teachers, and provided subtitles in our classrooms so we could have a whole week off to do it. The two of us participated. Then that summer there was a follow-up workshop. Then the following year, by choice, we had a kindergarten and two first grades in here because we wanted a K–1[1] grouping. By the middle of

the year, we had changed the room around in such a way that there was one center for everything. There was one art area, one science area, one reading area. It worked very well.

Despite the fact that it worked well from the teachers' point of view, there was opposition from the parents and the previous principal:

The first year we did it the parents had a great deal of apprehension that the children were never going to learn to read. We got called all sorts of names, like a 'zoo' and a 'barnyard'. The principal we had then was against it, but we just stuck it out. Then Dr Williams came, and he has supported us all the way. Now we have a K–1–2.

Dr Williams supported both open classrooms and classrooms which were more teacher-directed. He hired both kinds of teachers. One young faculty member hired by him came to Coolidge with good training in open education. She taught a second-third-grade class. The fourth grade had had two open classroom teachers the year before we were in Coolidge. However, as we have already mentioned, one of them was fired at the end of the year due to parents' complaints. The other, an Englishman trained in open education in Britain, had also been severely criticized by parents and had 'closed up' his room to protect his job. Of the two members of the fifth-sixth-grade open team, Nancy Stuart had had some open classroom training at the teachers' college where she took her Master's degree. Her young teammate, Manny Levine, had had no open education training of any sort. He said he just 'made it up as I went along'.

At Coolidge, when we observed, there was one open classroom at every grade level except the fourth – and at least two classrooms at each grade level which were not open. This pattern of organization, which might seem ideal in the light of our discussion of Southside, where no choice was provided for parents or teachers, actually caused great difficulty. The next chapter discusses these problems. This chapter takes a closer

188

look at Coolidge's self-designated open classrooms. We already know from both Johnson and Southside that the same label can be attached to very different classes or teams. Again at Coolidge, we found variability in the implementation of open classroom doctrine. But more important, we found something which we had not noted at Southside, possibly because we were now more experienced observers of these kinds of classes. Open classrooms at Coolidge usually did not maintain social fluidity. Rather, they developed peer groups with strong boundaries, the more so the older the children were. The same thing happens in the 'traditional' classroom, but in them the functions of the peer groups are more nearly confined to the extra-curriculum. In open classrooms, where children are permitted to choose their own associates for most activities, the peer groups often become the task groups as well. They take over many of the functions of the 'traditional' teacher; for instance, deciding what work to do and how much of it. The results are first, the emergence of interpersonal skill as the main basis of peer leadership, second, a 'hidden curriculum' which makes popularity with one's peers the highest value of the pupils in the day-to-day functioning of the class, and third, peer-determined norms which limit the output of academic work.

While the second-third-grade classroom and the fifth-sixth-grade team we shall describe differed widely in their conformity to open classroom doctrine – the second-third-grade classroom was a much better example of the type – both classes were strongly affected by the concerns of their pupil peer groups.

Carol Stone's multi-aged second- and third-grade class[2]

Carol Stone and her two student teachers had a class of twenty-four pupils, disproportionately made up of the children of doctors and psychiatrists. There were only two children in the room who were not upper middle-class. One of them was the daughter of a domestic servant, who was so embarrassed by that fact that she met her mother at the end of each day in front of the post office to avoid having her appear at the school grounds.

The classroom contained a rich variety of materials. Its space was divided into clearly defined areas, each used for specific activities. The children's work was kept in folders on the teacher's desk. Cuisenaire rods, Dienes blocks, math and language arts games, science and art materials all had definite places where they were stored. The walls, ceiling, and windows were used to exhibit children's work. There was an exhibit on American Indians, another on gerbils, a picture of Pegasus with a story to go with it, displays of the children's paintings and mobiles, and a window with their straw dolls pasted to it.

The physical arrangement of the room took into account the fact that small children do not like to sit in chairs all day. There are really only a few activities for which tables are required. Thus there were only a couple of tables to work at. There were three carpeted areas with dividers. One was for the class library. Another was the place where the children used math 'manipulatives' and math games, as well as checkers and chess. The rugged areas were protected enough to keep children from disturbing each other's activities as they moved through the room. The traffic patterns had been carefully thought out. There was also a large, three-sided, painted box, with the open side facing a wall, where one to four children could sit isolated and protected from the rest of the groups. It provided an opportunity for being alone and out of sight of the teacher.

Carol had no consistent daily schedule, but there were a few regularities which provided continuity and predictability for the children. As is common in open classrooms, a class meeting was held at the start of each morning to discuss the day's activities, class problems, and special events. For example, Carol might use this time to explain some new materials and how they worked. Another meeting was held after recess to help the children focus again on classroom activities after the excitement of the playground.

190

The other consistent element running through the schedule was the weekly work assignments. Every Monday, assignments for the week were distributed in folders to each child. Carol made up the assignments individually, no two pupils being assigned exactly the same work. The amount of work, type of work, and level of work were determined by Carol's conception of the child's ability and emotional needs. Children who had a hard time doing academic work had less assigned to them than those who did it easily. The work included maths, reading, language arts, and projects. Children had until Friday to complete their assignments, and were themselves responsible for arranging their time so it would be completed by then. Part of the idea behind this procedure was that the children should learn to budget their time.

However, the system did not work altogether smoothly. One difficulty was that about seven children – nearly a third of the class – were unable to work independently or with other children. A few could work for a while with an adult, but others seemed unable to work at all. Carol explained that these children came from problem homes and had emotional difficulties. She tried to take such difficulties into account in assigning work to them. However, this created the danger of a self-fulfilling prophecy. Carol gave less work to children who were either less able academically than others, or under emotional pressure, and by thus expressing her expectation that they couldn't do much work, she actually made it harder for them to experiment with how much they could accomplish.

The open education teacher is supposed to 'diagnose' what level of work a child is ready for by observing the child. There was evidence that Carol made several errors of diagnosis. She gave some children work that was too hard for them and others work that was too easy:

The pages showed different amounts of dollars and cents. Jack was supposed to count them out and write them down. He went through it very fast. Actually the work wasn't up to his capacity. He was doing it so rapidly and easily that it was clear he could have handled much more difficult material.

191

He seemed bored by it, but the teacher said he had to do two pages.

And on the other hand:

Some of the children have been given 'Reading for Concepts' books, and they have just dropped them because they couldn't do them. I have heard them say several times, 'Well, I don't know how to use it, so I just don't use it any more.'

One very bright child told the observer that he did his work very slowly over the course of the week, because if he finished early, he'd be given more work. On the other hand, one of the girls in the class completed her week's work in two days by doing some of it at home, and then luxuriated in having the rest of the week free for activities of her own choosing.

On Friday, the folders were collected. Children who had not finished were not permitted do to anything but their assignments until they were completed. Nevertheless, when we looked through the folders there were some enormous differences in the amounts of work they contained. Some were crammed with work, others had less, and some had almost nothing in them.

Carol's schedule allowed for flexibility so that special activities could occur without disrupting the children's work. And Carol provided a lot of special activities. There were frequent films. Visitors came in to share some expertise with the children; for instance, a mime, a clarinetist, and an architect. Children went on field trips to learn about some current topic. On one occasion, they went to the computer center of a nearby university.

While Carol's class was given constant exposure to the academic skills considered important for second and third graders, no single teaching method was employed. Children got a wide variety of language arts experiences ranging from comprehension readers and phonics activities to creative writing, dramatics, and charades. A very frequent activity was to have the children dictate stories which one of the adults in the room wrote down. (In addition to the student teachers,

192

there were frequently volunteer mothers in the classroom.) Because of this diversity, children had a wide variety of ways to gain a specific academic skill. This is in keeping with open education theory: children learn best when the same skill or concept is reinforced in many different ways.

Carol helped the children explore many topics in small groups or individually. These might be called interest groups. Thus, some children explored Greek mythology; others observed the changes in a tree outside the school, recording them through photographs; still others studied musical instruments. One girl did a project on moss. Two boys did one on different types of slingshots as weapons. Carol tried to integrate science, math, reading, and art into each of these projects. Children were encouraged to observe, question, and explore. Carol understood open education as helping children to formulate questions about the world, which they then tried to answer.

Carol spent a lot of her time moving around the room acting as a 'facilitator' of learning: telling a child or small group how to use a particular material appropriately, suggesting a new activity with some material, giving new information, asking questions, teaching a new skill. She constantly brought in new materials and offered new starting points for skills and projects. For instance, she brought in seeds for the children to plant and at the same time, put an exhibit on the structure of seeds which included cards for the children to write down what they had done and what was happening to their growing plants.

Carol believed that children also learn when the teacher is not directly teaching. However, she did not feel it was all right for a child to spend all of his or her time on one kind of activity for a long period. Rather, she thought children needed a wide variety of experiences, and she tried to see that they got them. Carol was helped in doing this and in making up her individualized assignments by the careful records she kept. For each child, she had 'academic' record sheets where she wrote down what the child had done in math, language arts, social studies, and science; and 'social-emotional' record sheets in which she took down observations of the child's social behavior. These records, combined with the child's folder containing his work, gave her a picture of every individual pupil.

In the realm of interpersonal relationships, Carol encouraged collaboration among the children. Children often taught each other. There was no stigma attached to a child's not knowing a skill. Rather, the norm was that children who knew something had the responsibility of teaching it to those who didn't. This is one of the important aspects of the multi-age classroom. The teacher utilizes the children's wide range of skills to have them teach each other.

If this were a full account of this class, it would seem an excellent example of the open classroom, except for the large proportion of pupils who were doing no work. However, it is not a full account. All through the period of observation, the children were carrying on an underground life of their own, largely on the playground, but also in the classroom, which preoccupied them at least as much, and probably more, than the 'official' activities. It was a life filled with competition and aggression, both verbal and physical. There was an intense struggle for control of a 'fort' which the boys had built on the playground. They would not let 'outsiders' in. Outsiders included all girls, everyone not in their class, and some boys in the class who were unpopular with the others:

> The fort consists of pieces of wood leaning against each other like a lean-to, with hay all across the top, like a house, and rocks along the side. Then there is an opening for children to crawl in. Actually, by the time other classes came out, there were about ten boys working on it, and there is only room for two or three inside. It has great symbolic value for the boys building it. Connie was totally ignored, and she was really angry. She said, 'It is not fair that the girls are not allowed on this territory. It is not their territory. It is the school grounds, and anyone should be able to go there.' I saw Lenny conferring with Sam. Lenny plays up to Sam a lot. Lenny was telling them, 'Remember,

we built up the fort and the fourth graders wrecked it. Now they think the fort we are building is theirs. We are going to attack them.' Jimmy said, 'Well, I'm ready to beat up anyone who comes over.' They were really spoiling for a fight. Then John came and said, 'Can I see Sam about joining the fort?' Lenny said, 'You can't see Sam without an appointment.' Connie threw a fit. 'That's really crazy. You have to have an appointment to get into this fort.' A group of fourth-graders came over and a fourth-grade boy said, 'You wrecked our fort, so we are going to wreck yours.' The boys in the class said, 'No, we didn't wreck yours; it was ruined by the rain.' The fourth grader persisted, 'We are going to come back and wreck your fort.' Carol's boys were very upset for a while.

The fort was the center of many episodes. Girls who tried to gain entry on one day were physically attacked by the boys, knocked to the ground, and had their coats torn off – in winter weather. The teacher in charge of supervising the playground at the time did not interfere. She said the girls enjoyed having the boys chase them. But the observer felt that many of them were frightened and some were physically hurt by these attacks.

A competing fort, built by a challenger for the leadership of the boys, caused a great many quarrels about the stealing of building materials and accusations about deliberate destruction of each other's handiwork.

Carol did not seem to be fully aware of the complex peer-group ramifications involved in the struggle for possession and leadership of the fort. She did know, however, that the children had taken exclusive possession of a part of the playground which belonged to the whole school. Several of the children pointed out that this was not 'fair'. Carol's style, in playing the role of the teacher, was never to give orders but always to discuss, explain, and persuade. She used these techniques to try to correct the situation, but to no avail. And she seemed incapable of simply asserting her authority to do what needed to be done. Instead, she allowed these aggressive children to keep their exclusive fort, taking advantage of the whole school, until the wind and the rain finally blew it down, and the children became absorbed in something else. This is the kind of teacher, extraordinarily reluctant, and even incapable of asserting authority, who, as Roland Barth (1972) pointed out, is disproportionately attracted to open classroom teaching.

Another observation we made about this class was that popularity with peers and working hard academically were negatively associated:

> Sam does very, very little work, even though he is the most popular boy in the class. (He is the leader of the fort in the playground.) The boys who really do the most work in the class, Richard and Peter, and the girls too, Pam and Shirley, are not the most popular. Richard is well liked by everyone, but he is very much a loner. Larry, who does almost no work, is also among the most popular ones.

Thus the anti-intellectual student culture described by Coleman (1961) for high schools is already present in the second and third grades, at least in this school. But the main point is that peer group subcultures are more important in open classrooms than in traditional ones. In traditional classrooms, work is individual; peer groups carry on their activities during recess, athletic periods, and other interstices of the school day. In the open classroom, children are permitted for most of the day to work with self-chosen groups. This means that the peer groups invade and influence the central dynamics of the classroom and affect the children's work in fundamental ways. That will be even more apparent in the next class we discuss.

A fifth-sixth-grade open classroom team

Nancy Stuart's fifth-grade class and Manny Levine's sixth-grade class were teamed. They occupied rooms located at right angles to each other in a corner of the second floor corridor.

196

There was no connecting door between the rooms, and since the fifth and sixth graders were not separated for most of their work, there was a constant flow of children through the corridor from one room to the other. Nancy specialized in teaching language arts and Manny taught math. Social studies was handled by one of the two student teachers, and science was not taught at all during the period of our observation.

By contrast with Carol Stone's room, or the K–1–2 open classroom at Coolidge, Nancy's room showed a great dearth of materials. There was a two-tiered loft where children could sit, play, and read. It had been built by a shop teacher with the help of some pupils. There was a pyramid-shaped castle, the walls of which displayed the children's writing. There were some art materials and a class library. There were cages for the hamsters and gerbils, but the cages were not well-made, and the animals kept escaping and dying in closets and other hiding places. Some placards on the walls suggested topics for stories children could write. There were two TV sets, a phonograph, and some tables and chairs. The space was not organized in any discernible pattern, so that activities would be clearly located in certain places, and traffic flow through the room would be facilitated.

The only new materials Nancy brought into the room during two and a half weeks of observation was some colored tissue paper. She showed the children a collage of fir trees in various shades of green and yellow that she had made by cutting out the tissue paper and mounting it on a white board. She said she was going to prepare some tissue paper and board and show anyone who wanted to learn how to do it.

Manny's room was a bit smaller than Nancy's. In the center, running from front to back, were three tables with chairs around them. A carpeted space on one side of the room was surrounded on three sides by mathematics games on shelves. Another little space had Manny's desk. There was a third space, a kind of alleyway made by a wall between the classroom and the clothing closets, in which children often sat on the floor and worked. The room had a display of mathematics books and math problems and puzzles on cards. There was a calculator as well.

Toward the back of the room was a box of miscellaneous materials – tools, fabrics, paper, foam rubber, styrofoam, nuts, bolts, buckles, and electric plugs – from which the children made diaramas in shoe boxes.

Manny's room was often overcrowded because the fifty children on the team spent more time there than in Nancy's room. They may have been due to the fact that the tables and carpeted spaces were well-suited to working in groups. The room was also tidier than Nancy's, which had a lot of trash on the floor, closets left open, and materials left around in disarray.

The team organized its work around a contract system. Each week each child made a contract with one of the teachers to do certain things. The children wrote the contracts themselves and had them approved by a teacher or student teacher. A typical week's contract had five tasks on it:

1 Write a story.
2 Draw a picture of anything.
3 Play chess.
4 Read a mini-library math book.
5 Do a math problems card.

Another contract read:

1 Read two books and do a project in connection with one of them. [that usually meant doing an illustration for the book.]
2 Math project. [Unspecified.]
3 Work in recycle center. [This was the center with all the materials.]
4 'Yellow.' [This meant playing a certain math game with another student.]
5 Write a story.
6 Work with Arthur. [This was a learning disability specialist who came to the school regularly.]
7 Fix room.
8 Work with arithmetic.

A third contract read:

198

1 Chips [a math game] and this was marked 'Finished. I played with John.'
2 Read a book and do project.
3 Play Quinto. [Another math game.]
4 Make a maze for the hamsters. This was marked 'Looks OK to me' and initialed by a student teacher.

We calculated that these contracts took up a little less than half the children's school time during the week. They went to gym classes, music classes, and art classes and had an afternoon of optional activities. Once or twice a week they received whole-class lessons in mathematics, and they also worked as a class on 'Man, A Course of Study', the well known elementary school social-studies curriculum.[3] Any remaining time the children had, and they had quite a lot of it, they were free to do what they chose. The classrooms didn't offer many possibilities for constructive independent work. There were several flourishing business enterprises going on among the children, which the teachers knew about and didn't interfere with. Some children drew pictures to order and sold them for a fee. Others bought and sold baseball cards. One boy constructed an ingenious spinning pointer on a dial which his clients spun for a fee; where it rested there was printed a 'fortune' for the client. Some fortunes were catastrophic and some were wonderful, but all of them were funny.

Children did not write their contracts individually. Rather, the members of a clique all wrote their contracts together. Sometimes there was cheating. For instance, a girl trying to curry favor with a popular child said to her, 'I wrote a report on the kidney. You want to read it? You could put a report on the kidney in your contract and copy mine.' It might seem surprising that the children could get away with this, but they could and did, because their teachers did not check carefully each week to see that the work in the contract was done. Rather, they 'took the kids' word for it' that they had completed their contracts. Manny told us that the children were truthful and trustworthy about this, but observation revealed that many of them were not. Many were not mature enough for the responsibility the loosely supervised contracts put on their shoulders. And others were not inventive enough to keep themselves occupied. One of the student teachers observed:

> I see a number of kids who are just sort of swimming around aimlessly all the time. Certainly not a majority of them, but enough of a minority so that I think this is a question of great concern. Maybe it's something inherent in the open classroom itself which requires a larger teacher-to-student ratio.

This contention, that open classrooms require a high adult-to-child ratio, was reiterated many times to us by open classroom teachers. Without at least one adult for every twelve children, American open classrooms do not seem to work. At least those we observed which had a lower ratio than that – like Abe Winner's class at Southside – were often disorganized.

A form of neglect that Nancy and Manny's pupils suffered was that their teachers hardly corrected their spelling, punctuation, or grammar. The children's writing was filled with errors to a degree quite surprising for their age, intelligence, and background in reading. The more formal fifth- and sixth-grade classroom teachers did correct such errors systematically, and it was our impression that their pupils' writing was more correct than that of the open classroom team. We do not believe it was so much a scruple about not stifling creativity, as sheer laziness, which kept Nancy and Manny from correcting the children's written work. Here are some examples of their writing from an exercise which was a blank page headed; 'I felt, I was, I am, I did, I learned, I improved, I experienced, I wish, I can, I tried, I overcame, I started, I finished, I know, I. . . .':

> this year I think I did pritty good. it was fun this year and I learned a lot of things in math and soashal studies. I did finish a lot of [s]peed math tests and I go[t] [a] fare number of them right. My contract work it satisfis me but I wish I had more freinds in schoo[l]. tried to do some things that

other kids did to see if I could make some more feinds but it didn't work. I feel like every time I walk in to the room every body walks out and never want to do any thing with me. and that is all I can say for this year.

This year I learned new kinds of math. But I did not improve in multipucation then I did in the Beginning of the year. I'm allrite in social stuids the Part I liked most was the Babons. I like the new class myths its rely fun. Im rely lousy in spelling as you can see. And same with my pucuation. contracs are fun most of the time I get them in late But I dont think Ive gotin any 8 ball notes. I love optionals on wed. They class I like the most is FolkDancing and this is my second time Before that I taoke weaving and folkdancing in writing I get good idears for storys But I never write them down good one story I wrote was about a candy maker who Bad a candy rocket that was one of the Best story I ever did in this class this year

This year was pretty good. I learned about the salmon and the Herring, gulles and the Eskamoes in social studies and the classes were pretty good but Gabriel [the student teacher] kept on taking a fit and we never got anywhere. I also like talking about myths and how they were maid up. Miss Marks teaches myths and she's really nice Gabriel teaches math and so does Mr L. but Gabriel teaches most of the time.

I think that this year is my best and I really like Mrs S. and Mr L. We have contracts and my contracts I think are pretty good. but some times I can't finish them in time and I get really frustrated. I am not so good In math or reading. in fact Im terrible. Some times my contracts don't get finished by Wednesday and I get scared I'm going to have to com back. I have never come back and I never got a 8ball note.[4]

This year I have met a lot of new Friends and this is the best class because all the teachers arn't like teachers There like Friends and that why I like this class. We have optionals and they are really great but the optional that I like best is the one I'm in now Entering Adolesens and it's great when we talk about having babies. I have done some book projects that I think are pretty good. And have had a wonderful year!!!!

I wish I could start the year over
I ttried to do better and projects
I was scar ed tha last weeks because of the play
I know that 6th grade is fun
I started I think with better projects
I did great thingstoo like ...the puppet show my ABC book,
Dictonairy vocabulairy I am happer I felt sad at the begging of the year
I can do a fractions I overcame being scared
I experienced being yelled at a lot
I finished my cross number puzzle book
Mrs Stuart said I improved behaveyor
I learnd how to make a teacher mad

Both Nancy and Manny said in their interviews that affective goals for pupils were as important to them as cognitive ones. An example was an agreement they had with the mother of one girl that they would try to help her overcome her excessive dependence:

Julie came up to Mrs Stuart and pointed out that a piece of furniture had half collapsed. Mrs Stuart said, 'Julie, I think you had better do something about that.' Julie went and fixed it; it was quite easy to do. The next day Julie asked Manny for some rubber bands and he said, 'You know where they are. That helplessness of yours is what your mother and I talked about.'

A floating substitute teacher in the school described to us how Mrs Stuart once had a fifteen-minute discussion with the class about the feelings of a boy from whom something was stolen. Nancy felt the child was upset and that others had had similar experiences; it was important to get these feelings out in the open and talk about them. Mrs Stuart was particularly skilled at leading such discussions. On another occasion, after we had delineated for her the sociometric structure of the team,[5] she decided to talk about cliques with the children. She began by asking them what was nice about having 'special friends.' The children talked a good bit about this, and then, spontaneously, they moved over to the question of what was 'not nice' about their cliques. They mentioned the pain of exclusion. They mentioned their own unkindness to outsiders. They mentioned the fact that they often hid their own true opinions in order to conform to the majority view in the group. Mrs Stuart did not draw any moral. There was no need to. The children themselves concluded that they had been grossly unkind to some new transfer students, who were excluded from the cliques simply because they *were* new.

The cliques also reported some of their norms of behavior. One girls' clique prescribed dungarees and body shirts as the sole acceptable costume for its members. A boys' group required each member to insult all the others once every day, and the insulted party was supposed to come up with a fast and witty retort. Games of ritual insult like this occur in many cultures. What this boys' clique at Coolidge did, resembled in many respects the way the black children at Johnson played 'the dozens'. In both cases the 'winner' is the person judged by the audience to have been coolest, fastest, and wittiest. However, youngsters at Johnson frequently 'lost their cool' and got into a physical fight in the classroom, corridors, or playground. Boys at Coolidge were more likely to maintain their aggression at a verbal level, though not always. Sometimes, a boy who went too far was 'creamed' on the way home from school.

Nancy and Manny worked more closely together than many of the other two-person teams in the school. In the non-open fifth-grade team and the non-open sixth-grade team, the teachers simply divided up the subject matter and each taught the two classes his or her own way, without consulting the other party, except for occasional chats about individual pupils. However, the very closeness of their collaboration created certain difficulties for Nancy, or so she said. She complained that Manny, who was in his mid-twenties, was very immature:

> He's a baby. And I find that very difficult. Up until this year he used the children for his own ego gratification. He was very dependent on their love of him. One day a girl who was in love with one of the boys told him a dream she'd had and he told it to the other kids and he had her sobbing. He played into emotions that he should not have played into with preadolescent children. He used to do that kind of thing all the time.

In contrast to the K–1–2 teachers and the 2–3 open classroom teacher, who spent evenings and weekends planning for their rooms and their pupils' work, neither Nancy nor Manny did much preparation. Nancy said she did some planning on Tuesday and Thursday afternoons when the children had gym or art or music. But she never brought work home, except for the writing of anecdotal reports to the parents, because she had her own two children who needed her attention. Manny said that he taught 'off the top of my head'.

Peer group functioning in the fifth-sixth-grade team

As one reads philosophical accounts of the open classroom, one gains the impression that children choose their activities individually, that those who have made the same choice form a temporary task group which dissolves when the activity is over, and that new groups re-form easily around new individual choices.

This suggests great social fluidity in the open classroom. The sociometric literature tells us that young children are more fluid in their social groupings than older children. However, one of the K–1–2 teachers at Coolidge told us about very strong peer groups in her room:

In last year's first-grade class there was a group of boys who were the closest thing to a teenage gang at the age of six I've ever seen. It was unreal. They were totally exclusive. Unfortunately, they were all very strong leader types whom other children like to emulate. We had enormous problems with children being very unhappy who were not included, and the group was being very nasty, very cruel to other children. This year we broke them up. We separated them. Now I have another situation this year which is a group of second- and first-grade boys who are just super kids. Everyone wants to be their friend. There are some children who are very unhappy that they are not really good friends with them. But they are not unpleasant; they are not nasty. Their support of and help to each other is just phenomenal to watch. We just try to use what happens constructively.

Question: 'In what way?'
Answer: 'We can use some children's desire to be friends to structure the situation so that they are at least communicating.'
Question: 'Do these peer groups present a different problem in open and traditional classrooms?'
Answer: 'Absolutely. In a traditional classroom they are there, but nothing happens within the classroom. It's mostly kept on the outside. In the informal classroom they are there in the middle of the classroom all the time.'

Each clique on the 5–6 team had a customary gathering place. This territory, which was usually a certain table or corner of the room, performed the same function for the children as the street corners they frequent perform for young adult gangs; they made it easy for the members to find each other.

The members of a clique collaborated on their weekly contracts. Children in each clique took care to sign up for roughly the same amount and kinds of work. The norm for a 'fair week's work' was indicated by such comments as, 'If you put that in, it will be too much.' It was indicated too by the comparisons among children of the number of pages of original writing they turned out each week and by the gentle or not so gentle razzing of members who had done 'too much'. We validated the existence of 'output norms' by examining the contracts themselves which, rather than being individual, were strikingly alike for members of the same clique.

The face that self-chosen peers did most of their work together on the 5–6 team had several consequences. First, the members helped each other. This was a desired outcome, except when it degenerated into feeding each other 'right' answers. Second, tasks which were meant to be individual became a group product – like writing a poem by having each member contribute a few lines. Third, and most important, there were large chunks of time when there was no clear-cut division between being 'on-task' or 'off-task'. The work was carried on simultaneously with purely social conversation. For instance, a group of girls sat around 'their' table. One was writing a book report; one was reading a book; one was drawing a picture; and one was doing a cross-number puzzle. As they worked, they discussed a slumber party they were planning for the following week. In the background there was rock and roll music on the class phonograph. The attention of each member of the group fluctuated continually between the work and the conversation, with the background music also claiming some attention. The children seemed able to fulfill contracts in a way acceptable to the teachers, while working in this manner. There is some question in our minds as to whether children who have worked this way for several years can easily learn to work any other way; viz., with their attention fully concentrated on the task. They seemed to be acquiring a trained incapacity to concentrate their attention. On the other hand, they were learning to work with others.

The larger and more enduring the peer group, the more likely it was to have a differentiated internal structure, with a leader and a hierarchy of influence and prestige. The main criterion of leadership was interpersonal skill. Popular children were described as being 'nice', 'never mean,' and 'never letting you down'. When very popular leaders were observed for a while, it became clear that they were helpful to and supportive of their followers. In order to be helpful, they had to be good at activities valued by the clique. One leader of a girls' clique was good at drawing and gymnastics. She was 'pretty' and 'into' boy-girl relationships. Above all, she had the requisite inter-personal skill. These criteria are like those Coleman described in *The Adolescent Society*. However, in the open classroom this girl's leadership extended to academic work. She was asked for her judgment of their work by clique members who were academically her superiors. On one occasion a girl in the clique complained to Manny that more work was expected of her than of the leader. Manny explained that that was due to the fact that she had greater skills. But the girl persisted in regarding the teacher's demands as 'unjust'.

Boys mentioned athletic skill and 'being a good kid' as the criteria of popularity. The importance of interpersonal skill among them was demonstrated one day in art class when each clique was working on a large painting. In one of these groups the outstanding artist at first took the lead in deciding what they would paint and how. But because he could not organize the activities of the others successfully, he quickly lost his place to the usual leader of the clique.

As in the 2–3 classroom, academic ability was not a criterion of popularity for either boys or girls. Best-liked youngsters tended to do little academic work, and youngsters who did a lot of academic work were not liked. Output norms were set by peer groups, and they were low.

This last point was an aggravated issue at Coolidge in the fifth and sixth grades. Teachers and students in the non-open fifth- and sixth-grade rooms both claimed they did much more work than the 5–6 open classroom team. Teachers and students on the team insisted this was not so. It seemed to us that it was so, but the explanation was uncertain. Since Nancy and Manny did not work very hard themselves, that might have been a sufficient explanation of why their students didn't work much either. It is possible too, that at the 5–6-grade level – which is very cliquish in any case – the centrality of peer groups in the open classroom, and the intense preoccupation of the preadolescent cliques with the requisites for social success, make it likely that pupils will do little academic work if the teachers let them get away with it.

While the fixed rows of seats in the traditional classroom encourage individual – if not individualized – work, the open classroom makes it somewhat difficult for a child to work alone. The degree of difficulty varies with the ratio of space to number of pupils. Open classroom teachers recognize the need for places in the room where a child may have some solitude and privacy, but it is not always possible to provide them in overcrowded rooms. Even when they are provided, the child working alone must be capable of doing so surrounded by intensive social interaction.

Not all children in an open classroom are members of a peer group. Among those who are not, it is necessary to distinguish between loners and isolates. Loners are children who prefer to work alone most of the time, but who are attractive to their classmates. We encountered several such loners at Southside. Usually they were highly able youngsters who did not wish to be pulled toward the peer groups' mediocre norms of achievement. They were liked because they emerged from their invisible shells periodically, and made themselves available to help others with work. Loners seemed to be left alone when they wanted to be, partly because what they were doing was too difficult for many others to share and partly because they gave off signals which indicated when they were ready to be approached, and when they were not. When they wanted company, they did not hesitate to take the initiative in seeking it. They knew they would not be rejected.

Isolates are children who are rejected by others. The isolate is the victim of verbal and sometimes physical aggression. He can often be seen on the spatial periphery of a group watching, listening, and attempting to participate.

To be an isolate in an open classroom is more painful than it is in a traditional classroom, where the life of the peer group does not color the whole school day and nearly all of the work.

One newcomer-isolate on the 5–6 team clung to the teacher for the support which was not forthcoming from his classmates. He was a good student who, out of ignorance of peer group output norms, did 'too much' work. He read 500 pages one week. The teacher publicly praised him for this, thereby worsening his situation with his peers.

While this particular isolate overproduced, it was more common for isolates to 'underproduce'. At first they were preoccupied with their social problems. Later they became depressed about those problems and the depression made working difficult. Maurice Gibbons and Katherine Cobb, who conducted an open classroom in English at junior high school and wrote about it as participant-observers, suggest that the need for companionship in the open classroom is so basic that compatible persons should be imported into the room if necessary for such children (1969).

All the open classrooms at Coolidge were strongly affected by the children's peer groups. In the 2–3 classroom and the 5–6 team, we observed this for ourselves. In the case of the K–1–2 team, we had the teacher's testimony that it was so. Yet the range of problems which peer groups can create are not discussed in the literature of open education. Open classroom teachers vary in their awareness of peer groups and their effects. Some know quite well what the membership of the groups in their rooms is, and others, like Nancy Stuart and Manny Levine, do not. Some, like the K–1–2 teacher at Coolidge, are aware of both destructive and constructive effects that peer groups can have, and they try to manipulate these as best they can. However, they are also aware that there are limits to what a teacher can do in influencing peer groups. 'You cannot legislate a friendship', as the K–1–2 teacher said.

Our hypothesis, deriving from these observations, is that children's peer groups take on added importance in the open classroom over and above the importance they have always had in school. In particular, to the extent that they are also the task groups, social considerations tend to interfere with and override considerations of academic effectiveness. Time after time, we saw children whose skills for a task made them the natural leader of the group for that task, displaced because the group would follow only its established leader. It happened to the best artist of the 5–6 team, when the task was to paint a mural. It happened when academic leadership was ceded to the most popular girl in the main girls' clique on the 5–6 team, although she was inferior as a student to many members of her group. In addition, in a classroom where much of the work is done in small groups, rather than individually or by the class as a whole, the child who is a social isolate not only lacks *social* companions, he has no one to *work* with and sometimes, thereby, is rendered unable to work at all.[6]

If our hypothesis is correct, open education has consequences not intended by its practitioners. By allowing children to group themselves spontaneously for work as well as play, they have admitted into the classroom – in the form of strongly organized and stable cliques – powerful social forces which are neither understood nor controlled.

Notes

1 Combining grade levels, as into a kindergarten and first grade, or a kindergarten, first, and second grade, is called 'family grouping'. The practice is a part of open education in England. It is a kind of limited nongrading which permits children to move ahead at their own pace and also allows for a great deal of teaching and learning to occur between children. In a K–1–2, only one third of the group changes each year. The 'old-timers' in the classroom give the teachers a lot of assistance in socializing the newcomers into the way things are done.

2 This classroom was observed by Laura Schorr and described in a first draft by Diane Levin. The final writing was done by the author, partly from Levin's paper, and partly from Schorr's field notes.

3 Created by the Educational Development Center, Newton, Mass.

4 Apparently an 8ball note was given by one of the teachers to a pupil whose contract was not finished on time. The pupil then had to stay after school to finish it. We never saw this happen.

5 Sociometric structure is a term sociologists use to describe the pattern of cliques, of isolates, and of popularity in a classroom,

depending on the answers to questions such as 'Whom do you like best in the class?' 'Whom do you like least?' 'Whom would you most like to have as a partner on an art project?' etc. We did not ask sociometric questions until after we had observed for a while, and then we did it as an interview with each child, rather than a paper-and-pencil questionnaire. Today there are some computer programs for deriving the sociometric structure of a class from data like those we collected in this team. We, however, used the answers to the questions only to check whether the groupings we observed day after day reflected fairly accurately the pupils' verbalized feelings of mutual attraction and dislike. They did.

6 The reader will recall this happened to a pupil at Johnson, who was isolated from her table for a while, as a punishment.

9

Black resistance in the liberal comprehensive

John Furlong

In 1974 Dhondy concluded, 'The behaviour of black youth in relation to the discipline machine can be considered nothing less than a crisis of schooling, (p. 44). As a consequence he prophesied a 'black explosion' in schools in the near future. Has his prediction come true? Are black youth more seriously alienated than their white counterparts? Do black pupils now pose a threat to the running of inner-city comprehensives? Most contemporary theorizing in the sociology of race relations
· would confirm Dhondy's expectation of a black explosion. Both neo-Marxist (Castles and Kosak, 1969; Nikolinakos, 1973; Sivanandan, 1976) and conflict theories (Rex, 1970; Rex and Moore, 1967; Rex and Tomlinson, 1979) lead to predictions of alienation and rejection by black youth of the dominant institutions of society, including schools. Yet despite the elegant theorizing, comparatively few sociologists have actually studied disaffected West Indian pupils in school (Tomlinson, 1977). Most have been content to speculate from the sidelines and suggest that because older black youth in the Rastafarian movement seem to have totally rejected white society then so

too must their younger brothers in school (Hebdige, 1976 and 1980; Hall *et al.*, 1978; Garrison, 1979). The starting point of the research on which this paper is based was the observation that this was not in fact the case, at least not yet. In reality West Indian boys at school – however they may appear to their teachers – do not reject their education, but instead take up a contradictory approach to it. It will be shown that even those who are seen by their teachers as the most seriously troublesome at school are not consistently alienated from it and are in many ways deeply committed to it.

The research presented comes from studying a small group of disaffected West Indian boys in a London comprehensive. The argument relates to boys and cannot be generalized to girls who appear to take up a somewhat different stance in relation to school (Fuller, 1980). The fieldwork was part of a study examining disaffection in six schools. The seven boys discussed here attended one of the schools and formed a close friendship group. Most lived near the school and had been friends since primary school. In the school's terms they were all low-achievers. All were British born and entirely British educated, but none of their parents was born or educated in this country. The school which was in a well established working-class district of East London, had approximately 50 per cent non-patrial pupils, the majority being of West Indian descent. Research contact was made with these pupils during their fourth and fifth years and involved a combination of techniques, including semi-structured and unstructured individual interviews, group discussions and classroom observation. (For a more detailed account of the research as a whole and the methods employed see Bird *et al.*, 1980.)

These seven boys constituted a regular problem for their school and demanded constant vigilance from their teachers. Their school records revealed that each of them had had a turbulent school career involving regular confrontations – both verbal and physical – with teachers and over the years almost every form of pastoral care and discipline had been tried on them. By the fourth and fifth years, during the period of

213

research, they were involved in almost daily skirmishes with the senior staff and these frequently developed into more serious confrontations which resulted in suspensions and/or parents being called in. From the outside it looked as though these boys were engaged in a constant war of attrition with their teachers, continually sniping at those who showed any signs of weakness but never managing finally to defeat the enemy. If any group of West Indian pupils were to provide evidence of the widely predicted alienation and rejection of school then surely these boys would.

Contradictions?

Initial contact with the group began with one boy, Wesley,[1] interviewed in the spring term of his fourth year. He had been nominated by a number of teachers as a major problem in the school. Described as rude, awkward and aggressive to teachers and sometimes physically violent, Wesley seldom did any school work and was always to be seen wandering around the school when he should have been in lessons. Yet in interviewing him it became clear that there were considerable contradictions in his attitudes to school: he was both for it and against it, he wanted to achieve but was unwilling to work, he wanted control but rejected its imposition.

Wesley generally believed in school and achievement in exams, for example:

> JF: Well, as we're talking about exams, what do you think of them? Do you think they are important? I mean some kids think they are a waste of time and some kids think they are very important.
>
> Wesley: Well, they're the only thing that'll get you a job – get you a good job.
>
> JF: Do you see any of these subjects as relevant? How about maths?
>
> Wesley: Yes. I find it relevant, but I don't seem to be doing well in it. It's important because they can get you a job, maths and English, they're the most important things.

214

These opinions were typical of Wesley's high evaluation of formal academic achievement. Later in the term contact was made with the group of six other boys with whom Wesley spent most of his time. Despite their low record of achievement they too shared his relatively high academic aspirations. Yet when it came to school work these boys did virtually nothing. For example, they would turn up late to lessons.

> Wesley: English – that's good, but I usually turn up late.

The same was true for maths.

> Wesley: Well, maths I come late as well. Well, when we've only got a single period, I'm late. I come about ten minutes from the end. Well, about twenty minutes late.
> JF: Does the teacher say anything?
> Wesley: Well, I don't really care if he does. He says he's going to tell Mr ——. I don't know if he does or not. I don't know what he does, but I don't seem to get into trouble for it. No, I always come late.

When he actually arrived at a lesson Wesley seldom seemed to do much work and, at least from his own accounts, spent most of his time talking.

> Wesley: When I'm there (in class) I work. Oh well, sometimes I work, if the girls is messing about and they're talking to me, then I talk to them and we get into long conversation and do no work. When I start talking I don't finish.

Although Wesley and his friends valued school – and it was more than merely paying lip service – they never did much. They stood in marked contrast to many disaffected working-class boys and girls contacted during the same study, who seemed to reject the whole notion of the legitimacy of school, even in an instrumental sense (Willis, 1977; Bird *et al.*, 1980).

A similar and interrelated contradiction concerned the attitude of these boys to authority and discipline. On the one hand they appreciated teachers who were 'strict but good', saying that they did a lot of work in some lessons and gained a considerable sense of satisfaction and pride in their achievement. Yet they revelled in the chaos of classes where the teachers could not control them.

JF: So what happens in (that teacher's) classes?
Wesley: (laughing) Oh, a lot of things.
JF: Like what? Is it chaos, or what?
Wesley: Yeah, yeah. He can't control it.
JF: Do you join in when every one else starts mucking about?
Wesley: Yeah, yeah. Well, he can't control *me*.

Wesley liked control yet revelled in its absence and, as his records showed, he would even hit a teacher who tried to impose it.

These contradictions between work and misbehaviour and between accepting and rejecting authority are seen as typical of West Indian pupils by many teachers. To understand and explain this contradictory approach to school it is necessary to utilize a rather different theoretical tradition from that common in contemporary race relations: the theory of a culture of resistance.

The study of cultures of resistance both amongst pupils at school and amongst youth in general has a long history (see Furlong, 1985). Whether the focus has been on school or on society at large, cultures of resistance are seen growing up either consciously or unconsciously in response to the 'problems' members feel they face. Those studies which have concentrated on pupils picture them as constructing their own cultures in order to solve the problems thrust upon them by the school. (For example, Lacey, 1970; and Cohen, A. 1955.)

Willis (1977) has demonstrated how cultures of resistance can have both an institutional and a broader logic at the same time. He argues that the very structure of society is mediated through the school and that school resistance amongst working-class youth can therefore be seen as a form of class struggle. In constructing their culture of resistance, Willis

216

shows how a group of white working-class boys exploited features of normal school life and 'reworked' them so that they became symbols of resistance: a uniform worn in a slightly different way could be clearly subversive; arriving late for a lesson could imply a direct challenge to authority. He suggests that pupils selected particular symbols and combined them with elements from popular culture – particularly music and clothes – to form a coherent culture of resistance. Elements were chosen because of their 'resonance' with the pupils' experience of their class location both inside and outside school. Certain actions 'seemed appropriate', certain clothes or songs 'felt right' precisely because they helped to articulate, if only in a symbolic way, the pupils' experience of a structured society as mediated through the school. In this way the pupils' culture of resistance grew up in a conscious way – its elements were freely chosen – but at the same time the pupils were only partially aware of its full import, for it partially penetrated the reality of their position in society.

If the culture of resistance of these seven West Indian boys is explored we can see that they too drew selectively on popular culture, parental culture and aspects of their institutional life in order to create their own unique cultural resistance. But unlike Willis' boys, the reality of their situation was obscured from them. The liberal policies of the school, in combination with their families' lack of experience of the British education system, meant that they were able to maintain their aspirations for high educational achievement despite all of the evidence to the contrary. Some form of resistance was essential – in comparison with their peers they were failing – but the full reality of the position was not revealed to them until their mock CSEs during the fifth year, by which time they could be gently eased out of the school or their absences ignored. Until that time what they wanted was a partial culture of resistance that would allow them both to accept the school and the possibilities it held out to them for upward mobility while at the same time rejecting it, because they were indeed failing. This was precisely what their culture allowed them to do.

The culture of resistance – its theme and form

This section will outline the main *theme* of the sub-culture that these boys subscribed to, that is their concern to establish a reputation as a man, and it will then go on to describe the *form* of their group life. In both of these matters – the theme and the form of group life – these West Indian boys were quite different from white working-class boys. Both black and white male cultures of resistance are often concerned with activities that relate to masculinity and both talk of 'hardness' as an essential feature of that masculinity, but the word 'hard' is used in different ways. Amongst white working-class youth, hardness has predominant overtones of physicality and strength. Although being able to 'handle yourself' was important for these West Indian boys too, the way they used the word hardness was essentially different and much more closely associated with 'style' and maturity. The concern was to establish a reputation as a 'man' through style that informed how they dealt with all the central aspects of their lives: their music, their dress, their girlfriends and their relationships with the school.

In this sense the theme of masculinity strongly parallels the argument put forward by Wilson (1969) who, in a review of Caribbean anthropological literature, argues that it is the need to establish and maintain a reputation that underpins the social organization of all male life there. Traditionally, he argues, West Indian society has been seen as entirely matriarchal with women dominating the family, and taking precedence in any formal institutional community life such as the church or the school. Wilson argues that women's concern to pursue the more universalistic values of 'respectability' makes them more visible by their community involvement, to western anthropologists, so most researchers have overlooked the far more localized and informal peer groups that make up male social life. Unlike the universal values of 'respectability', the particular concerns of male groups vary considerably. Some may centre on drinking, others on gambling, and so establishing a reputation for masculinity is dependent on intensive verbal interaction by small groups.

Wilson's description of Caribbean male peer groups parallels the form of social life established by this group of boys. They too engaged in an intensive verbal form of social interaction. Being at school was predominantly about being with friends, and being with friends involved a continual dialogue. The theme of a 'reputation' for masculinity and the form of intensive association that characterized this group's life were therefore essentially true to traditional male West Indian society. Their interests were modern (contemporary popular Dub music and Rasta) but on another level they had rediscovered and reworked established forms and themes of social behaviour in developing their own particular culture of resistance to school. In reality it is impossible to distinguish the theme of reputation from the form of association through which it was lived, for every demonstration of hardness or style, be it verbal or otherwise, was also valued as part of the process of association and vice versa. Nevertheless, for analytical purposes the two will be presented separately.

Reputation

One of the central concerns of this group was music which illustrates how the boys appropriated items in a particular way that fitted their culture of resistance. The music they were interested in was a particular derivative of Reggae, Dub as they called it, and they would travel considerable distances to hear it. Discussion of Dub illustrates their concern with hardness and style.

JF: Is it a particular form of Reggae?
P: Dub, you know what I mean?
JF: No.
P: You know a guy called Bob Marley, but he's commercial, so we don't think much of him.
P: But higher than Bob Marley, right?

219

P: 'Cos Marley too soft, you know what I mean, soft? It's commercial, all them records commercial.

P: Why don't you play him Dub?

P: Yeah, bounce a record for him.

P: Cool, cool, cool.

(They turn on a portable cassette recorder)

P: This is a classic example of what we play in our Reggae clubs.

P: Strictly rockers.

(Music plays, voices over)

P: Good there.

P: Strictly rockers.

Competition over hardness was central to what went on in the clubs that they went to. Instead of disco units they were called 'sounds' and each 'sound' had a distinctive style and band of followers.

P: All of them is roots – they play Reggae but it is the one who can drop the hardest record from Jamaica ... from roots.

P: Or sometimes they cut their own records, you know what I mean?

P: And when they drop one against Shaka – say Coxon dropped one against Shaka.

JF: I don't understand.

P: He don't understand. Listen, listen. He play a record, right, and he has to challenge that record to see who's got the better record and that the people likes.

P: Scene, scene, scene. (i.e. hear, hear)

JF: You get two systems?

P: Four sometimes, four....

P: You get four, one in that corner, one in that corner, and they've all got boxes, all lined up.

P: The records come from Jamaica, cos that the roots of Dub music, you know what I mean? So Fat Man Hi Fi. This man name Fat Man, he's one of the sounds, he went over and bring back this (name of group I can't hear) that everyone like – they're rankin', they're rankin'. Know what I mean?

Not all the boys were Dub fans. One boy, Steve, was a 'Soulie'; that is he listened to soul music. During the interviews there were a number of very heated arguments about which was better, but the dispute was about which was harder. Despite the differences between the Soulie and Dub boy, they both seemed to agree on the central value of hardness.

> P: The reason why I like Reggae – Dub I call it – Reggae is what the old people call it – it's harder. . . . You see, Soul to me it's – too fast – it's stupid, you know what I mean? . . . It's kinda womanish.
> P: Scene, scene.
> P: It's got nothing to it. You know what I mean?
> P: Womanish.
> P: Soul is American. Dub is rockers – Jamaican, you know. ('Jamaican' in this context is an accolade.)

Steve, the Soulie, disputed this description of his music.

> Steve: You think most of them are weakhearts, don't you? Weakhearts.
> P: Yeah, most of them are.
> Steve: You don't know nuttin', you don't know nuttin'. . . .
> P: You know they more peaceful than us.
> Steve: If you peaceful that mean you weak, we ain't weak.

Although on one level Soul and Dub cultures were used in a similar way by these boys (both appropriated as part of a culture of resistance to establish a traditional reputation of masculinity) on another level the two cultures are quite different. Both stem from the unresolved problem of the black community's relationship with white society (Campbell, 1980). The Soul culture with its emphasis on fast cars and lavishly stylish clothes seems to take the value of conspicuous consumption implicit in western society and 'out-do' white society by being even more stylish and even more extravagant (Cohen, P., 1972; Hebdige, 1980). Dub culture, with its associated

221

theology of Rastafarianism, is altogether more radical. Rather than taking a value from white society the Rasta movement eschews commodity fetishism, celebrates the West Indians' blackness for its own sake and emphasizes black identity and heritage (Troyna, 1978).

As many of the songs the boys liked related to Rasta texts it is not surprising that they were interested and knew about the Rastafarian movement, but here too they appropriated it in a particular sort of way – they were interested in Rasta dress and hairstyles (locks), but not in the less stylistic aspects of its philosophy. They had appropriated aspects of the Rasta movement that were in line with their own needs; they were interested in its possibilities for establishing a reputation as a man – hence the concern with style – but at this stage in their development were less concerned with its theology. As argued below, a more complete involvement with the Rasta movement was not appropriate for these boys until they left school and the reality of their position was clear to them. While in the protected environment of school the Rasta movement only meant style and maturity.

Rasta and Dub were interests that lay outside the school, but the theme of reputation for masculinity provided the basis of their relationship with every aspect of school life. For example, it influenced the way the boys looked at other pupils.

> P: They're, they're youtish, 'cos things they do we wouldn't do. Now I see them one time playing with a frisby, now I wouldn't do that, 'cos that a bit youtish. I would just fling it, just like that, but I wouldn't go flinging it and catching it, flinging it and catching it, you know what I mean? That's a bit youtish.

A great many traditional activities were proscribed by the importance of being seen as hard and this often included playing sports for the school, even when the boys were good at it.

> P: I used to do a lot (of sport) for the school, but I don't do it any more. I can't be bothered to do things after school, I'd rather go and watch and not take part.

What was important for these pupils was their particular form of socializing which would allow them to develop and maintain a reputation for hardness. In some significant way this was not possible on the sports field.

This theme was particularly influential in how they felt they should conduct themselves with teachers. Discipline was only acceptable to the boys if it did not compromise their sense of dignity. Relationships with authority always had to be conducted on their *own* terms.

> P: If I hit a teacher my mum would tell me off, but if it was something like the teacher hit me and I hit him back and I got suspended, then my mum wouldn't say nothing, because at my other school the teachers used to hit me and I never used to do anything.... But *now*, if the teacher hits me – I hit him back.

If teachers were rude or aggressive or in the boys' eyes 'shamed' them in front of their peers then they would withdraw their support and become openly hostile, aggressive and even violent.

The theme of reputation therefore frequently brought them into conflict with their teachers, but at the same time it also committed them to education, for reputation was fundamentally involved with the occupations to which they aspired. In discussing future careers with these boys it became clear that their aspirations were quite different from their white counterparts. For example, it was apparent in the following discussion that the idea of being a dustman, whatever its financial rewards, was entirely unacceptable:

> JF: There were some kids I was talking to recently who said that what they wanted from work was money and they didn't mind being a dustman.
>
> All: (Cries of derision.) Shame.
>
> JF: The reason they wanted to be dustmen was that they could work from seven until twelve and they could then

go on and do another job, so they could get a lot of money.

Wesley: Yeah, well, what if you pick up the bin and your mate comes out of the house? (Indignant laughter.)

P: Or see a girl, see a girl, and she goes, 'I say you. You picked up my dustbin, didn't you?' – No man, shame.

Wesley: No man, you ain't got no pride.

JF: So, is that more important than money?

All: Yeah, yeah. Very!

P: Yeah, like I don't wanna work in a factory.

JF: For the same reason?

P: Yeah.

Jobs, like dress and ways of 'handling yourself', were closely bound up with a sense of style and taking a low-status job was something to be ashamed of; it would have to be concealed from friends and particularly from girls:

JF: Supposing you were offered £200 a week to work in a sweet factory?

Leroy: £200? I'd take it!

Steve: I'd take it, yeah.

JF: What? Even if it was routine?

Tony: I'd take it. I'd take it – £200 – you'd be mad to refuse it! But I wouldn't tell people what I was doing.

Leroy: Yeah! I wouldn't tell anyone what I was doing, especially girls. I wouldn't tell girls that I worked in a sweet factory.

The jobs considered valuable by these boys included all kinds of skilled manual work, but most particularly the work of a mechanic:

JF: Well, what sort of jobs do you think are good?

Leroy: Well, clerical, and mechanical. You can say you're something, not just a factory worker or on the dole. Anything mechanical.

Tony: Say someone asks you, like, what's your job? You can say a mechanic, right? You can say it straight out, right? Or your mum, if she's talking to her friends, can say, 'My son's a mechanic', you know, 'working for a firm' and all that – British Airways or something. But if you say 'My son's working down the factory', that's nothing to boast about, is it?

The jobs to which these boys aspired demanded considerable entrance qualifications and there was therefore an essential congruence between what the school felt it could offer these boys by way of certification and the sorts of jobs to which they aspired; but it is here that the heart of the contradiction lies. Although the boys aspired to employment that demanded entrance qualifications and therefore examination passes, a reputation for style within the school could not be gained by being conformist and settling down to work. Even the most ambitious black boys seemed to engage in a precarious balancing act. To maintain their sense of dignity they had to work hard in class *and* flout the rules of the school and develop a reputation as a man. Unlike their white counterparts, they did not see unskilled work as an acceptable alternative path to adulthood and independence. Their rejection of school could therefore never be complete because they were always tied to a recognition of its importance.

Association

If the main theme of this culture of resistance was reputation for masculinity constructed around various aspects of school life and popular culture, its 'form' was one of a particularly intensive association. For these boys, school was about meeting friends and talking and this was what they spent a great deal of their time doing – talking in lessons, talking on corridors between lessons, hanging around at lunchtime and sitting on the wall outside school talking at four o'clock. On the surface this may not seem different from many white groups, but in reality there was a unique and particular form of interaction that distinguished it. White working-class groups of delinquent boys are far more concerned with 'action' and the emphasis on language is less pronounced – when something 'happens' it usually involves a fight, a confrontation or being chased by angry neighbours or the police. These West Indian boys' distinctive form of association was illustrated by the group interviews which were important social events in themselves. There was a continual dialogue amongst the participants: they talked incessantly, sometimes excluding and sometimes including the researcher. They spoke in a range of accents from standard London English through various West Indian accents to complete Patois, and they used language creatively for running jokes amongst themselves, or jokes against the researcher as an outsider, and also as a demonstration of their own hardness.

Many of the jokes were on the researcher, for example, this was said by one boy in a heavily exaggerated English accent when asked what he did at school with his friends: 'Come on, come on, how about the kid we're going to duff up tonight?' (The phrase 'duff up' was very much out of context here.) They also used extra long words as a joke on the researcher as well. 'I live adjacent to the school, supplemented to.' (Hysterical laughter from everyone.) They used this sort of subversion amongst themselves as well. For example, one boy had coined the word 'immature' to describe the other pupils in the school. He pronounced it carefully and tentatively and others copied him at the same time, then it became a joke with someone else saying, 'The analysis of substantiality is crackers.' (More hysterical laughter.) Here is another one:

JF: What clubs do you go to?
P: Go all round, we go all round. You know, Balham, Streatham.

An undercurrent voice is saying:

Surrey, Jamaica, Cardiff, Ethiopia. (As his voice gets louder everyone breaks into laughter.)

This sort of banter was incessant, continual and seemed to form a major part of what it meant to be together. The theme

226

of hardness itself was continually demonstrated and created through talk. One particularly common way to be hard was to talk in heavily accented 'cool talk'. Supportive statements like 'scene, scene' and 'strictly rockers' were often shouted when boys agreed with what someone else had said. Yet this too would often finish up as a joke, with speakers trying to talk so cool that they would end up mumbling at which point everyone could laugh at their own coolness.

For this group of boys, being together seemed extremely important. There were many important issues to discuss: music, Rasta, girls, the teachers, the politics of race. Observations around the school showed they did indeed spend a great deal of their time discussing them and often arguing about them quite violently. As a form of social life, theirs was quite distinctive and, as Wilson has suggested, heavily dependent on social support. It is because of this form of association that the notion of private time and territory within school became so important to them as a group. It was this, more than anything, that brought them into conflict with the school authorities.

Private time, private space

One of the most unusual and distinctive features of this group of pupils was that their subculture was so much school-based. The territory of the school was absolutely central to their lives. They virtually never took days off, they spent most lunch hours and quite frequently time after school simply hanging around the premises. If they missed a lesson, which they did occasionally, then it was not to leave the school premises, but to wait around in lavatories and odd corners to meet their friends. This was from a conversation with Wesley:

JF: Do you ever bunk off a whole day?
Wesley: No.
JF: Do any of your mates?
Wesley: No.
JF: What do they do?
Wesley: I don't know. Well, I don't know about a whole

227

day – they do bunk a whole lesson.

JF: Well, some kids you don't see for weeks.

Wesley: Yes, but most of my mates don't bunk a whole day, just an odd lesson.

JF: When you bunk, you usually stay round the school, do you? You're not round someone's house?

Wesley: No, no. I stay round the school, usually round by the toilets. I'm always in school.

This was in marked contrast to some white disaffected boys contacted in the same study. For them 'home' was a small estate where they lived – it was here that they spent time – it was here that things 'happened' in evenings and weekends. It was their territory which had been won and defended through disputes with other children and other tenants, and was marked out as a defensible space by grafitti and acts of vandalism. To them school was not central in the same way and if they bunked off a lesson (or more practically a whole afternoon) then they would certainly not spend the time at school. For the West Indian boys though the school premises were absolutely central. School was their territory where things would happen, and what 'happened' was association: making friends, chatting and chasing girls. (In contrast to the white boys studied, amongst whom an 'event' was more likely to be a fight, an act of vandalism or doing a 'job'.)

In order to make the territory their own, and in order to have time to enjoy it, these West Indian boys had to put considerable time and energy into exploiting the weaknesses of the school so that they could create the 'social space' for their particular group life. One exploitable resource was the school building: it was old and disorganized. Innumerable twisting and turning stone staircase led to three floors. There were so many different outbuildings and huts that new pupils took nearly a term to find what they all were. Here was superb material to be exploited. The building was impossible to patrol effectively and, because there were so many staircases and corridors, even if they were caught out of a lesson by a teacher it was quite easy to make a getaway.

Pursuing subcultural goals at school for these pupils was often the matter of appropriating private time. The official routine of the school meant moving quietly and quickly from one lesson to another when the bell went. The boys were in so many different teaching groups they should only see their friends at break and at lunchtimes. In fact, they put a great deal of creativity into making more private time for themselves by arriving late and leaving early:

JF: Quite often you are five minutes late, are you?

P: Five minutes, is that all?

JF: Well, five or ten.

P: Usually ten – ten to fifteen minutes late.

JF: And what are you doing during those ten to fifteen minutes?

P: Talking with Velma and (names several of his friends).

JF: So they are out of their lessons too? And where would you do that talking?

P: Usually down by the boys' toilets.

This account was backed up by observation. At every lesson change these boys engaged in the most furious socializing. During the five minutes when it was more or less legitimate to be on the corridors, they were often to be seen running round and round. Sometimes they would circumnavigate the building two or three times – meeting people, chatting to friends and even more frequently chasing (and catching) girls. As more and more of the other pupils moved back to their classrooms, these boys moved towards the toilets. This was a private space *par excellence*, for it was always partially legitimate and could provide a plausible account of why they were out of lessons, even to sceptical teachers.

Of course, it was not possible to miss or turn up late for every lesson. These boys were acutely sensitive to those teachers with whom they could get away with it and those teachers they thought so little of that getting caught did not bother them. These boys seemed intent on exploiting every

229

possible weakness in the school's armour to find time and space to celebrate their own cultural values. At times they would even wander into other teachers' lessons so that they could chat to friends or make some excuse to wander out of their lesson just to see who was hanging around.

Conflict was therefore inherent in the very form of association the boys adopted. Establishing their public sense of identity as a group demanded that they be together and maintain an essentially school-based territory. They nearly always came to school, but in order to achieve identity they had to 'redefine' school time and space and this inevitably brought them into conflict with their teachers.

Why did the boys remain at least partially committed to education despite the daily evidence at school that they were failing? And why, despite the fact that they explicitly recognized themselves as part of an oppressed minority in a frequently racist society, were they less alienated from school than many of their white working-class peers? The answer to these questions lies in the specific context in which their school culture arose.

The context for a culture of resistance

Rex and Tomlinson (1979) confirm the widely held belief that West Indian parents traditionally have high expectations of education for their children. Most of the parents in Rex and Tomlinson's sample had not experienced secondary schooling themselves as they had been educated in the West Indies, but they had a strong belief in the possibility of upward occupational and social mobility that could be achieved through schooling. None of these boys' parents had been educated in this country either and all the boys reported that their parents placed considerable emphasis on school achievement.

> JF: What about homework? Where does your mum stand on that? Does she make you do your homework?
> P: Yes, yes. She says, if it's school work I have to do it. If

it's going to help me take the exam and pass it then I've got to do it.

In this context the boys' relatively high occupational aspirations, despite their low achievement, are not surprising. Like their parents, they were committed to the possibility of upward occupational mobility and saw the school as a primary means of achieving this (Foner, 1975). Such attitudes to education and employment shared with their parental culture provided an important part of the context of their school subculture. Their actual experience of the school structure provided another.

The school was typical of many modern comprehensives with its liberal rejection of explicit streaming, its policy of a wide option choice system around a common core of subjects – in this case maths, English and science – and its comparatively open examination entry system. These factors in combination meant that despite their evident low academic achievement these boys were shielded from the full impact of academic stratification until the last possible moment. English and maths were taught in sets in the fourth and fifth years, but most of their other subjects were taught in mixed ability groups. Yet even in English and maths the pupils were often unaware of which set they were in: top, middle or bottom. Considerable effort in the school had been devoted to developing CSE and 'O' level syllabuses that were compatible. It was therefore possible for pupils to be taught CSE and 'O' level within the same class and in the fourth year at least the possibility of 'O' level was held out to all of the pupils. It was only as the pupils moved towards the mock exams at Christmas in their fifth year that the distinctions were made explicit. The full force of pupil differentiation and stratification was therefore obscured from the pupils for as long as possible.

This process was also aided by a liberal examination entry policy. In some subjects, failure in the mock exams meant that pupils would not be entered by the school, but other teachers in an attempt to encourage their pupils to work harder adopted a more open approach and were willing to enter those who achieved only very modest marks. Even in those subjects

231

where the rules of examination entry were most rigidly applied there was always the possibility that pupils could pay for themselves to enter the exam. Once again the reality of examination failure was partly obscured.

Finally, this school, like many others since comprehensivization, had developed a broadly based curriculum around a common core. Everyone had to take maths, science and English, but for the less academic the rest of the timetable could be filled up with more practical subjects, like motor maintenance, fabric craft, jewellery or even outdoor pursuits. For those unable or unwilling to opt for the more traditionally academic subjects like languages or a further science subject, a more practically based timetable was available. These boys partially recognized that the traditional academic subjects were going to be important in securing their entry to work. Yet, each of these boys took a heavy dose of practical subjects, so that academic, and hence occupational, stratification had in effect already taken place in their option choices, but the full implications of this selective process was unclear to them. Neither they (nor their teachers) really knew what status a CSE in outdoor pursuits would be granted in the labour market and they would be unlikely to know until they actually came to get a job.

All of these factors shielded the pupils from the full reality of their academic failure. These boys knew they were not successful *within* the school. Like all pupils they were constantly evaluated against each other every time they answered a question in class and every time they gave in their homework to be marked. They therefore recognized their own lack of ability in relation to their more successful peers, but the school had learned the lessons provided by social science in the 1960s. It had abandoned explicit streaming and had broadened its curriculum and the pupils were therefore shielded from the full reality of their *public* evaluation on standards established outside the school by examination boards and eventually employers.

These two factors (their high valuation of education as a potential path to upward occupational and social mobility, and

232

the liberal policy of the modern comprehensive school) provided the fundamental parameters of the boys' educational experience and therefore the context for their particular culture of resistance. They developed a culture of resistance because in one sense they knew they were failing – in comparison with their peers they were less successful and saw this every day – but the full reality of that failure was concealed from them. They therefore needed a culture of resistance that would allow them to maintain the myth of the possibility of success.

In this sense these boys were quite different from many of their disaffected white counterparts in the same school. Many white working-class boys and girls already know from their parents that unless they are particularly bright then education will not provide the path to the alternative future that it promises. Even though they may see certain high-status occupations as desirable and recognize that for some education is a means of achieving them, they are willing to accept that if they fail academically then there are other paths to alternative futures which seem equally valuable and which do not demand educational certification as an entry requirement.

This point marks a key difference from Willis' (1977) work. Willis suggests that his 'lads' positively aspired to manual work. It was their 'celebration' of anti-academic values that delivered them to the unskilled labour market. The evidence of this research (Bird *et al.*, 1980) suggests that most under-achieving white working-class pupils did in fact appreciate the advantages of high-status occupations, but recognized the impossibility of their ever achieving them. It was in this light that they developed alternative values and devised alternative futures for themselves. Such an observation seriously challenged Willis' 'voluntaristic' model of cultural reproduction. There was a moment of voluntarism, but it took place within a far more constrained context than that implied by Willis. For them, the mystification of the modern liberal comprehensive is irrelevant. Many such white pupils have decided early on that schooling is not for them and by the time the fifth year comes have already voted with their feet and begun to truant. These low achieving black boys had yet to learn that lesson.

To understand the position of all groups of black pupils in school – boys and girls, successful and unsuccessful – a clearer understanding of the impact of school in obscuring and revealing the realities of wider society is therefore needed. This demands an examination of particular practices and patterns of organization in particular schools.

Yet studying the structure and organization of individual schools will in itself not be enough. A more thoroughgoing analysis of the cultural location of different groups of pupils is also needed. For example, both black and white boys in this particular school were subject to the same formal school organization; their relative failure or success in relation to a stratified society was equally obscured or revealed by the school's examination and curriculum practices.

Yet the responses of these two groups were typically quite different. However a school is structured, the way it is experienced by individuals is itself influenced by their specific cultural location. Different cultural groups – blacks, whites, boys, girls – will of necessity, develop different perceptions of their experience and, if necessary, develop quite different cultures of resistance. At present we know all too little about the changing educational values being transmitted to boys and girls by different groups of ethnic minority parents.

Epilogue

The culture of contradictions developed by Wesley and his friends lasted until the mock CSE exams at Christmas in the fifth year. It was only at this point that the reality of their situation began to press itself on them. Even then it was still possible for them to maintain the fiction of success: the hope that employers might be impressed with three CSEs, or the possibility of going on to further education. Nevertheless, despite these let-outs, their attitudes to school began to change. They began to truant for the first time in their school

234

careers and became increasingly hostile to school.

One boy in particular was especially bitter when he realized in the mock CSE maths exam that he had covered virtually none of the syllabus:

> Chris: Now look at this exam paper. Lots of the things on here we haven't done. You compare this with what I did in my exercise book (he shows page upon page of neatly written addition, subtraction, multiplication and division) and you will see that lots of the things we were asked to do in our mock exam was stuff that we hadn't done at all.

Chris' teacher had been 'successful' in keeping him interested and motivated in maths despite his obvious low ability, but his resentment and feelings of being let down were that much greater at the end. By the end of the fifth year these feelings of frustration and anger had begun to grow.

> JF: I want you to look back at what you have done at this school.
> P: Nothing! This last year I've done nothing.
> P: Haven't learnt nothing at this school!
> Chris: They haven't got no proper good teachers. They give you maths in the classroom but when you get to the exam it's all different.
> P: Yeah, yeah! Anyway you need too much education in this country to get somewhere, too much education. You need 'O' levels and things.

By this stage these boys were posing a growing threat to the school, but once again its liberal policies protected it from the worst of their aggression. Pupils did not have to attend lessons for subjects they were not taking exams in. They could undertake 'private study' in the library. From April onwards they were only required (and in many cases only allowed) to attend school on those days when they had examinations. Finally, fifth formers were no longer required to return after examinations and therefore school effectively ended for them in May. These boys were therefore 'squeezed out' of school at the same time as they were understanding the reality of their position. Real disillusionment for them would not have hit them until August when they saw their examination results (the best got three low-grade CSEs) and tried their luck in the employment market. It was perhaps fortunate for the school that by this stage the boys were no longer its problem.

These seven boys, like many of their black peers up and down the country, were committed to education and believed its promise of success and upward mobility despite their low level of achievement. It was not until they left the protective and concealing environment of the school that the reality of a hierarchically structured employment market was thrust upon them. If their experience is typical then it is not surprising that the Rastafarian movement mainly attracts black youth over school leaving age. Unlike the culture described above, Rastafarianism totally rejects participation in conventional white society, but it is not needed in a liberal comprehensive. There a more ambivalent culture is appropriate. By contrast, white working-class youth learns its lessons from its parents and its flamboyant cultures of resistance – mods, skinheads, punks, which embody a complete break with the value of education – centre on the last years of schooling and the early years of employment. For the blacks, the lessons of the British educational system are yet to be learned and predictions of alienation and rejection at school are premature. Unfortunately for schools and teachers, once these lessons have been learnt by the black community resistance will be that much stronger.

Note

1 All names are pseudonyms.

This section parallels Chapter 5 in *Interaction in the Classroom*. The first two papers deal with initial encounters, the second pair with patterns of interaction where routines have been established. David Hamilton, represented for the second time in the volume, here describes the very first school experiences of four- and five-year-olds in a Scottish private school. Pupils are, in this extract, learning their role. The introduction to secondary schooling, where the general role is known but its particularities have to be learnt, is revealed in the paper by Beynon and Atkinson. Together these chapters present Scottish and Welsh data, *and* show how pupils face up to schooling.

The balance between young children and teenagers is repeated in the material on established relationships. Lisa Serbin describes the sexist pattern of interaction in kindergarten, and shows how it can be altered. Stephen Ball shows how several different teachers cover the same material in various ways. The four papers together reveal the richness and complexity of classrooms, and of classroom research.

10

First days at school

David Hamilton

Abridged from David Hamilton (1977) *In Search of Structure*, Chapter 4. London: Hodder & Stoughton.

*   *   *

To understand fully the significance of a classroom event it is not sufficient merely to observe its enactment, it is also necessary to be aware of its history, to be alert to its possible outcomes and, above all, to be sensitive to the thoughts and intentions that guide its participants. In short, it is necessary to move much closer to the day to day world of teachers and pupils.

This essay – which focuses on a class of five-year-olds during their first days at primary school – attempts to make such a shift. That is, it is concerned not only with the turbulent stream of classroom events, but also with the reasons, strategies, patterns, and processes that lie beneath its surface.

The decision to study this age group was based on two related assumptions. First, that a child's attempts to come to terms with the distinctive features of schooling are likely to be more visible at this age than at any other time. And secondly,

239

that the beginning of a new school year is the occasion when experienced teachers are usually most explicit about the codes of practice (rules, standards, sanctions, etc.) which they use to regulate the social diversity of classroom life.

The core data were gathered on nine of the first fourteen days of the school year. A longhand record was kept of the general flow of classroom events and day by day a typed transcript of these notes was returned to the teacher for her reactions. These initial data were then augmented by interview with at least one parent of each child and by the observer's experience of teaching the class for two days later in the term.

Thus, the evidence in this account is drawn from the fieldnotes and the parent interviews, whereas the interpretative commentary is derived from a dialogue between the teacher and the observer conducted over the remaining weeks of the term. To simplify the reader's task, the commentary can be read independently of the evidence.

Day one

At 8.20 am on Tuesday, 26 August, Mrs Robertson arrives at school for the first day of the autumn term. (It is not only the start of her fifth year of teaching since leaving college, but also the start of her fifth year in the same school.) The class area already shows signs of her presence. Pictures are displayed on the wall; games and maths equipment are laid out on two trestle tables; paper, crayons, and plasticine are arranged on some of the low tables; and the house, library, and painting areas are carefully rendered attractive as well as accessible.

Stephen and his mother arrive while Mrs Robertson is in the staff room. In the meantime, Miss Downie (an assistant head teacher) takes Stephen under her wing and shows him round the class area. Mrs Robertson returns and takes over from Miss Downie. Michael arrives with his mother and father. Both boys are shown where to put their coats and schoolbags. At Mrs Robertson's prompting, Stephen and

240

Michael choose a game or activity and are shown to one of the small tables. They are left to fend for themselves as more children arrive. While being shown around the area each child is drawn into conversation by Mrs Robertson ('What is your name? What would you like to do?')

Michael gets up from his chair leaving a large wooden shoe (used for learning how to tie laces) on the table. Noticing this, Mrs Robertson shows him how to put it back in its 'proper' place (i.e. on the high table). Meanwhile Nicola is rolling the plasticine on a table instead of on a board. Like Michael she is shown how to follow the correct procedure.

At 8.50 am the last few children are waiting to be taken round the class area. By nine o'clock all the children who are due to come on the first day have arrived. Three are sitting at the plasticine table; two are working with jigsaws; one is assembling unifix (maths) blocks; and three are just watching. The children begin to talk among themselves (e.g. 'At nursery school we had to play on the floor with bricks – but we didn't have to do sums with them.').

COMMENTARY

(1) From the outset the class area is deliberately laid out to be attractive and eye-catching to the children, and to facilitate their circulation and access to equipment and materials. This state of readiness did not arise unheralded. In practical terms, it was created during the previous week when Mrs Robertson spent three full days at school.

(2) Mrs Robertson's initial contact with the children is deliberately built on a person-to-person rather than a teacher-to-class basis. This not only makes it easier for her to learn about the children individually but also minimizes the chances that they will be overwhelmed by a more formal approach.

(3) Although there are only nine children present on the first day, Mrs Robertson is unable to attend to all of them at once. As a result, she tries to provide activities which the children can do with the minimum of direct supervision.

(4) The children are deliberately introduced to a set of rules about tidiness; that is, they are taught certain conventions about the use and replacement of equipment. These rules, however, do not necessarily meet with immediate acceptance. They may conflict with patterns of behaviour established elsewhere (e.g. at nursery school). Thus, the children may have to unlearn old ideas before they can learn new ones. (All the children come from professional families and have spent at least one year at nursery school.)

(5) The children have come to school with all sorts of expectations about what will take place when they get there. To the extent that these expectations are unfulfilled the children may become disoriented. (Interviews with the parents later revealed that disappointment was the most frequent negative reaction shown by the children during the first days of term. For instance, one child (in the words of her mother) was 'bitterly disappointed' that she did not learn to read and write on the first day.)

. . .

9.20 am Keith puts his picture in a schoolbag. Mrs Robertson suggests that he puts it in his drawer. She shows him where the drawer is located. At 9.25 am the children are shepherded into the home base ('What's that?' one of the children asks). The stragglers receive special reminders ('Are you remembering to put the paint brushes back properly?') Shortly afterwards a joiner arrives to replace a cupboard lock in the base.

Mrs Robertson changes her plans and takes the children to the unisex toilets. At 9.45 am the children return to the home base and Mrs Robertson asks all of them individually about their families. Michael receives a reminder about not interrupting other people. Stephen is sent to look for the milk bottles. The children are lined up and led to the milk crate. Mrs Robertson asks them to take their milk to an empty table ('We don't want milky plasticine') and then shows the class how to open their bottles. When they have finished she also indicates where they are to put the tops, straws and empty bottles. The children return to their earlier activities. Someone has left out a yellow crayon. Michael finds his way into Mrs Nuthall's area (next to Mrs Robertson's) and works with some toy cars. Other children are shown the outdoor sandpit and are left to work there unsupervised (but overlooked by other teachers).

COMMENTARY

(11) Athough this episode contains the first occasion when the class are taken as a group, the teacher's attention is still focused on the attributes of individual children. For the children, however, it becomes a real class (i.e. group) situation: while the teacher elicits information about their home circumstances (e.g. family size), the children begin to learn how to take their turn in a group discussion.

(12) The class teaching later that morning is quite different. The main flow of information is from the teacher to the pupils. In this sense the children are the receivers of knowledge, whereas previously they were the transmitters.

(13) Although, ostensibly, Mrs Robertson merely shows Keith the location of his drawer, her action has much more than transitory significance. First, she is aware that Keith may not be able to read his own name and therefore must learn to recognize his drawer by non-literate means (e.g. by its position in the drawer unit). Second, she tries to discourage the children from putting completed work directly into their schoolbags since, at a later stage, she intends to monitor their work before they take it home. (When they start to use notebooks Mrs Robertson will indicate special places in the home base for the children to put work that is to be marked (see Day 10).)

(14) Despite being interrupted by the joiner, Mrs Robertson switches without difficulty to another activity. Furthermore, having organized the children into a group for the first time, she deliberately retains this form of organization rather than

letting the children return to their individual activities.

(15) At this stage the children have neither learned the 'boundaries' of their class area nor the composition of their class group. Thus, the more adventurous of them take advantage of the attractions to be found in other class areas (and the willingness of other teachers to receive them).

(16) The children are deliberately taken to the sandpit since it is not visible from the class area. Mrs Robertson is interested not simply to see whether they can work on their own but also whether they can work at such a distance from the class base.

> At 11.35 am Mrs Robertson gathers the children together in the home base and tells them the story of the three bears. Some of the children keep interrupting. Eventually Michael is told that 'When I'm telling a story, you sit quietly and listen'.... Before letting the children return to their individual activities, Mrs Robertson reminds them to bring their pinafores the following day... Douglas and Michael become noisy; Mrs Robertson takes them 'for a walk' while the rest of the class continue with their drawing, painting, etc. Meanwhile Miss Dean (another primary one teacher) comes into the area to report that the toilets are awash. When she returns Mrs Robertson takes her entire class back into the toilets and reiterates the correct procedures (e.g. 'turn the taps on gently'). At 12.25 pm the children are asked to find their schoolbags and put on their coats. Peter is sent with Julie to show her how to put off the lights. When the children have gathered in the base Mrs Robertson reminds them about the toilets. Finally, she says a formal 'Good afternoon' to the children. Their reply is ragged. She asks the children what her name is and then repeats the greeting. Their response is more appropriate. At 12.30 pm the children pick up their schoolbags and move out into the communal area where their parents are waiting.

COMMENTARY

(17) Mrs Robertson's decision to recount a story that the

children already know is deliberate. She tells it 'for security, not newness' (see Commentary, note 2). Nevertheless, this decision also relates to another purpose. As Mrs Robertson expects, some of the children have not yet learned how to listen to a story. Unwittingly they contravene two important rules. First, that listening is a passive activity; and second, that unless their questions are to the point, they should be asked at the end of a story rather than in the middle.

(18) Mrs Robertson maintains her policy of talking to the children individually. Thus her reaction to Michael and Douglas's noisy interaction is to take them quietly outside the class area, not to make a public issue of it ... As this incident suggests, Mrs Robertson's strategies for maintaining classroom control vary widely from situation to situation. Indeed, the most invisible strategy – that of observation rather than intervention – is probably the most pervasive at this stage in the school year.

(19) The pupils' day is built round very short units of time and a generous supply of activities. In catering terms the curriculum is rather like a smorgasbord. The children help themselves from tables laden with attractive dishes produced earlier in the day....

(20) By asking Peter to show Julie the location of the light switch, Mrs Robertson begins to capitalize on the fact that the children can teach one another. Again, this is important to her overall style of individualized teaching. She also uses a similar chain-message technique to spread information around the class. For example, she is able to gather the entire group in the home base without ever addressing them publicly.

(21) The fact that Mrs Robertson has to take her class for a second formal visit to the toilets is the first evidence that her teaching strategies are not always successful. Repeatedly throughout the year she had to retrace her steps and 'start again'....

(22) Mrs Robertson's rehearsal of the formal greeting ('Good afternoon') at the end of the day is not merely for her own benefit. She realizes that there will be other occasions in the

coming weeks when the children are likely to receive a similar greeting from an unknown (outside) visitor. By stressing this activity, Mrs Robertson hopes not only that the children will be well-prepared for such an eventuality, but also that no one (herself, the visitor, or the children) will find it embarrassing.

Day two

(This and later extracts from the fieldnotes have been chosen selectively to illustrate new and changing features of the classroom context.)
By 9 o'clock eighteen children are present. . . .

> 9.50 am While the new children are at the toilet, Emily and Nicola reconvene the tea party. Michael, Keith and Douglas join them. A few minutes later (9.53 am) Douglas and Michael start a mock knife fight at the tea table. Keith watches and the girls carry on preparing the party. . . . Douglas puts down the knife and starts to pass the toy iron over Michael's hair. . . . The toilet group return and Mrs Robertson reminds the boys in the tea party to behave more appropriately. She then moves into the painting area. The knife fight becomes a sword fight. . . . (10.08 am) Douglas moves out of the house and begins to wave his knife in front of Peter who is seated at the plasticine table. Mrs Robertson intervenes, smacks Douglas's bottom once with the palm of her hand ('I'm very cross with you'), and makes him sit on his own. Christina wheels a small pram through the class area while Mrs Robertson reminds the remaining members of the tea party about the noise-level of their 'playground' voices. Mrs Robertson then takes Laura for a walk round the painting area. . . . At milk time (10.20 am) Christina asks 'Do we have this every day?'.

COMMENTARY

(27) The 'knifefight' and its eventual resolution is a turning point in Mrs Robertson's relationship with Douglas. Her

246

decision to smack him was taken in the light of the knowledge she had accumulated over the preceding two days. On balance she felt that the gravity of the situation justified the intensity of the remedy. Later that day Douglas told his parents about his experience. They came to see Mrs Robertson and, upon hearing her explanation, endorsed the action she had taken. They, too, were concerned about their son's behaviour. While at nursery school Douglas had suffered from asthma. As a consequence, his broken attendance record allowed him to contravene the standards that were normally applied to other children. In addition his nursery teacher had been reluctant to enforce such standards for fear of reactivating the asthma. In the parents' own words (as recorded during an interview) Douglas had become 'uncontrollable' at nursery school. Although he continued to be a regular focus of Mrs Robertson's attention, Douglas's general demeanour became much more subdued after this shared experience.

(28) The fact that Mrs Robertson chooses to take Laura into the painting area illustrates a dramatic shift in her attention. Unlike Douglas, Laura does not place any overt demands on the teacher (see Commentary, note 25). Nevertheless, Mrs Robertson is quite aware that Laura has not previously shown any apparent desire to paint. Thus, although certain children apparently receive more attention than others, this does not necessarily mean that the remaining children are beyond Mrs Robertson's field of vision.

(29) Christina's question 'Do we have this every day?' indicates that while some children (especially those with older brothers and sisters) may be fully conversant with the nature and conventions of schooling (see Commentary, note 5), there are others who find it a significant source of wonder and amazement. . . .

Day three

The entire class are present for the first time (ten girls, thirteen boys). . . .

9.02 am Mrs Robertson walks round the tables and ask the children to tidy up and go into the home base. The experienced class members are asked to help the new ones. Emily tells her neighbour: 'You have to push your chair in.' Ewan points towards the home base and asks 'Is that it?' A boy and a girl from another class come into the area and ask Mrs Robertson if they can paint. . . . (9.08 am) In the home base, Mrs Robertson reiterates her jigsaw policy (viz. they should be replaced on the high table but not before they have been reassembled.) She then says a formal 'Good morning' to the class and, for the first time, marks up the register. When Julie (the second person on the register) is asked 'Are you here?' she paused and then replies 'Yes' in a tone of voice that suggests she finds the question totally pointless. (As if to say: 'Yes, of course I'm here today.') After registration, Colin is asked whether his brother is older or younger than himself. He is unable to reply. 'Is he bigger or smaller than you?'. Colin gives an answer. . . . Mrs Robertson reads the 'Mr Happy' story to the class. There are very few random interruptions although some children mistake pauses in the story for invitations to ask questions. . . . (9.26 am) The experienced children are told about choosing their activities: 'You don't need to ask. If you want to paint and there's an easel free . . .'. Morag starts to cry and is taken on to Mrs Robertson's lap.

COMMENTARY

(33) The arrival of two children from another class to ask if they can paint reinforces the idea that the children have not yet developed a strong sense of classness.

(34) Julie's amazement at being asked 'Are you here?' when Mrs Robertson marks the register is a unique event never to be repeated in the context of that class. By the time the registration has been completed she has learned – like all the others – how to give the appropriate response ('Yes, Mrs Robertson'). At all levels, teaching is characterized by the repeated use of 'pseudo questions' (i.e. questions which are not

designed to be treated literally). As this illustration indicates, children are not always aware of the real meaning of these questions. At the same time, however, it also reveals that, if shown, they can rapidly learn their real purpose.

(35) The discussion between Mrs Robertson and Colin about his family is a good illustration of the fact that discourse between teachers and pupils is multi-layered. For the teacher's part she not only learns about Colin's home setting but also about his competence with mathematical relationships, his knowledge about family structure (e.g. brother, sister), and his ability to keep to the point of a discussion.

(36) This is the first time that Mrs Robertson reads a new story to the children. To control them without constantly interrupting the story Mrs Robertson varies the inflection of her voice. Nevertheless, some children still misunderstand the messages that she conveys by this means. Her dramatic pauses are sometimes taken to be opportunities to ask questions.

Day five

9.28 am (in the home base). Mrs Robertson produces 'Hamish' (a matchstick man made from pipe cleaners). She then gives each child a book made of sheets of drawing paper stapled together. Different shapes have already been traced out at the top of the pages in the book. The children leave the home base, put their books on the small tables and then sit on the floor facing the blackboard. David has to be reminded to put his book on a table. Mrs Robertson leads the children in making shapes in the air. The children then return to their seats. Christina points to her name on the book and asks Mary 'What does that say?' Douglas and Nicola begin to trace out the shapes using crayons. Mrs Robertson interrupts them. They are asked to put their crayons back in the tins and, with the rest of the class, put their hands on their laps. The children are requested to point to their names at the top of the page. Mrs Robertson scans the class. David has his book upside down. Three

249

children are moved to different seats (so that all the left-handed children sit together). David has already started. The children are asked to choose a pencil and trace out the shapes, starting from 'Hamish's red dot' (a matchstick man marker on the left-hand side of the page). When the children have finished Mrs Robertson demonstrates the next exercise on the blackboard.... (9.48 am) The children are then asked to sit on the floor around the drawer units.... Each child has the same number on their tray as on their writing book. One by one they put their books away under Mrs Robertson's supervision.

COMMENTARY

(37) The distribution of writing materials represents the first time that the children are seated as a class group for a book-orientated activity. For approximately the next ten days Mrs Robertson uses this all-class approach for the introduction of new topics. It is a 'dinner party' not a 'smorgasbord' (see Commentary, note 19). A fixed, no-choice menu is followed by all the pupils in a definite sequence. The teacher sits at the head of the 'table' and the courses are brought out at the same time for each child.

(38) Although Mrs Robertson has spent a great deal of time in preparing this writing activity, not everything goes to plan. Nevertheless, this outcome is not entirely unexpected. Each time she has previously introduced this topic it has produced new and unforeseen difficulties. Mrs Robertson is quite prepared, therefore, for the widely different degrees of competence shown by the children. However, to bring the activity to a relatively tidy conclusion, Mrs Robertson deliberately chooses a follow-up activity which retains the whole-class form of organization (see Commentary, note 14) but which, by contrast, is relatively simple and easily completed.

(39) During this episode (which lasts less than twenty-five minutes) Mrs Robertson moves the whole class through four different positions (home base, in front of blackboard, seated

at tables, in front of drawer units). She makes the maximum use of available space but, most of the time, keeps the children very close to her. Again this has implications for the monitoring and control of individual children. By her close proximity to the children, Mrs Robertson can see and hear much more than in a dispersed situation. For the same reasons, her own behaviour is much more visible to the rest of the class. Furthermore, in this position she can use techniques (e.g. touching children) which are inevitably (or conventionally) ruled out in a dispersed teaching situation. . . .

(10.25 am) Mrs Robertson announces that this will be the last time that the class take their milk all together. She explains that in future the children can take their milk whenever they wish. Michael asks 'What happens if we don't know when to go?' When Michael has finished his milk Mrs Robertson talks to him about the grouping exercise. When he asks 'What is maths?' all of a sudden, someone else replies 'work'. After milk the class are assembled in front of the blackboard and then introduced to 'Dick' – a cardboard figure stuck to a magnetic board. Mrs Robertson writes 'Dick' on the blackboard and asks the children what it says. She then tries 'dock' and 'dish'. . . . While the class are putting on their coats to go out to playtime, Michael bursts into tears: 'I want mummy'. . . . (11.50 am) Mrs Robertson requests the class to 'Stop and listen' (twice). She then asks the children to try to work more quietly. . . .

COMMENTARY

(42) Day five is the last occasion when the children take their milk all together as a class. As far as milk consumption is concerned, the 'dinner party' is over. On subsequent days the children follow a self-service system and take their milk whenever they wish. The patterns of class organization that Mrs Robertson uses at milk time tend to run ahead of those used for other activities. Thus, the whole class consumption of

milk is abandoned at a time when such patterns are just being introduced for other activities.

(43) Although the children have already begun to learn the basic skills of writing, this is the first occasion when they are required to recognize word shapes (a prerequisite for reading). Furthermore, this is the first time that Mrs Robertson has written on the blackboard; a cogent reminder that it is a literate medium.

(44) When Michael burst into tears at playtime he has misunderstood the nature of the occasion. The fact that the other children were putting on their coats reminds him of home time. He has not fully learned the routine of the school day. . . .

(46) Mrs Robertson's double call for the children to 'Stop and listen' and her subsequent reiteration of the classroom rules is one indication of the fragile stability of classroom life. Although at any given time the overall atmosphere may appear to be stable it is, in fact, more accurate to characterize it as a state of continual oscillation: at times the children set the pace, at other times it is the teacher who takes the initiative. On this occasion Mrs Robertson feels that the children are moving too far ahead of her. To restore the balance, she decides to remind them of the core rules that govern the use of furniture and equipment. . . .

Day nine

Over and above the regular choosing activities the children complete the last page of the writing book. Emily complains that she hasn't got a page eight (she has) and David writes on the wrong page. . . . A final sorting group is convened. . . . At 10.20 am Mrs Robertson rehearses the number work that she has introduced on previous days. 'How do we make one?' The children chant 'down' and make an imaginary stroke in the air. She then brings out a set of cards featuring the number 'Two'. When the children have answered her questions (e.g. 'How many boots are there? How many eyes has the cat?'), she makes them practise the shape in the air. Before letting the children find a seat to work at, Mrs Robertson distributes the number books by holding them up and waiting to see if the children can recognize their own names. The number books are very similar to the writing books. They are home-made by the teacher and comprise spirit-duplicated sheets stapled together by Mrs Lee, the auxiliary. The children trace out the number shapes page by page and also use their crayons to colour the diagrams that go with them. This activity continues after playtime.... After a further period of choosing, the children gather again in the home base. Mrs Robertson continues to tell them about the seasonal events of autumn (e.g. fruits and seeds). While the children are still in the home base, she introduces them to 'Fluff' (the cat owned by Dick and Dora). She then sits by the magnetic board and 'plays a game' with the children by matching (and mismatching) the words against the pictures (Dick, Dora, Nip (the dog), and Fluff). The children correct her when she makes a mistake. Andrew asks if they will be 'getting Dick and Dora books'. When Mrs Robertson sends the class to fetch the colouring books from their trays there is a period of confusion since not all the children find the correct book (i.e. the one with their name on it). The children are asked to colour in one picture of Fluff and one of Nip. There is some difficulty because there are not enough black and brown crayons to go round all the children. (12.15 pm) Some of the children have finished so Mrs Robertson asks them to take their schoolbags to their seats. Colin complains that James is sitting in his seat. Mrs Robertson explains that he doesn't have his own seat. He finds another but wanders out of it. Morag takes it. Colin returns to say to Morag: 'I was there first.' Mrs Robertson helps Morag to find a new seat....

COMMENTARY

(50) The fact that the number activity spreads over playtime is

253

the first occasion that Mrs Robertson has allowed this to occur. Previously all class activities have been drawn to a conclusion before the children go out to play.

(51) Three different kinds of classroom procedures co-exist at this time: individual choosing, specialist groups, and whole class teaching.... These procedures are not insulated from each other. At different times they will be applied to the same part of the curriculum.

. . .

(53) The episode when there were not enough black and brown crayons for all the children to use them is a specific but rare instance where the teaching strategy used by Mrs Robertson runs up against a (relative) shortage of resources....

(54) The seating policy followed by Mrs Robertson is that the children can sit wherever they wish. (The only time this convention is breached is when she asks individual children to sit on their own – usually because they have been interfering with someone else's work.) Thus, each child may use several work places during the day....

Day twelve

At 10.20 am the class are engaged on the following activities: building with woodblocks (6), milk (1), painting (3), jigsaw puzzles (2), unifix blocks (4), drawing (3), reading (1), observing (2)....

. . .

COMMENTARY

(60) ... Although Mrs Robertson's teaching is individualized, she also has responsibility for up to twenty-two other children at the same time. Thus, before she can develop person-to-person teaching she must also design activities for the rest of the class. In this sense her overall unit of organization still remains the entire teaching group, not the individual child.

11

Pupils as data-gatherers: mucking and sussing

John Beynon and Paul Atkinson

First encounters

Ethnographers who study organizations like schools are always enjoined to pay very particular attention to their 'first days in the field' (cf. Geer, 1964). It is during the initial phases of such a research project that key lines of inquiry are established. The sensitive fieldworker is enjoined to pay close attention to the 'strangeness' of a newly encountered research setting: such strangeness indeed provides the necessary analytic distance and perspectives. Social anthropologists often refer to the analytic and personal significance of 'culture shock', while sociologists who work in their own society talk of the difficulty of rendering familiar settings 'anthropologically strange'. George Spindler, for instance, writes that he came near to giving up his first attempt:

> I sat in classes for days wondering what there was to 'observe'. Teachers taught, reprimanded, rewarded, while pupils sat at desks, squirming, whispering, reading, writing, staring into space, as they had in my own grade-school

experience, in my practice teaching in a teacher training program, and in the two years of public school teaching I had done. . . .   (Spindler and Spindler, 1982, p. 24)

Research workers are not the only people who face strange situations in unfamiliar settings. Members themselves have to learn the ropes and establish their working knowledge of persons, rules, routines and the like. Recruits and novices also have their 'first days in the field', during which they have to find their feet. These early phases may be of considerable significance for the members' success or failure, and their 'moral career' in the organization.

This paper reports on research where the ethnographer's methodological concerns overlap and coincide with those of the members. It is based on a period of participant observation and recording in Victoria Road School – a boys' comprehensive in South Wales. The research focused attention almost exclusively on the first few weeks experiences of the eleven- and twelve-year old boys who were embarking on their secondary school careers at Victoria Road. The boys in just one class were observed for the first half of the Autumn term, and their lessons were taperecorded.

In addition, extensive interviews and conversations were conducted with the pupils and members of the staff – both individually and in groups. This paper will draw primarily on the interviews and conversations, supplemented by some interactional data. The names used throughout are all pseudonyms we have given the boys and the teachers. (We have used their surnames in referring to them: this reflects usage in the school.)

Although they were by no means strangers to schools and the role of school pupil, these Victoria Road boys had to learn how their new school operated. In particular, they had to discover how their new teachers operated – what 'made them tick', what behaviour they would tolerate and so on. Their teachers, of course, were confronted by a similar need to discover the characteristics of this new cohort of pupils.

Teachers and pupils are thrust together in enforced intimacy

256

in the classroom. In that arena they negotiate working relationships, and classroom identities are developed. Teachers and pupils alike are engaged in sizing each other up. Teachers acquire reputations in the eyes of their pupils. Pupils' characters and abilities are weighed up by their teachers. Teachers share and collaborate in the production of pupil identities, while pupils collaborate in the discovery and exploration of teachers' classroom behaviour.

Such exploration and mutual evaluation between teachers and pupils goes on from their very first encounter. Indeed, identities and reputations start to crystallize from the very outset. In the course of the first lesson between a teacher and a new class, important clues and interpretive frameworks may be established.

The investigation of such initial encounters is thus a potentially fruitful approach to a more general task of understanding the sentimental order of schools and classrooms. More generally still, it will inform our exploration of the formal topics of professional-client interaction, organizational careers and so on.

Despite such analytic value, initial encounters in classrooms have not been subjected to a great deal of systematic scrutiny. Ball (1980), who is one of the few ethnographers to have done so, has suggested one familiar methodological reason for such relative neglect. It is a well established generalization about ethnographic fieldwork that gatekeepers (like head teachers) are often keen to steer the fieldworker away from apparently sensitive periods and places. If researchers are to be granted access at all, then their presence will normally be encouraged only when things are running smoothly. Fieldworkers themselves may implicitly collude in such organizational impression-management by tactfully avoiding trespass on such occasions. Ball recognizes that teachers themselves may be reluctant to have researchers present during the earliest days of the school year, continuing, however, to argue that

the reasons for the teacher's reluctance are exactly the reasons why the researcher should be there. These earlier

encounters are of crucial significance not only for understanding what comes later but in actually providing for what
comes later. (p. 144)

As Ball also points out, these very early periods of classroom
interaction can quickly lead to recipes and routines of action
which are persistent. He refers to a 'process of establishment',
which involves

an exploratory interaction process involving teacher and
pupils during their initial encounters in the classroom
through which a more or less permanent, repeated and
highly predictable pattern of relationships and interactions
emerges. (p. 144)

As the observations at Victoria Road confirm, initial encounters can be characterized by a very great deal of 'exploratory
interaction'. The recordings and observations of the early days
at Victoria Road are replete with instances of such action, and
– as we shall see – some such 'exploration' can be vigorous and
far-reaching.

Ball's own observations lead him to suggest that the initial
explorations fall into two phases. During the first, 'passive'
stage, pupils rely primarily on the observation of their
teachers' behaviours in order to establish working hypotheses
about what kind of teacher they are confronting. During the
second stage the pupils adopt a more active stance, in order to
develop and test their hypotheses. During this more active
stage, the pupils not only test their hypotheses, but simultaneously test out the teacher. In the course of this, as Ball
phrases it, some pupils can be 'real horrible'.

While we do not wish to contradict Ball's general characteri-
zation of initial classroom encounters, our data from Victoria
Road suggest some pupils all but dispense with the initially
passive stage of observation. Some of the boys reported in this
paper adopted a much higher profile from the very first,
challenging, probing and testing their teachers. We are,
however, in agreement with Ball's assessment of the overall
significance of this process. During the coming weeks and

months the pupils and their teachers will be engaged in intense social interaction. Interactionally speaking, school lessons are extremely busy places. The participants are recurrently engaged in rapid decision-making. They must assess each other's temperaments, interests and abilities. Teachers have to manage the whole class as a cohort, and monitor and manage each individual member of it. Often this implies a delicate assessment of pupils' attention, motivation, stock of knowledge, politeness, demeanour, verbal skills and so forth. Likewise pupils have to assess and respond to teachers' questions and instructions – or decide to disobey, be cheeky and so forth. In order to accomplish such detailed interactional work, therefore, teachers and pupils need to build up reliable assessments of each other which can serve as predictors of their actions and reactions. Ball again suggests, for example, that pupils' assessments permit them

> to weigh up the amount of satisfaction to be obtained from the commission of a 'deviant' act against the dissatisfaction likely to be involved in the teachers' response to it, if any. This may in fact account for pupils' often stated preference for 'strict' teachers. Strictness usually also provides for a highly structured and therefore a highly predictable situational definition. (p. 154)

Several authors have documented the range of pupils' typifications of their teachers, and the social construction of teacher reputations (e.g. Furlong, 1976; Gannaway, 1976; Nash, 1976). It is certainly the case that pupils routinely express a preference for teachers whose classroom behaviour is relatively stable and predictable, so that you 'know where you are' with them. Such stability forms part of the 'working consensus' (cf. Hargreaves *et al.*, 1975).

Pollard (1979) suggests that the working consensus of the classroom is established within the limits of 'unilateral' acts by teachers or pupils, which are open to censure by the other:

> Actions within the parameters of the working consensus can be classified both for teacher and children as either confor-

mist behaviour or as routine deviance. Unilateral acts lie outside such understandings. Interestingly both teachers and children see each other's unilateral acts as semi-mindless or uncontrolled – the teacher goes 'mad', the children 'act daft' – yet they each see their own unilateral acts in terms of recouping dignity – the teacher 'shows who's boss' whilst the child 'proves he's tough'. (p. 84)

The limits of censure are, of course, in no way fixed or predetermined. Hence teachers and pupils have practical interests in negotiating such boundaries. In particular, the boundary between 'routine deviance' and behaviour which is beyond the pale is a crucial one. Pupils also need to monitor how, on each occasions, individual teachers will interpret and apply the tacit norms of working consensus. Hence they need to inspect their talk and demeanour for behavioural clues as to 'mood' (cf. Pollard, 1979).

Any classroom action has three sorts of potential consequence, all three of which are closely interrelated. A pupil's act, for instance, and the teacher's response (or lack of response) to it will have implications for: how the individual pupil is perceived by the teacher; how the teacher is perceived by the pupils; how the pupil is perceived by other pupils. On the basis of such actions and reactions classroom identities and reputations are constructed.

As we shall outline and exemplify in the remainder of this paper, then, early encounters between teachers and pupils are often characterized by varieties of strategic interaction. There may be a complex process of mutual weighing up and testing out. This often takes the form of disruptive behaviour on the part of the pupils (cf. Woods, 1983). Whereas teachers at Victoria Road tended to see such activities as pathologically mindless, the boys themselves were acting in accordance with their own versions of rational decision-making and information-seeking.

We do not wish to over-emphasize the extent to which mucking about in class was directed towards the conscious testing of teachers' classroom behaviour. To a considerable extent, disruptive behaviour was valued for its intrinsic merits

– of relieving monotony, and 'having a laugh'. It provided escape mechanisms from classroom routine, and a form of guerilla warfare or resistance against teachers' authority. Nonetheless, a good deal of the early interaction between teachers and the class was coloured by the attempts by some of the boys to 'suss out' their new teachers.

In the next section of the paper we shall provide some evidence of the extent to which pupils' own accounts reflect the rationality of sussing out. We shall then go on to indicate some of the strategies the boys used in their accomplishment of classroom mucking.

As has been illustrated elsewhere (Beynon and Delamont, 1983), the Lower School at Victoria Road was characterized by high degrees of antagonism. The data are full of instances of verbal and physically aggressive behaviour between teachers and pupils. We shall report accounts by the pupils themselves to suggest that such action is to be seen as part of a strategic process of data-gathering about the dispositions of their teachers. These accounts suggest that – for some of the boys at least – this can be a highly self-conscious process.

Mucking and sussing

Boys at Victoria Road were able to provide accounts of mucking about in class which portrayed it as a rational activity. Amongst other things (such as alleviating boredom) it provided the principal means of discovering what the boys regarded as essential knowledge about the school, their teachers, and fellow pupils. It was, as they put it, a way of 'sussing out' in order 'to know where you stand'. Successful mucking about could simultaneously accomplish several things: it could reveal how teachers would react under pressure; it could enhance the reputation of its instigator; it could flush out accomplices in the classroom and provide occasion for joint subversive action.

Such sussing out provides useful information not only for the pupil who is engaged in mucking about, but for the audience as well. Two boys expressed it in this way:

261

Levy: In the early days King became a big star – he just acted stupid and everything he said was daft! He started up the very first lesson we had with Miss Floral.

Green: He and O'Mally were always messing, talking, and acting a bit thick, testing teachers an' that. I didn't do much of it, but I watched them.

J B: Did you enjoy all that?

Green: Yea. I mean someone had to do it.

J B: Why?

Green: To find out about the school, the teachers and see who your mates were. You got to know where you stand.

Likewise, the following boy's account suggests a degree of calculation in observing the effects of mucking. The staff saw him as an innocent dupe, led astray by King and his troublemaking. Robert Morgan, on the other hand, offered a very different rationale:

JB: Did King have a hold, an influence over you? Did he use you?

Morgan: Oh no, I used him!

JB: Meaning?

Morgan: Well I mucked about with King because I wanted to, not because he forced me or anything like that. We mucked around together and it was fun. But I made sure I did my work as well, whereas I could see he wasn't doing anything.... I let him copy because I knew it wasn't going to make any difference, he wasn't going to take it in because he hadn't done the work for himself.

These two extracts both refer to one particular member of the class – King – who established himself as a ringleader from the very first encounters of the school year. King himself was quite clear and precise on some of the functions of mucking, in particular as it related to the differential evaluations of teachers and classmates:

JB: How do you impress teachers?

King: By neat work, getting on and being quiet. Teacher's pet, an' that.

JB: How do you impress fellow pupils?

King: By larking around in class, having a good muck.

JB: Any other ways?

King: Well, standing up for yourself and being all hard. And in sport, football. But mostly mucking around in class.

Likewise, Levy, a conformist high-achiever, himself rarely fooled or mucked in class, but recognized the valuable service provided by King and his clique. They sussed out teachers on their own behalf, and did so indirectly for others:

With some teachers if you talk now and again they don't mind, but if you talk all the time they tell you off and tell you not to talk. You find out what you can get away with. With Mr New in 1Y, if you used to ask him if you could take your jacket off he'd say 'There's no need to ask. I don't ask you when I take my jacket off and so there's no need to ask me.' You see other people and they do something to a certain, say, degree and then you see how much they get told off and you know not to do something in one class but you may be able to do it in another.

King and his immediate circle were themselves well aware of the fact that other, more 'conformist' pupils were able to trade off their mucking. Such awareness contributed to their pride in being good 'muckers' and reflected on their reputations and status in the eyes of other pupils:

King: We plays up the teachers and they share the laugh. We're good muckers, we are!

JG: What do mean by 'they'?

King: The quiet ones an' that . . .

Ginger: Kids like Fuller who are all quiet and reserved. They make you want to throw up!

King: Yea, all the wankers and little girls, the ones who never join in or anything. (Pause) I mean we does all the mucking an' that and discover who are the hard teachers that'll pull your hair out and who are all soft and, I mean, they benefit as well 'cos they're there all quiet watchin' and listenin' aren't they? I mean when they know a teacher's soft then they join in then 'cos they know there's no danger. Kids like Levy and Pale even they plays up the soft teachers.

Ginger: We buggers the hard ones up as well though, don't we, Dave? We're good muckers!

King: Yes, the best! (Laughter)

Mucking methods

In general, the methods used by the boys were those of a guerilla campaign, exploiting limited resources, with skill and inventiveness, in having a laugh, disrupting lessons and challenging teachers. Again, the boys themselves could be quite explicit about their actions:

JB: So what are the best ways to annoy teachers?

Blond: By shouting across the classroom, throwing paper, writing on desks, kicking the person in front of you, and writing foul things on the books! (Laughter)

Green: And by telling jokes and laughing at the back where we all sit, a big group of us.

The precise methods used depended on the perceived characteristics and weaknesses of the individual teachers.

Roland: We sussed out all the teachers at the start of the year, didn't we?

JB: How?

King: Talking, messing about, whistling, funny noises, shouting your head off when they're not looking, firing paper balls through an empty biro pen, bits of rubber an' that. When the teacher's not looking you shout your head off and he turns around and says, 'Who's that?' I like firing things around like bits of paper and laughing your head off when other people get into trouble. We started throwing paper aeroplanes around in Union's Maths

lessons – old foureyes - but you can't fool with him much
'cos he'd send you out into the corner. You had to be
careful of Mr Pickwick as well. When you're in class he's
patient, in' he, but he sometimes goes really mad.

In addition to such general activity, the boys in King's group
would also openly refuse to respond to a teacher's request or
command if they thought they could get away with it. The
female teachers they had for Drama, Art and French were
special victims of such challenges.

> King: I make silly noises an' that. I always make silly noises
> in Mr Union's class, dun I! I whistles, dun I, and he
> shouts his head off trying to find out who it is. (Laughter)
> And I make funny noises an' that, and then rolls marbles
> an' that.
>
> JB: What else did you do in those early weeks?
>
> King: Cheek and answer back. Say she says, 'You do that'
> and I say 'No, I can't do that, Miss, it's too hard!'
>
> Long: When they say to draw something, you say 'No, we
> can't draw that, it's too hard.' I didn't used to do all that
> Art homework. I refused.

The King fraternity had clear ideas as to when and how to
suss. They would go for teachers' vulnerable points:

> King: You go for a teacher's weak points, don't you. When
> they're working really hard on the board an' all that, you
> starts up whistling and he turns round and goes mad.
> Course then you're looking all innocent!
>
> Roland: Yeah, that makes them mad.
>
> King: And they goes 'Who done that?'
>
> Roland: Early in the morning or right at the end of the day,
> that's the best 'cos you know they're tired after a day's
> work.

They would also talk about the development of new ways of
mucking. Teachers' responses were not fixed, and they were
thought to get tougher or 'harder'. In response King and his
circle would develop new strategies. They took pride in the

creative improvization of novel challenges. In the following interview extract, King himself talks of his developing experience and creative flair:

King: I always fools around when someone else is – when they're shouting at someone else I starts up! I've learnt a lot this year about annoying teachers, gettin' them mad an' that.

JB: In what sense?

King: 'Cos teachers have got hard on you. At first you think it's going to be a pushover, they seem all soft at the start of the year. They have to be nice to you so as to get to know you, but when they get to know you are a fool, they get hard on you. They're really hard on me now.

JB: So you're not allowed to muck now?

King: I finds new ways, like kids look at you and you laughs your head off. Last week I got this massive big screw-driver that was in the yard – the caretaker must have left it – and I drilled around and I made this 'orrible big hole in my desk. And then in class this chair was broke so I smashed it up even more and snapped the legs off! Crack! Crack! Crack!

JB: Why did you do that?

King: Well I knew Miss Floral would do her nut and she did! She was scared in case Mr Changeable found out 'cos she knew he'd give her a right bollocking! She hid all the pieces in the corner and no one would tell it was me what had done it. If anyone had squeaked I'd have smashed their heads in, but they're good kids like that in our form, they keep their mouths shut, they don't grass.

The successful accomplishment of disruptive, guerilla tactics may call for a degree of prior planning, and collaboration among the participants.

JB: Do you plan things ahead?

Ginger: O yea, like we plans to stick our hands up [in Mr Union's class] and make funny noises like . . . (he whistles like a bird, then burps).

JB: So you work it all out beforehand?

266

Ginger: Yes, before we gets into the Maths class 'cos we always mucks around in the class. We talks all the time when he's not looking and when he looks around he's looking to see who's done it. We mucks him no end.

Long: Me and Blond planned something the other day, about two weeks ago on a Tuesday when we were in the English room before we went to Maths with Cobweb [the teacher's nickname]. Blond goes, 'If he starts on me today, I'll ask him for a fight!' Blondie was going 'Sharrup!' [mimicking Mr Union] and making all funny noises and I did the same. We worked it out before the lesson started. We enjoyed it – it was a good laugh.

In a similar vein, the development of mucking depends upon collaborative work between pupils. Pupils rely on verbal and non-verbal communication in collective mucking and setting each other off:

O'Mally: I started laughing and so the teacher told me off again. Everyone made you laugh, they sort of looked at you and made you laugh. They think, 'Oh he's being told off!' They all smile at you and you can't help laughing, you can't stop yourself.

Blond: That's it! It's like if you've been told off in, say, Mr Union's class when you're told off there's King and he goes like that (laughing gesture) and as soon as you've seen him he laughs his head off and, well, you just can't stop it. You start giggling and you can't stop.

JB: How important is eye contact?

Ginger: Very, very important. You've got to catch people's eyes before you can muck around. And if you, say, saw them do that (winks) then you'd know that the teacher was watching you, or something like that. It's like dropping a pen and when your friend goes down for it you tell him then.

Blond: And mouthing words across the class and signing with your fingers. You can pass all sorts of messages around like that.

It would be wrong to overemphasize the nature and extent of self-consciously purposeful sussing. It will already have been apparent that the same boys' names reappear in the data extracts illustrating this paper. By no means all of the boys in the class contributed to classroom mucking. As has already been indicated, quieter boys could benefit from the disruptive and challenging behaviour of others. In the class observed, one particular boy, King, and his fraternity, were the prime movers. They constituted a sort of 'forlorn hope' in the assault on teachers' authority. Our focus in this paper has therefore given this small group of boys undue prominence, and has highlighted their activities.

Likewise, we have stressed the extent to which the mucking had a data-gathering function. It would be wrong to conclude that this was the boys' only motivation. To a considerable extent, the generation of classroom laughter was an end in itself. Pupils' humour could be used to challenge and suss teachers while simultaneously alleviating boredom.

> Long: If you couldn't have a proper laugh now and then there'd be nothing to do in school. It's very important to. . . .
> Ginger: Yea, I mean there'd be no point to school if you was stuck in your desk all day being all quiet. You've got to have a laugh, a bit of a muck-around now and then.
> JB (to King): What do you feel?
> King: You've got to have a laugh or you'd go bleedin' daft!

From the teacher's point of view, much of the pupil's classroom activity seemed aimless and inexplicable. This is evident in early assessments of the ringleader King:

> 'The way I look at it, King is a little mad, a little unbalanced.'
> 'King is as mad as a hatter! He's a fruit and nut case!'
> 'In my view there's something seriously missing with a large number of boys in this school. I'll go as far as to say some of them are mad. Their upbringing has made them like that.

King, for example, you couldn't describe that boy as a normal, healthy eleven-year-old, could you? Physically he is, but mentally he's what an American friend of mine would describe as a "goof ball"!'

As we have tried to illustrate, however, there was clearly more than a little method to the 'madness' displayed by King and those who mucked with him. Moreover, King and boys like him contrasted their own rationality with the 'madness' of teachers:

> King: I just shouts out words and plays 'em up, dun I Mike! You've got to see if they'll come out and hit you an' all that. Like Mr Stern – I've shouted there sometimes, 'aven't I, I don't know why 'cos he comes and picks your hair out like that. He goes mad and pulls you around by your hair, dun 'e?
>
> JB: Unless a teacher bashes you around you don't respect him or her – is that what you're saying?
>
> King: No, I'm not saying that. But some teachers gets on your nerves. They're so hopeless you've got to play 'em up otherwise you'd go round the bend yourself. They're mad and they're trying to make you like they are.

Mucking in action

We have concentrated in this paper on the presentation of boys' accounts of their classroom actions. We have done so in order to emphasize the extent to which they were willing and able to produce rational reflexive accounts of their disruptive behaviour. These accounts display the extent to which the boys of the Lower School at Victoria Road maintained a strategic interest in mucking and sussing as data-gathering techniques. In the course of this one paper there is not space to devote full attention to their actual behaviour in class. The fieldnotes and tape-recordings of classroom interaction contain numerous examples of disruptive activity, and display a rich variety of mucking techniques. The culture of 1Y was characterized by repeated use of individual and collective challenges to teachers' authority – both verbal and non-verbal. It should not be thought, therefore that the interview extracts presented here reflect only the boys' bravado: they were not simply bragging. The following extract conveys something of the tone of such classroom exchanges:

> Mrs Paint (who teaches Art) is guillotining large sheets of art paper at a side table. Boys are in groups talking and painting. The noise builds up and peaks with an outburst in the far corner, with kids laughing and dodging around the table.
>
> Long (shouting): Sir, Sir, King is throwing water around.
> Mrs Paint: I'm Miss. My name is Mrs Paint.
> Long (cheekily): Hey, Mrs, King is chucking water around.
> Mrs Paint (shouting as she walks to the scene): STOP IT! Stop throwing water around. RIGHT NOW! Look at the mess!
> Green: He (Ginger) wet himself, Miss. (Laughter)
> Ginger: It's piss, Miss. (All boys collapse into laughter.)
> Mrs Paint: Get the sponges and mop this lot up, QUICK-LY! (She hits King across the head and pushes him, none too gently, towards the door.)

This incident occurred during the first week of the term, and was part of a barrage of open cheek that this teacher was subjected to. It illustrates how the female teachers – who were suspected of being 'soft' – were challenged by the boys. It also shows how various boys can collaborate in the escalation of verbal challenging and cheeking. The boys themselves referred to such joint productions as 'build-ons' – as they put it 'joining in with the lip' and 'helping your friends'. The following extract further exemplifies such collaboration:

> Mrs Calm: What are you doing, King?
> King: Hanging from the rail. (Laughter)
> Bright: He thinks he's a monkey. He's a nut!
> Blond: King's a monkey nut!
> Long (sings, to the tune of The Milky Bar Kid): The

monkey nut kid is big and strong. (Laughter)

Mrs Calm: Right, quiet. (Claps hands) If he's a monkey then all of you lot ought to be in the zoo with him.

Blond: We are! (Animal noises and laughter: a cacophony of moos, growls, hoots, etc.)

Mrs Calm (shouting): That's enough, I said THAT'S ENOUGH!

Verbal sparring and challenging such as these were highly significant face-winning, face-retaining, and face-losing contests. Subversive laughter became both a means of unsettling teachers, and sussing them out, and of acquiring enhanced prestige among peers in the class. To retain credibility a teacher had to deal competently with such challenges: to be able to forestall challenges, deal with them and terminate them in what the boys considered to be an appropriate manner. A proper response could involve both physical and verbal violence (cf. Beynon and Delamont, 1983). Teachers who were deemed 'hard', on the basis of their retaliation, were given little trouble; 'soft' ones were likely to be tormented, and to be subject to the challenging behaviour suppressed in less lenient classes. 'Soft' teachers thus suffer what Woods (1979) has termed the 'sponge rubber' effect.

Conclusion

The strategies of verbal and non-verbal mucking at Victoria Road were many and varied. In this paper we have not attempted to document and detail that complex variety. Rather, we have concentrated on the boys' accounts of their activities, and the inferences they draw from their effects on teachers. During the early days and weeks of the school year this process of data-gathering is of special significance. The pupils need to know where they stand. Teachers and pupils alike need to establish the negotiable boundaries of tolerable classroom behaviour, and to establish the calculus of response to infractions of such boundaries. During these early days and their initial encounters, teachers and pupils generate mutual typifications, while classroom characters and reputations crystallize. In this rather general paper we have not attempted to demonstrate the chronology of these processes. The data indicate, however, that characters and reputations take root and develop from the very first moments of initial classroom encounters. We do not intend to imply that this process is a temporary affair. It is particularly intense during initial and early classroom encounters, but the activities we have described continue to be part and parcel of the daily enactment of school lessons.

12

Teachers, peers and play preferences: an environmental approach to sex typing in the preschool

Lisa A. Serbin

Originally published in Barbara Sprung (ed.) (1978) *Perspectives on Non-Sexist Early Childhood Education*, pp. 79–93. New York: Teachers College Press, Teachers College, Columbia University, © 1978 Women's Action Alliance, Inc. All rights reserved.

*   *   *

In every classroom there is an unofficial curriculum, a part of the learning experience that is determined by the teacher's attitudes and behavior rather than by a formal syllabus. In regard to sex typing, much of this unofficial curriculum is 'hidden'; teachers themselves are often unaware of their own expectations and behaviors that effectively sustain and reinforce conformity to sex-role stereotypes.

The research in which my colleagues and I have been engaged for the past five years has focused on differences in the educational experiences of boys and girls during the preschool period. By observing the actual daily process of classroom learning, we have attempted to describe the different ways in which boys and girls receive attention and instruction and the different ways they are taught to behave in learning situations.

We have also tried to determine objectively the consequences of these differential experiences, and, finally, to develop effective programs for reversing sex-stereotyped behavior patterns that had previously been maintained in the preschool environment. I am going to summarize some of the results of our research and to describe the implications of these findings for classroom programs.

I personally became interested in preschool sex stereotyping after an experience I had when I was a graduate student. In 1971 I was observing a nursery school in New York City. It was around Easter time, and the teachers were having an Easter celebration with the children. I watched during music time, and the first thing I saw was the teacher asking the little boys to stand up while 'Here Comes Peter Cottontail' was played on the piano. All the boys were bunnies. They hopped all over the room. After the boys had had their turn and had all been Peter Rabbit, they sat down, and then it was the girls' turn.

This time the teacher played the Easter Parade song, 'In Your Easter Bonnet'. The girls paraded around the room. At the end, the teacher at the piano stood up and looked very solemn. She said, 'Ladies, that isn't the way we have a parade. When we have a parade, we all walk very nicely, and we pick up our feet so we don't make lots of noise on the floor, and we all walk like little ladies. Now let's do it again.' She sat down and played 'In Your Easter Bonnet' again, and the little girls went very quietly tiptoeing around the room. Then they sat down.

A little boy raised his hand and said, 'The girls got to go twice. Don't we get to go twice?' The teacher sat down at the piano and played 'Here Comes Peter Cottontail'. The boys hopped all over the room and made quite a good bit of noise, but nobody said anything to them about being 'gentlemanly' or quiet or making 'nicely' restrained movements.

This little incident bored into my head over the next weeks and months. I started thinking to myself, what are these children learning? Is this something pervasive or was it just a

274

quirk of this particular teacher? It seemed to me that if this was a pervasive aspect of the preschool curriculum, something different was being taught to boys and girls, something about what is expected of them. Girls were being taught to restrain their movements, boys were encouraged to use their large muscles and move around freely. And I thought, maybe this is pervasive. Maybe it doesn't just affect how they behave when they have music time; maybe it goes on beyond this.

About this time I started my internship. I'm a clinical psychologist. I did my internship at a county mental health clinic, and there I noticed something very odd. Among the children five times as many boys as girls were being referred for psychological problems. The most frequent reason for referring these children was some kind of disruptive or aggressive behavior. In most cases a teacher was the original source of referral and had complained that a child was unmanageable and/or inattentive in class. Ultimately the child was sent to the clinic.

The other thing I noticed that seemed very odd was that my adolescent and adult caseload was very different. Instead of seeing primarily males at these ages, we were seeing females. Females outnumbered males by about three to one in the adolescent and adult caseload. I wondered why there was a 'flip flop' at about age thirteen or fourteen. In all of my clinical training nobody had ever pointed out this phenomenon. I wondered if it was a fluke of our particular clinic, but when I looked at the statistics, I found that the same phenomenon exists nationwide.

The incident at the nursery school came back to me at that point. I wondered if there was something about the socialization boys and girls receive that results in these differences in psychological and emotional difficulties. I certainly wasn't naive enough to think that the nursery school was the primary source responsible for this, but I thought, 'Maybe there's a culture-wide, pervasive indoctrination children are receiving that, in extreme forms at least, is resulting in this strange imbalance – more boys having problems in elementary school years, more girls in high school and adult years.' At this point I went back to my graduate school readings on sex-role socialization, looked at the patterns that had been reported there, and found two characteristics that have been widely reported. The characteristics of male and female sex roles include aggressive behavior on the male side and dependent behavior – dependency and passivity – on the female.

It seemed clear to me that if one trained children to an extreme degree to be either aggressive or passive and dependent, they were likely to have problems. But how does this come about? If something about boys' socialization is teaching them to be aggressive, they're going to have problems in elementary schools. If something about girls' socialization is teaching them to be dependent, they're not going to have such noticeable problems in elementary school, but they are going to have problems when they become adolescents, and are suddenly expected to be independent and to begin to function as adults. When they've been socialized as youngsters to be dependent on others, this could lead to tremendous conflicts. In fact, there is a good deal of literature relating dependent personality characteristics to all kinds of psychological problems, especially fears, anxiety-related problems, and depression.

Aggressive behaviors

I decided to go and look in the preschool *before* children enter public schools and the behavior problems reported for boys begin to result in psychological referrals. In this first study, we observed systematically in fifteen different classrooms at four schools. Over the entire semester this involved over sixty hours of observation time that included children and teachers from a variety of socio-economic backgrounds. (A detailed description of the methods used in this study may be found in Serbin, O'Leary, Kento, Fonick, 1973.) The project focused on the children's behavior and also on the teachers' reactions to what the children did. Were there different contingencies in effect for boys and girls, contingencies that might shape sex differences in behavior, if they weren't there already? And if sex differences *were* there already, were the teachers reacting differently in ways that would maintain these differences or strengthen them?

The first thing we examined was teachers' responses to disruptive classroom behavior, including their responses to aggression, to children who ignored their directions, and to children engaged in deliberate destruction of materials. How did the teachers react? The results we obtained were very similar for all three forms of disruptive classroom behavior. I'll illustrate what we found with a story, one I find especially dramatic because it involved not only the teachers but also the other children in the room.

One morning we were observing a class of four-and-a-half-year-olds during free play. We saw a group of little boys playing with tinker toy materials. One boy reached for another child's piece of tinker toy and tried to snatch it away from him. The second child hung onto the tinker toy and resisted. The first child lifted his hand, obviously ready to strike. Instantly there was a chorus in that room: 'Mrs Jones, John's hitting.' There was John with his hand up in the air, and all the other children were shouting, 'John's hitting him'.

Mrs Jones said, 'John, I told you. We don't hit in here. What is going on over here, boys?' She walked over to them and said, 'What was it? Oh, Billy wouldn't share the tinker toy. Well, okay, Billy, you know you have to share with John.' The whole class was standing there watching this. The incident had now become the central focus of the classroom. 'John, we don't hit when we want something. You'll have to wait your turn. I'm sure Billy is going to share with you, aren't you, Billy?'

We recorded this incident. The observers put down 'John, aggression'. One tally mark in the aggression column. 'Teacher, loud reprimand'. (Loud reprimand was defined as a comment the rest of the children could hear.)

A little bit later in the same classroom, three little girls were playing in the kitchen corner. One little girl tried to take away a set of dishes that another girl was playing with. She snatched for them. The second little girl pulled away her dishes. The first little girl raised her hand, and this time actually followed through with a slap. The second little girl looked at her, pulled the dishes farther away, and moved two steps down the counter. At least two other children saw this. Nobody said anything. The teacher didn't say anything.

After our observations in all fifteen rooms, it became clear that there was a relatively low probability that anybody would react when a girl hit. Seventy-five percent of the time that boys struck someone else, or even moved their hand in that direction, teachers would intervene, most of the time with a 'loud' reprimand that everyone in the room could hear. Only 25 percent of the time that girls were aggressive did teachers say anything and most often gave a 'soft' reprimand, audible only to the girl herself, when they responded at all.

Why do teachers react differently to boys' and girls' aggression? Obviously, teachers may be responding to sex differences in children's behavior. If you ask teachers about these patterns, they'll say, 'Boys hit more often. We're much more sensitized to it. Also they hit harder. They're bigger. We just notice it a lot more, and we're more worried about it, because we know that they have a problem in this area. So we intervene.' But what is the result of this type of intervention?

John, in that instance, learned that he can (1) get a tremendous amount of attention and (2) eventually get to share that tinker toy by hitting another child. At the least, he knows he'll get a squeal from the victim. If you're angry and frustrated, that could be reinforcing right by itself, to hear somebody else get upset also. For girls, there's no response. It just doesn't work for a girl to try to hit somebody. At least, it doesn't work very often. Teachers quite inadvertently seem to be strengthening the pattern they're trying to discourage in boys, while teaching girls that physical aggression is not effective.

It should be obvious at this point that different treatment of boys and girls hurts boys as much as it hurts girls. I think that this is often underestimated in talks about sexism in the classroom and sex-role stereotyping.

Dependent behaviors

Let me turn now to girls, because I think disruptive behavior and other school-related problems more typical of boys have been studied a great deal. Dependent behavior as a problem area is usually ignored, because a quiet child does not receive the same kind of attention from a teacher as a disruptive child. A girl who is socialized to be passive and dependent may be perceived as a good student, since she is quiet, compliant, docile, and so forth. I do not think these children have received the attention that they deserve, because a child who is socialized in this mode may well have trouble later on when conflicts resulting in emotional problems emerge in adolescence and adulthood.

The antecedents of these problems seem to develop during the preschool period when patterns of dependency and passivity begin to develop. In our study we examined teachers' reactions to dependent behaviors. We observed how teachers interacted with children who were immediately proximal to them versus a little farther away (the other side of the table or elsewhere within eye and ear contact). Here we found a very subtle and interesting pattern. Little boys received approximately constant levels of teacher attention, praise, comments, and instruction, regardless of whether they were beside the teacher or farther away (these were all unsolicited comments). In other words, teachers would notice what a boy was doing, find it interesting, and interact with him. With girls, there was a differential attention paid according to how close they were to the teacher. Girls were learning, 'I can stay near the teacher and I'll get attention. If I go farther away, I'm going to be ignored.' To the boys, no such message came across since teachers noticed them and talked to them from a distance as well as when they were playing immediately beside them.

Why do teachers do this? Is this pattern deliberate? I don't think so. I don't think they're deliberately teaching little girls to 'hang around'. In fact, our teachers complained about it saying, 'I don't like it. They're just not as interesting as the boys. They hang around. They don't get into their own things. They don't explore.' We sat down with these teachers and showed them the observation records. They were quite honestly not aware of their own reactions. They did not see that they were socializing the very dependent behaviors in girls that they found so irritating and uninteresting. Why did they respond differently? Boys' behavior may be more salient. The teachers argued that it was, that it was more noticeable, that boys did things in a 'bigger way'. Boys have more trouble doing things. They aren't as well coordinated. The girls could be trusted to 'pick things up on their own'. However, the effect of reacting in this 'natural' way to differences in boys' and girls' behavior may be to exaggerate, reinforce, encourage, or maintain whatever sex differences in independence, motor coordination, and learning abilities are present when children walked into the room.

In this study, we also looked at attention given to the children when they were behaving appropriately. They were not clinging nor hitting; they were just doing what they were supposed to do during free play. Many earlier studies on this topic are difficult to interpret because they don't take into account what the children may have done that elicited differential responses from teachers. For example, if boys raise their hands or call out more than girls, obviously they're going to get more attention.

In our study we observed differences in the children's behavior and tried to allow for them. Given that a child was playing or working appropriately, what was the probability the teacher would become involved? We found this pattern: more interaction with the boys, more praise, and, one of our most interesting findings, a difference in the kinds of instruction given to boys and girls. Boys received more detailed step-by-step instruction in how to solve a problem or how to do something for themselves. Eight times as much instruction was given boys as to girls. Eight times! When we asked teachers about it, they replied, 'Boys need that kind of instruction much more than girls do. Girls pick stuff up on their own.' Perhaps the teachers are right. I'm not willing to abandon the hypothesis that girls at that age may be better socialized and better coordinated. Maybe they *can* use scissors without being taught how to use it before boys can. But what is the effect of boys receiving that much more step-by-step instruction, that much detailed analysis, that much modeling? What is the effect on children's learning how to do things for themselves and learning how to analyze a problem?

Teachers, of course, are not the sole or primary enforcers of sex-role patterns. Parents, peers, and media are all major contributors. Nevertheless, these teachers were reinforcing patterns of sex-role learning that are pervasive in American society.

What happens when these patterns are shifted around? We tried to reverse some of the reinforcement patterns for dependency we had observed and set up controlled designs to evaluate the effectiveness of reversing these patterns. We found that when teachers did not reinforce proximity seeking by little girls and attended to the children essentially at a constant level, regardless of proximity, initially there was an increase in clinging. But this dropped off within a few minutes. We found that proximity seeking, hanging around the teacher, by both girls and boys reduced sharply. Not only did girls work at greater distances from the teacher, but they also increased their exploration of the room and played with more toys. We also found an increase in task persistence. The kids worked for longer periods of time on their own without trying to involve the teacher in their projects. These were very encouraging results, and really all it took was a teacher being aware and making sure that the children received attention when they were working a little bit farther away, rather than primarily when they were right beside her.

Sex typing and cognitive development

We also focused on the development of cognitive and learning skills that may be hindered by the sex typing process. One of the primary goals of a nursery school is to encourage children to explore new roles. Children are at nursery school to learn to do new things, to be exposed to new experiences, to learn to interact with people they haven't met before, people from other groups and other backgrounds, and to explore, trying out new things, new toys, new behaviors, and new activities. Schools also function to help children develop their individual abilities to the greatest possible extent, to provide opportunities for them to grow in new directions where they haven't yet had the impulse or opportunity to explore.

It is widely believed that the activities in which children engage in preschool will have an impact on the roles they will practice and the skills they will develop. Blocks are in the room for a very specific purpose. Playing with blocks helps eye-hand coordination and teaches children to build in three dimensions. Similarly, dolls are in the classroom for a specific reason also – practicing nurturant roles. However, as anyone who has observed a preschool knows, toys that children actually play with in the classroom are very definitely affected by sex-role stereotypes.

Children do not come in and randomly play with every toy in the room. By the time children walk into the nursery school classroom, sex preferences for specific toys and activities are already present. As a result of this, children do not take the opportunity to explore every toy in the room but rather play with certain toys and develop certain skills according to the sex-typed labels they have learned.

As early as age four, there is a definite relationship between conformity to 'masculine' and 'feminine' activity preferences and specific patterns for cognitive development. For example, visual-spatial problem solving ability is believed to be an important factor in mathematics and science achievement, and sex differences in both these areas appear later on in the school years. We found that preschool children who play primarily

282

with 'boys' toys' such as blocks, trucks, and climbing apparatus showed stronger visual-spatial problem solving abilities than children who play primarily with 'girls' toys' including dolls, housekeeping materials, and fine motor activities. Sex differences in visual-spatial ability are not yet present during the preschool period, but these data suggest that sex-typed activity patterns may contribute to later sex differences in problem solving ability and achievement.

Sex typing of play activities

In one study we asked teachers in nine classrooms to introduce three new toys to their classes. A fishing set had been labeled 'masculine' by adult and child raters, sewing cards as 'feminine', and a third, a counting puzzle game, was rated non-sex-typed. We asked teachers to show each toy to their class and to call on several children to help demonstrate its use to the other children. The teachers responded to the sex typing of the toys, introducing the fishing set with stories of 'going fishing with daddy' and the sewing cards 'like when mommy sews on a button'. In addition, the teachers called on many more boys than girls to demonstrate the fishing set to the class, and, when introducing the sewing cards, also reacted in terms of the sex stereotypes. Only when introducing the non-sex-typed toy did the teachers call on boys and girls indiscriminately.

The effects of sex-typed introductions and use of male versus female models to demonstrate specific toys has been shown in many laboratory studies (Liebert, McCall and Hanratty, 1971; Montemeyor, 1974). Children readily learned whether a toy is sex 'appropriate' or 'inappropriate' from such introductions. The fact that nursery school teachers introduce activities in this manner suggests that they are providing children with sex-typed labels for these activities. Children are learning that the teacher expects either boys or girls to play with a particular toy.

Another observational study focused on a more subtle pattern that tended to prevent exploration of new toys. Beverly Fagot and

Gerald Patterson (1969) found that teachers interacted with children of both sexes primarily when activities were female-preferred. In other words, their time with boys and girls was spent in the activities girls like, so that their interactions with boys were primarily in female sex-typed activities. Now this seemed puzzling. If teachers are reinforcing boys by engaging in girls' activities (which is one way of interpreting this finding), why don't boys start to play with these toys? Doesn't this argue that reinforcement doesn't have much of an impact?

Here's a different interpretation of this data.... Teachers, perhaps because they are socialized as females (and these were female teachers), have certain interests in a classroom. They're also trained to focus on certain things. Traditionally teachers have been trained to encourage fine motor tasks. In a free play situation teachers will spend a good deal of their time sitting at a table interacting with the kids who are making things: craft activities, drawing, and so forth. How much time do preschool teachers spend with the trucks and blocks? Relatively little.

Since teachers seem to focus on certain activities as a result of their own interest and training, the question asked in this particular study was, 'Is it possible that girls do not explore certain areas because they have been socialized to follow the teacher around?' I described above how we observed teachers reinforcing proximity seeking by little girls. Is it possible that the reason girls don't get into the blocks and the trucks is because the teacher doesn't get into the blocks and the trucks either? To find out, we did a very simple study: we asked a teacher to simply place herself in the block area for a little while. This is what happened.

First the little boys were in the block area. When the teacher joined them, they continued with what they were doing. A little girl very shortly wandered by and looked around. She was holding a doll. This happened to be a little girl we had never observed in the block area before. She was a 'follower', one of the proximity seekers. She stood there for a little while and then picked up a block and began to play. Gradually other little girls drifted in. After ten minutes that whole block corner was occupied by boys and girls; half the children had never been in that area before.

We also asked the teacher to do the same thing with dolls, with the same effect. This time little boys who had not played with dolls before entered the doll corner. Again their hesitancy was interesting. They hung around for a while and looked. It took them about five minutes to really become involved in playing with the dolls. No 'coercion' was involved at all. The teacher never said, 'Bobby, why don't you come over here?' She just sat there. It was quite dramatic.

Now the interesting thing to us was that both sexes responded; both girls and boys ventured into the others' sex 'territory'. But perhaps more interesting from a theoretical perspective was that girls responded about twice as much as boys did. In other words, these results provided strong support for the idea that girls' interests are being developed by the fact that teachers spend their time in certain areas. Girls are more likely to follow their teachers no matter where they are in the classroom.

We have since repeated this study with both male and female teachers (the first study involved only a female teacher) and found that girls again tended to follow teachers wherever they went. Boys, however, were particularly responsive to modeling of traditionally masculine activities by the male teachers. For example, a male teacher in the block area was a much more powerful model for boys than the same male teacher in the doll or kitchen area, or than a female teacher in either type of activity. For this reason, I believe it is especially important for male teachers to be aware of where they spend their time in the classroom. If they stay in the vicinity of traditionally masculine activities, this will effectively keep the boys in these areas also.

Our conclusion from these studies is that teacher presence and modeling is an extremely powerful factor in determining children's activities. If female teachers stay in the 'feminine' areas, while male teachers focus on 'masculine' activities, their classrooms are likely to reflect their own (probably sex-typed) developmental and educational histories. However, we have

285

found that when teachers are made aware of these patterns, they are willing and able to diversify.

Peers and play preferences

Peers, of course, also influence sex typing in classrooms. Children seem to conform not only to their perceptions of teachers' expectations but to peer expectations as well. To demonstrate the power of this effect, we recently did a study in which children were taken individually to a playroom containing a variety of male and female stereotyped toys.

Initially the children were very stereotyped in their toy selection choices. But when we left them for a little while, they started to explore. A boy would play with the dishes and the doll; a girl would throw airplanes around the room. However, this relaxation of stereotypes didn't happen when another child was present in the room, and it especially didn't happen when the child was of the opposite sex. A little boy sitting coloring a picture at a desk in the room was enough to keep little girls with their dishes and dolls. We found the same effect in reverse for boys. A little girl coloring a picture in the room kept them with their trucks and planes. We concluded that just the presence of a peer, especially an opposite sex peer, is likely to make a child conform to sex-role stereotypes. In a classroom, it is easy to see that children may avoid certain toys and play areas they have learned are sex-role inappropriate if other children, especially of the opposite sex, are nearby.

Rates of cooperative play between boys and girls are typically much lower than between same sex children. This may also keep children from exploring particular toys. In other words, if boys and girls primarily play separately rather than together, it is likely that boys will continue playing primarily with 'boys' toys' and the girls with 'girls' toys'.

Fortunately, we found that this pattern is not difficult to reverse. When teachers indicate that they expect and approve of cross-sex, cooperative play, by simply commenting on it when it occurs, boys and girls do begin to play more with each other. Comments such as, 'John and Cathy are building a very high tower with the blocks' effectively convey to children that playing with someone of the opposite sex is not disapproved of (a message they are likely to have received pervasively from sex-stereotyping indoctrination outside the classroom).

Freeing children from sex-role stereotypes

Children come into a preschool classroom heavily 'programmed'. They have already learned that different characteristics, activities, and behaviours are expected of males and females. They will conform to these sex roles in the classroom unless the teacher makes an active effort to communicate different expectations and values. If children are to be freed from stereotyping, they must be treated as individuals, rather than as members of a classified group. Teachers will have to make special efforts to introduce all toys to all the children. They will have to encourage children to take turns at all the activities, to explore new activities, and to engage in cooperative play with both boys and girls. We've shown that these things can be done effectively, but teachers will have to offset powerful home, peer, and media influences. It's certainly a long-term project – you can't expect it to happen in a morning or even in two weeks.

The process of freeing children from stereotypes will have to counter children's own tendencies to stereotype. For example, one day the children in our nursery school were running round the track at our university. They love to do this and to 'time' themselves, to see how fast they are. After all the children had run and had been timed, Michele was acclaimed the fastest in the class, and all the children took a final sprint around the track with their teacher. While they were running, they were passed by a female student who was running on the track. One of the boys looked up at the teacher with a very puzzled look on his face. He said, 'What's she doing here? Girls can't run!' Chucky was running next to his teacher, who was also running and was a female, and Chucky had just acknowledged that the fastest child in his class, Michele, was a girl.

Children do seem to filter out information that runs counter to their expectations or to their stereotypes. To change these, children will have to be taught that specific behaviors, specific roles, and specific interests are not part of 'being a boy' or 'being a girl'. Being a girl does not mean that one has to be passive and not able to run very fast. Children have to learn, have to be taught, that specific activities and specific roles are not exclusively assigned to one sex or the other.

Conclusion

To summarize the findings I've reported, we discovered that teachers reinforce sex-role stereotypes in many subtle ways of which they are frequently not aware. We also found, however, that teachers can reverse these patterns effectively when they become aware of them. We demonstrated that increased independence, cooperative play between boys and girls, and exploration of all classroom activities by children of both sexes can be accomplished, if a teacher wishes to do so.

Will this mean a great deal of artificial programming or coercion? I don't think so. After all, teachers, like the rest of society, are already heavily 'programmed' to train and enforce traditional sex roles, which place arbitrary limits on the direction and extent of each child's individual development. Actually, I see the role of the preschool teacher as a powerful force to combat some of the pervasive stereotyping that children receive during the preschool period. As psychologists and educators have long been aware, this is the period when sex roles are learned. Learning during the preschool period may also, thus, be a key to introducing children to more flexible, rather than sex-role determined, patterns of behavior. The preschool period may, in fact, be a critical time for prevention of the cognitive and emotional handicaps that can result from conformity to rigid sex roles. From our data, it is clear that teachers will have to do more than 'not enforce' traditional sex-role stereotypes in their classrooms if they wish children to be free to develop as individuals. They will have to play a most active part in the process.

The methods I've described involve little that could be labeled 'coercive' or 'manipulative'. Teachers simply introduced toys to *all* the children, or 'modeled' a greater variety of activities, or stopped responding differentially to passivity and aggression by boys and girls. These methods do, however, require an active awareness and involvement. Teachers will have to be loving enough and concerned enough to analyze their own behavior and, if necessary, make some changes.

13

Mixed ability teaching
at Beachside Comprehensive

Stephen Ball

Extracts from Stephen Ball (1981) *Beachside Comprehensive*, pp. 197–234. Cambridge: Cambridge University Press.

Stephen Ball, whose work concludes the book, studied a comprehensive he calls Beachside. In the extract which follows he compares how different subject departments at Beachside adapt to the introduction of mixed ability classes. Ball contrasts Geography, Sciences, Foreign Languages, Maths, History and English, showing both departmental variations and differences between teachers within departments. The extract which follows includes Ball's analysis of Science, Foreign Languages and History only.

* * *

The Sciences (twenty-six mixed-ability lessons observed)

In the case of the Sciences, Chemistry and Biology prepared their own worksheets for use with the first year, but without essentially redesigning the syllabus. One Chemistry teacher commented:

> The Chemistry Science course is too staid and academic for
> me; there's not enough entertainment or project work in the

290

course and we've got kids who have scientific hobbies at home who are doing very badly in Science at school. And we haven't changed anything for mixed-ability really, it's more or less the same course as Band 1 had.

And the head of Science explained:

We just don't have the time to organize any sort of comprehensive reform of our syllabus.

In relation to this, both these sciences failed to act upon their report recommendation.

In the Chemistry lessons I observed, the prepared work-sheets were used only occasionally, and one member of the department was never observed to make use of them at all. For the most part the teachers continued with teacher-centred 'chalk and talk' methods, and, when they *were* used, the sheets became a guide to experiments to which the teacher referred. The head of department explained this in describing his teaching of one mixed-ability form:

I'm doing something that I never thought I would do with this form and that's class-teaching; it goes against all the preconceived ideas of mixed-ability groups but I find with experiments like this that they can all understand and find their own level in their written work.

FIRST-YEAR-CHEMISTRY: LESSON NOTES

The teacher had intended to spend the first part of the lesson giving a test, but as several members of the form were at a school choir rehearsal, the substance of the lesson came first.

T: OK, so let's go round. What did we do last time when we were heating things?
P1: (Untranscribable)
T: What colour is copper to start with?
P2: Brown. Well, goldish brown.
T: Yeh! It's shiny; all metals are shiny; that's one of the

things that makes them metals. It was a brown colour and you heated it and got this coating. Anything else happened, just to remind ourselves before we move on?

P3: It melted and . . .

T: *Yes*, it did melt, when did it melt? Did it melt straight away?

P4: No, after a little while it was red hot first, then it started.

T: Yes, anything else happened?

P5: (Untranscribable)

T: Just copper . . . last time did we heat anything else?

Chorus: No!

T: Right, so working in your two's or on your own again, some people, because some people are away or because people are in the choir practice, will obviously have to be working on their own. Get out a bunsen burner and an asbestos mat and a pair of tongs.

Two or three minutes pass while the pupils collect their apparatus and assemble it. The teacher then begins to pass out a worksheet.

T: Once you get a worksheet read it through to remind yourself what you are doing. . . . One thing you mustn't do – it won't do you any harm *now*, but it might later on – if you've got a pair of tongs like this chappie has here, instead of sort of playing with it and going like this and sticking it in your ear put it in the middle of the bench there and don't play with it. Sooner or later you'd play around with a thermometer or something and break it and cost you and me a great deal of money. . . . Has everybody got one? . . . Here, give one to this chappie here.

Right, some of you have only just got hold of your worksheets I can see; the thing to do with these always is to remind yourselves what you were doing last time. This one is for, is going to last us about three or four weeks. There's an awful lot of work which we've got to do. This is one of them. Look towards me now; you can finish reading about that before you do the experiment, make sure you do that though. . . . You've perhaps heard about this stuff (holding up a small bottle of chemical) and some of you may have seen your Junior School teachers using it. . . . I was talking to Mr Baldwin from Iron Road and he was saying he does a fair bit of Science work with his people and it's magnesium ribbon – you might possibly have seen it before; magnesium is a metal, the only thing that'll mean to you if you rub your finger along it, it can be seen to be shiny, and I did say before that something shiny is often a metal.

The teacher talked for a further *five* minutes before the experiment was begun, the period of the experiment lasted for *five* minutes and then the pupils were called to attention again by the teacher.

T: Right, stop, hush, turn your bunsen burners on to luminous, like that . . . right, there's no air on, the flame's luminous, it doesn't make any noise. And sit on your stools and look forward to me. . . . Come on, Tracy, we're waiting for you. . . . Now . . . all sorts of things have been said to me going round.

The lesson continued in this fashion with two further experiments. In each case the metals were introduced by the teacher to the whole form and discussion of findings was also done in a class-teaching situation, although the teacher also discussed the experiments while they were in progress with small groups of pupils as he walked around the room. But in every case the interpretation of the experiment was discussed with the form as a whole.

T: We are left with ashes – so we are. If you notice, actually if you look in the air at the moment, if you look around the air at the moment you see it's a bit foggy, it's not mist because mist is wet, isn't it? It's a bit foggy, there's the dust, it's just the same as the ashes left on the end of your

293

pair of tongs, have a look and see.... Now just for this once we're going to do this exercise all together, because I'm going to give you quite a few more to do now, if people finish one and write it up properly they can have another one. Just for this once I want you to fill in your table.... I shall just clear a space on the board here, you can do this on your own, but I'm just going to give some important spellings, some important words.... Right, well, let's put some important words down ... MAG-NESIUM ... RIBBON.... Right, use that when you are filling your table in.... What else could we say. It was very very hot for anybody here who knows what that means, it was that hot, 2000 degrees centigrade.... Right.... You also saw light given off, didn't you? I'll put that down for somebody who wants some words to use, OK, and it left you with white ash?

A period of writing followed.

  T: Right, if you've finished the write-up, come and get one of the test-tubes.... Right, one and one again, I'll give you some of this stuff, don't touch this with your fingers.... A straight line.... Don't start heating till I tell you to.... Now before you start doing anything, look this way, look at your worksheets ... it tells you, 'Put a measure of one chemical in a test-tube. Make a note of the name and what it looks like.' So you'll forget the name if you don't note the name, I'm going to have to tell you the name of this substance, we've just done magnesium. This one's called Iodine. Now Iodine used to be used by doctors as an antiseptic, does anybody know what antiseptic means?
  P: It keeps things clean.
  T: Yes, it kills germs, doesn't it? And keeps things clean. Something like that. It used to be used mixed with alcohol, actually, because Iodine itself is a solid.... Now I want you to heat that very gently. But you will need something to hold the test-tube with, a test-tube holder.

Can you two please go round and give one of these to each person with a test-tube. As soon as you get that you can gently heat the Iodine using again a medium flame, let some air into the flame. And once you've done that you can have the next one. I'll put the name of Iodine here.... Stop a minute, please, one thing I forgot to say very important, when you heat something up don't point it at everybody...

There was a further period of experiment with instructions being given to the whole form.

T: Don't make it too hot.... Take it away from the flame now.... That's enough at the back there, you don't want it too hot.... Turn the flame down now and just put it back in ... but don't make it too hot.

This was typical of most of the mixed-ability Chemistry lessons observed. When used, the worksheets played a secondary role in the pupils' relationship to the subject-matter. Invariably, the preparation of experiments and the de-briefing afterwards were done by the teacher to the whole form. The pupils only worked on their own during the actual 'experimenting', and the pace and timing of activities remained completely under the teacher's control. The pupils' experiment work was begun and ended on the teacher's command. His talk dominated the flow of the lesson and the responsibility for the transmission of knowledge clearly remained with him. Here the worksheet was used simply as a guide to experimental procedures and a reminder of work done. But there were differences from the banded lessons, particularly in the extent of pupils' participation in experiments, and the head of Chemistry certainly felt that his department had moved significantly away from traditional science-teaching methods.

As mentioned above, one of the Chemistry staff did not make use of worksheets in any of the lessons observed. She explained that:

When we were preparing for mixed-ability we produced lots

of workcards and projects, but I haven't felt that they have been necessary. I feel that we can stretch the brighter kids by stimulating their minds in open-type lessons.

The open-type lessons to which she referred followed essentially the same pattern as that of the Physics lesson described below. The teacher would do the experiment and then the pupils were asked questions. This particular teacher was also different from her colleagues in that she operated a system of streaming *within* the classroom.

> They're organized here roughly, by the benches – the brighter ones at the back, the average ones on the middle bench and the slow ones on the front bench. I gave them a rough test at the beginning, and then I sometimes move them around. But they don't know this – I can keep some idea of the level at which I should be pitching my questions.

In another sense it could be said that this was an attempt to create a more individualized learning experience in a class-teaching situation. But overall in Chemistry the introduction of worksheets did not in itself involve any more than a marginal move towards the individualization of learning, and the frame of lessons remained strong.

In Biology, worksheets were also used. Despite the fact that they normally consisted only of detailed instructions for experiments, rather than substantive lesson material, in the Biology lessons observed it was apparent that the teachers spent much less of lesson-time in addressing the whole form than had been the case with banded forms. Most of the teacher's time was spent in talking with individual pupils and answering questions and problems.

FIRST-YEAR BIOLOGY: LESSON NOTES

The pupils are given out their books as soon as the form is assembled.

T: Now then, in an orderly fashion I want you to go to the

bench at the end and collect a worksheet, then one person from each group should collect a microscope, a slide and a mounted needle. And please be careful with the microscopes, they are very expensive to buy and we cannot replace them if they are broken. Before you begin your experiment you should read, CAREFULLY, through the worksheet. Now are there any questions? Right, off you go.

Almost the whole of the rest of the lesson is taken up with the experimental work by the children and then their attempts to interpret and make sense of what they observed. For the first part of the lesson the teacher was engaged in solving the technical problems created by the microscope, and the use of the slide and needle. Later, there was much discussion of the drawing of the cells and with some groups the description of the experiment. As pupils finished, some prepared slides were brought out to be looked at through viewers and drawn to compare with the human cells drawn first.

With ten minutes of the lesson remaining some pupils were also finishing the second task, most of the others were just beginning this.

P: What shall I do now?
T: You can sleep quietly for the last ten minutes.

More than in either of the other sciences, the lesson format in Biology had changed for mixed-ability; the teachers talked much less to the form as a whole than they did under the banded system, and the pupils had much greater involvement in the substance of the lesson through experiment. The nature of these experiments tended to release the teacher, who could circulate and talk to small groups or individuals without being primarily concerned with the progress and safety of the form as a whole. Thus, the frame of the lesson appeared to be weakened considerably, and . . . this method of organization of learning tended to give the teacher much greater opportunity to monitor the pupils' involvement with and understanding of lesson-material.

In Physics there was a state of affairs rather different from that among the two other sciences. From the time of the original vote to introduce mixed-ability in the summer of 1972 until the arrival of the first-year mixed-ability cohort in the autumn of 1973, there had been a complete turnover of staff and the department had its third head. None of the departmental report recommendations was implemented; there were no work-cards prepared and no revision of the syllabus. Indeed, there was little change either in methods or presentation of lessons for mixed-ability forms. There was much greater reliance on teacher-demonstrated experiments than in either of the other sciences, and this approach generally maintained a high degree of traditional teacher-talk in Physics lessons.

> We don't use a real-mixed ability course here, it is a version of the band 1 course which is a pity. But making a proper mixed-ability course that they could work through at their own pace would involve someone in the department in a great deal of time and effort. We could make use of the combined Science Course but the department don't seem to be keen on it. (Physics teacher)

The following lesson may be regarded as highly typical of the mixed-ability Physics lessons observed.

FIRST-TIME PHYSICS: LESSON NOTES

The form are sitting in rows at the dark brown benches; the lesson begins with a recapitulation of the work done in a previous lesson.

> T: Who can tell me which of these two examples will exert the least pressure [a stiletto heel or an elephant's foot]?
> P1: An elephant's foot.
> T: Can anybody explain why?
> P2: Because of the area of the surface.
> T: Good boy.

The teacher goes over the theory on the board explaining with an example how to work out pressure per square metre.

T: If the weight is six kilos and the area is three square metres what is the pressure?

The same few hands are raised as before.

T: Yes?
P3: Two.
T: Two what? . . . Yes?
P2: Two kilos per square metre.
T: Right.

She now puts up a series of problems on the board to be worked out individually; the form work quietly; three boys are given individual help by the teacher.

T: Anyone not finished put up your hand.

Everyone looks around to see who has not finished; there are only a few of the form without their hands up, predictably those who were also answering the questions; the teacher begins to organize some equipment that the lab. technician has placed on her desk.

T: Anyone not finished put your hand up. (It is just a handful now, including those boys who had been 'helped'.) If you have finished read over what I've given you and sit quietly.

She spends some more time with one of the boys who is having trouble.

T: OK, leave that now – you can finish them off at home; I want you to gather around the desk at the front.

The teacher demonstrates a pressure experiment with water and asks questions.

T: Why does the jet at the bottom go further from the rest?
P1: Because it is under greater pressure.
T: Good boy.

Finally the experiment is to be 'written up'.

> T: I shall leave the conclusion for you to do for homework: I want you to explain what you think the experiment shows.

After the lesson the teacher explained to me:

> They are a nice form to work with. I haven't really found any problems this year, although I have this fear that I am going way over the heads of some of them. I feel that if I tested them people like Graham Jones would not know anything. But it has not been too bad this year; I am not sure about what will happen next year. And I certainly would not want to teach Maths and French to a group like this.

Without any teaching alternatives, except when equipment was available for pupils to do experiments, all the Physics lessons I observed approximated to this structure.

The teacher interacted individually with less than half the form and the majority of these interactions were by question and answer; the lesson was centred on the teacher's explanations and demonstrations. The pace was determined by the contents of the one lesson and a median pupil-speed. The 'knowledge' of the lesson was presented by the teacher in a traditional explanation-question-reinforcement format. Thus framing remained strong and there was little difference between the conduct of this lesson and the typical banded Physics lesson.

It is possible in the Sciences to account for the processes of implementation, to a great extent, in terms of the teachers' perspectives and their subject-identities. The head of Physics and the other Physics staff were against the introduction of mixed-ability and, as we have seen, they did little or nothing to change teaching methods to accommodate the new situation. The Chemistry staff, however, were in favour of mixed-ability, at least in the first and second years, and made changes in the organization of lessons. Although these changes appeared to be superficial in terms of altering the locus of control over subject-

300

knowledge, they did not involve a shift in the pedagogic basis of Chemistry teaching. In both cases, the teachers' view of the subject, as involving conceptual evolution and linear progression, was an important limiting factor in the degree of change.

It is not possible to account for the situation in Biology in the same way; although two of the three members of the Biology staff were in favour of mixed-ability, the head of department was decidedly against. Nevertheless, a shift in pedagogy was evident in the Biology lessons observed. It is certainly the case, though, that the Biology syllabus was less difficult to adapt to mixed-ability teaching than either Physics or Chemistry. It did not require a large financial outlay to introduce the more pupil-centred methods, whereas an equivalent redesigning in the other sciences would have been extremely costly. Neither did the changes in Biology involve the same safety hazards or problems of classroom organization as they would have done in Physics or Chemistry.

Perhaps most of all the departments, the Sciences were presented with considerable problems with the introduction of mixed-ability grouping, for any major changes in pedagogy and syllabus would also require the purchase of new equipment and materials. The department had considered the possibility of Schools Council Science but the cost of re-equipping proved prohibitive.

Languages (twenty-one mixed-ability lessons observed)

Given the strong opposition to mixed-ability within the French department and the particular subject sub-culture identified with it, changes were not to be expected. Indeed, the lessons observed indicated little change in teaching methods from a typical band 1 lesson. As anticipated in the departmental report, lessons continued to be of a traditional book-based, teacher-centred variety, following much of the syllabus and pace of the previous band 1 first-years. It was clear from the recommendations in the departmental report and the head of department's comments, presented in the previous chapter, that no method other than traditional class-teaching was ever seriously considered.

The teacher is already in the classroom; she has had her previous lesson there. The first arrivals of the new form hesitate at the door when they see her.

    T: Come in.

They enter and place their belongings – all are weighed down by briefcases and bags and books – but do not sit down. The form is in quickly; there are no stragglers, but two boys, seeming not to notice the others, do sit down.

    T: Some people seem to have forgotten their manners. (The two boys get quickly to their feet.) That's better. Bonjour mes élèves.
    Chorus: Bonjour, Madame Oakes.
    T: Asseyez-vous.

The form sit waiting silently.

    T: We started last week to talk about endings, and how in French the endings of words that are adjectives change. Can someone tell me when they change?

Half a dozen hands go up.

    T: Stephen.
    P: For masculine and feminine ...
    T: And also for?
    P: Plurals.
    T: Good. Now let's try some examples on the board.

Colours and other descriptive adjectives are used as examples, with the children putting their hands up to provide the correct endings, the answering is confined to about ten of the form and the more difficult 'irregular' endings go to just two or three

302

pupils, who thus answer a high proportion of the questions between them.

> T: Now, let me see what I have in here. (She searches in the drawer of her desk and produces a paper bag.) Ceci c'est un sac de papier ... What does 'sac de papier' mean? (No answers.) Someone guess. (She repeats the sentence.)
>
> P: Paper bag.
>
> T: That's right: 'paper bag'. (She repeats the sentence again.) Now, let's see what's inside. (She plunges inside and her hand comes out wearing a monkey glove puppet.) Celle-ci c'est Fifi.

She repeats the sentence in English, moving the puppet with her fingers; the form is entranced. The monkey now disappears into the paper bag and emerges holding a small plastic banana.

> T: What is it?

Hands up.

> P2: A banana.
>
> T: And in French?
>
> P2: Une banane.
>
> T: Fifi likes bananas! Can anyone say any more about it? Paul will you sit up straight, please.
>
> P1: Elle est une petite banane.
>
> T: Oui, très bien. Can anyone say any more about it? Remember what we have just been doing on the board.
>
> P3: Elle sont ...
>
> T: Elle?
>
> P3: Elle est.
>
> T: That's it.
>
> P3: Elle est une jaune banane.

This is repeated with a series of fruits produced by the monkey from the paper bag; the questions again tend to be answered by the same group of pupils; only occasionally do other pupils put up their hands, but sometimes the teacher asks someone who has not volunteered.

T: Allen, stop talking to your neighbour, please, that's very bad manners when I am talking. Now what is this, did we say?

Allen: Orange.

T: Just orange?

Allen: Petite orange.

T: Yes, but that wasn't what I meant. What goes before the word *in French*? The boy looks blank.

T: Who can help him out?

P2: Une orange.

T: Oui, une orange.

The lesson follows a rigid question-and-answer pattern, the teacher supplying a model statement and persuading the children to grasp the principle by repeating similar statements. The pace of work is totally dominated by the teacher in the oral interchange with a minority of pupils in the whole form, the French that has been 'learned' within the lesson is that displayed by the competence of this minority. The lesson is centred entirely on the teacher, and the 'knowledge' of the lesson or 'that which is to be learned' is presented within the pattern of explanation-question-reinforcement. (Also, the teacher constructs her definition of control in the lesson so as to include not only behaviour, but also manners, attitude, concentration, and health – she made frequent references to sitting straight so as to take pressure off the spine, to keeping fingers out of mouths to avoid picking up germs, and so forth.)

In one sense, this lesson is highly untypical. The use of puppets was not a method employed by any other teachers observed. However, in another sense, it represents an almost stereotyped lesson format for mixed-ability French lessons. Pupils would be presented with some kind of stimulus and introduced to new or previously-covered grammatical rules, and new or previously-covered vocabulary. In other lessons a textbook or slides were used to provide these stimuli. There would then be some oral work usually of a question-and-answer type, and then written reinforcement through book exercises. Pace was always determined by the introduction of new rules by the teacher or through the book, and always involved the whole class at once; the pupils would start and finish new work at the same time. The frame in these language lessons remained very strong.

. . .

History (twenty-five mixed-ability lessons observed)

The following observation notes and transcript materials are all taken from History lessons with mixed-ability forms; one transcript is presented from one lesson by each of the four members of the department. The History department provides an interesting case for examination, in that all of the four full-time members of the department were wholeheartedly in favour of mixed-ability, and had unanimously agreed to introduce home-made worksheets for mixed-ability teaching. However, the four transcripts presented below illustrate a range of different methods and forms of learning-organization covered by the notion of 'using worksheets'. It is clear that a commonly agreed terminology was used to explain and describe a variety of different classroom practices. Sharp and Green (1975, p. 175) discovered a similar situation with regard to the terminology of progressive primary education; they found that, 'If unprobed, the vocabulary (that teachers use to describe and justify their classroom practice) may legitimize a wide range of different personal categories used in their classroom practice.' This more detailed analysis of the implementation of mixed-ability in one department will also allow the exploration of some of the material constraints, as well as the ideological parameters, which impose limits upon the range of options available to the department, and to individual teachers, in the organization of learning in the classroom.

SECOND-YEAR HISTORY: LESSON NOTES (MR WHEATLEY)

The teacher arrives before the form and opens the book cupboard.

T: Please give out these.

He gives books to some of the boys as they come in; he also hands out the worksheets personally. Different members of the form are on different worksheets, and the teacher seems to be aware of the differences in individual progress.

T: You've finished that one, haven't you?
T: I want to have a word with you in a minute, don't I?
T: Yes, you had done that.

The form is quickly organized and quickly down to work. The teacher marks some books of those who have been 'first finishers'; he is standing over them at their desks; they get feedback from his questions and a follow-up on their work. He asks questions which question their understanding of what they have written. Within the first twenty minutes of the lesson, the teacher has interacted individually with every pupil in the form. He is always moving around the room, answering questions, solving problems of organization and procedure, as well as difficulties in understanding.

T: You read through that and see if you can find out and I'll be back in a minute.

The teacher is checking too.

T: How are you getting on, Robert?
T: Are you all right?
T: Which question are you on?

He is monitoring the understanding of the pupils and their progress and learning-difficulties. He returns to the 'I'll be back in a minute' pupil. He asks more questions and the pupil explains to him. The teacher addresses a boy sitting on his own in the corner.

T: Why are you sitting over there now, why don't you sit with them any more? (Pointing to a group of boys on the other side of the room.)
P: They're too noisy.

306

The lesson ends with the collection of books and worksheets. The teacher has not once sat down at his desk during the lesson.

The teacher has organized the lesson to allow a considerable flexibility in the speed of coverage of material; three different worksheets are being used in the lesson; he interacts with pupils individually both at his own instigation and at theirs; and he seems to be aware of the progress of individuals. The worksheets are written in a form of 'discovery learning', so that the pupils must search for answers in the three textbooks that are available to them, but the teacher seems concerned with checking 'understanding' as well as coverage.

This way of organizing learning makes available to the teacher a great deal of the pupils' 'self'. Teacher-pupil interaction takes place on a one-to-one basis in a number of dimensions through the process of the lesson itself.

Learning here is also 'socialized'. The pupils are allowed to talk among themselves and there is a considerable amount of discussion about the worksheet questions.

'What does it mean when it says . . .'
'I can't find a bit about . . .'
'What did you put for B . . .' etc.

I shall discuss the role of the worksheet in the framing of the History lesson at the end of this section.

FIRST-YEAR HISTORY: LESSON NOTES (MR FOOT)

The teacher stands by the door as the form enters and sits down. He catches two boys as they come in to give out work-cards and books; when this is done and the form is sitting down, he signifies the formal commencement of the lesson.

T: Right. (This is loud and sharp; there is total silence.) You should all have work-cards and books, I want you all to try to finish Section A today and I expect some of you

307

will get on to question 2 or 3 in Section B; remember what I said last week about checking in more than one book before you answer. Off you go.

The form begins to work in silence. The scratching of pens and turning of papers and pages are the only sounds. The teacher is sitting at his desk at the front of the room marking a pile of books. The silence continues for ten minutes; then a chair scrapes and someone goes to the front of the room; there is a quiet interchange and the teacher explains something; two of the girls at the back begin to talk.

    T: That isn't a sign for the rest of you to start talking, he barks.

The silence goes on for the rest of the lesson. Seven pupils go up to the teacher during this time and once he leans across to the boys in the front desks and points something out in their exercise books; there is one more rebuke to two boys.

    T: I don't think there's any need for you two to be talking to each other, is there?

The form continues to work after the bell has rung, until the teacher interrupts.

    T: Will the boys who gave out the books and work-cards collect them in again. The rest of you pack your things away.
    T: Off you go.

Within certain limits – 'I expect everyone to finish Section A today' – each individual is left to work at his own pace, but there is no interaction between pupils, and very little between teacher and pupils. The nature of the organization of learning in the lesson does not encourage this. The teacher explained the rationale behind his organization of the lesson in this way:

You can't have them chatting all the time, they never get

308

any work done. I just establish a scene in which they can get on with their work and they get a lot done in that way.

This, then, is the opposite extreme from 'chalk and talk' in the pedagogic role of the teacher. The teacher here has withdrawn from a transmission-role almost entirely and the pupils are left to interact individually with their worksheets. The worksheets in this lesson are used to establish solitary learning; the pupils are privatized from each other and the teacher. They have little opportunity in this learning-context to make the teacher aware of what they feel and think. Interaction is confined to a very narrow range of pupil activities, and little of the pupil's self is available to the teacher. He monitors their progress and production only indirectly in the marking of their books.

SECOND-YEAR HISTORY: LESSON NOTES (MR WRIGHT)

The form comes into the hut without noise; the teacher has arrived first. He has come from a free lesson and they have been on the other side of the school. The pupils do not sit down but stay standing behind their chairs, waiting and quiet. The teacher speaks to them quietly when everyone has arrived.

T: Sit down.
T: Go immediately to the question you were on last week.
T: Put up your hands those who have got as far as question 4 – not yet up to question 4.

The teacher makes no comment – he appears just to be collecting information; the form is quickly at work. The teacher goes to the pupils to check their work, but he is approached only occasionally; he has time to stand behind his desk at the front and look around the room. After twenty minutes, the teacher stops the individual work.

T: Put your pens and pencils down for a minute.

There follows a question-and-answer session for the remaining five or ten minutes of the lesson; the teacher is going over the work already done, highlighting and elaborating some points and clarifying terms.

T: What do they mean in the book by 'emigration'?

Hands up.

T: Pauline.
P: When you leave your country and go to live in another one.
T: Right, and what is the word they use to describe someone who does this?

Hands up.

T: Henry.
H: Emi ... emigrant. He struggles over the word but makes it.
T: That is good, emigrant, emigrant ... and can anyone think of any countries that people from this country, from Britain, do emigrate to, today?

About twenty hands.

T: Sally.
S: Australia.
T: Right, anyone ... June?
J: America.
T: Sometimes, not so much these days though, it's pretty full up now.

The teacher shares the pupils' laughter at this.

T: Another place, like Australia ... Terry?
T: New Zealand.
T: Yes, that's it, New Zealand.

The bell goes.

T: OK, before you pack away, it's your homework tonight?

It's not, sir, two girls volunteer.

T: No?
The girls again: Tomorrow.

T: OK then, I believe you, off you go.

Here, part of the lesson is dominated by the worksheet, but there is also a period of 'class-teaching'. All of the History staff did spend time class-teaching, even Mr Wheatley and Mr Foot. But each transcript so far represents a lesson typical of the particular teacher, both in terms of lessons observed and from the teachers' own descriptions of their organization of learning. There are obviously similarities between Mr Wright's classroom and Mr Wheatley's, but there are two general points of difference. The first is that Mr Wright always made a point of doing some oral work in every lesson: 'I like to expose them to different stimuli; their worksheets and books is only one way.' But because of the number of different worksheets normally being done in his lesson, Mr Wheatley rarely addressed the form as a whole, and when he did so it was usually only in reference to general points of technique – 'Don't forget to check in all the books' – or administration – 'Does anyone else need a new book?', etc. The second difference is that in Mr Wright's and Mr Foot's lessons it was usual for the whole form to be on the same worksheet and to go on to a new worksheet all at the same time, thus making it possible for them to ask questions, or lecture to the form as a whole, knowing that everyone would be working on that topic. For example, Mr Wright found that he was able to ask the whole form, 'What do they mean in the book by "emigration"?', a word which appeared in question 4. Mr Wheatley, on the other hand, maintained up to three worksheets in use at any time in his lesson, and pupils were able to move from one worksheet to the next in their own time.

The fourth full-time member of the History department is Mr Card. A long transcript is presented from one of his lessons, together with his own written description of the lesson and his comments on the transcript recorded sometime later.

FIRST-YEAR HISTORY: LESSON NOTES (MR CARD)

The teacher is five minutes late but the form is sitting quietly talking when he arrives – not working, but not misbehaving, either. The teacher quickly organizes the giving out of worksheets and textbooks; he then gives back exercise books which he has been marking. He walks round the room and gives each one back personally with comments.

T: Right, settle down, please ... and some for you. (He is giving out books.) I didn't have a book from you ...

P1: Mine's not here, either.

P2: I gave it in.

T: All right, see me later in the lesson ... (To the whole form) Very good, generally very good indeed.

T: Good. (To an individual as the book is returned)

T: Very good. (Again)

T: Not bad. (Again)

T: Did I see your book?

T: Karrie, outstanding; if I read out all your work that was good I would read out every page.

T: (To the whole form) As I was working through the books, most of your work is good, but what some of you are doing, in fact, is not really finishing off the question. Some of you are starting the question and then you, er ... I don't know, you get to the end of the lesson half way through a question and you're coming back the next day and you've forgotten that you've got to do it ... (There follows a long explanation about the shortage of exercise books and how much they cost and the need to use every space.)

Mandy: (Holding up her book) Shall I use this?

T: No, no, I don't mean a line like that, dear.

P3: I've got 'See me'.

T: Yes, I'll see you during the lesson ... er (He looks at Barry and Michael) Could you give out the worksheets, please?

Period of confusion.

T: Right (noise dies away) ... just start reading this worksheet. ... The one you finished off last week was the

312

Saxon village, wasn't it? Saxon Village life. Now, what I want you to do is to finish off any question that you've got to do. I want you to finish that off at home, please. Don't start anything now on THAT worksheet, but if there's anything you can do, finish it. Yes, Steven?

Steven: I was drawing.

T: What were you drawing?

Steven: Saxon buildings.

P4: So was I.

T: From the book?

Steven: Yes.

T: I'll lend you a book.

Desmond: I need a book.

T: What do you mean?

Desmond: I've got to read the book, then write.

T: OK, see me later.

P5: I'm doing Saxon buildings, too.

T: I'll lend you a book. Now then, about the Moot; the Witan Moot was not a man – some of you wrote, 'They went to the Witan Moot and *HE* was a most important person.' It was not a man. What was the Witan Moot? (Hands go up) The Witan Moot. (More hands) Yes, Nicholas?

Nicholas: The actual meeting.

T: Yes, the actual meeting of a number of men. Now which men? Do they go there to discuss Farmer Giles's cow or something like that, that the farmer next door said he owned or something? (One hand is up.) Klarisa.

Klarisa: The King's men.

T: Yes, yes, the King's men, the Lords, people like that. And they decide what? What might they decide? The Moot, this group of people who made up the Moot, what might they decide? (Hands up) Lennie?

Lennie: The new King.

T: Yes, who the new king would be if the king died and his son wasn't good enough. Michael?

Michael: Whether to make war or fight another country.

T: Yes, whether there would be war or peace, or something like that.

Beryl: Whether to have a new king or something. If one was bad they might choose another one.

T: Yes, right! important decisions. Whereas the Village Moot was just about the village, wasn't it? Just about the village. OK, you must remember that.... Now we can move on the next worksheet. 'The Spread of Religion in England'. Now, have you all got that one? ... slightly different from the worksheets you've done so far, inasmuch as you've got three sections. OK. Two questions in Section A, you've got to answer both of them; and then in Section B, six questions on that, so you answer all of them as well; and then we go on to Section C, if you make it in time, and you can do whatever you want of those. So, all Section A, all Section B, before you have a choice in Section C.

Michael: What's the difference between Section A and B?

T: Well, the only difference is in terms of time, because this is such a long theme we are doing, not just the Romans or the Saxons, but religion in the period from 450 AD right up to 1200, and we go through the Vikings and the Saxons and then the Normans, we go right through just talking about their religions.

Beryl: Do we have to LEARN the dates?

T: What do you mean LEARN the dates?

Beryl: Remember them.

T: What do you mean – roughly?

Beryl: Well, because it says from early Saxon times, 450 AD.

T: Well, obviously if it's early Saxon times it helps to know what you're talking about, doesn't it? It's all very rough, though, it's not exact dates.... Well, number one ...

The teacher now talks for the whole of the rest of the first half of the double period, interspersing his monologue with occasional quick questions. Most of the time is spent on the story of St Augustine, and the Vikings.

314

T: ... and now we are moving on to how it was – question 3 section B – how it was that the Church became very important in people's lives, you see – it became important for the way people lived; it taught them things, it helped the poor, helped the sick, it was more or less the largest, most important part of the town or village. OK. Anyway, we will come to that later.... OK, you can start on section A then, section A, put the heading 'The Spread of Religion in England', leave yourself some space if you've got to finish a question.

There is a period of discussion with individual pupils. Three books appear to be missing. The teacher leaves the form to get on while he goes to look in the staffroom. Four minutes later he returns without the books. The form has worked quietly while he was away. Most of the rest of the lesson is given to the various 'see me' pupils and some initial problems with the new worksheet.

Here is a lesson which is for the most part dominated by the teacher's talk and by traditional class-teaching on the question-and-answer method; the frame is rigid. The pupils are to finish the previous worksheet at the same time, although they would have completed different amounts of it, and there is some overlap by work 'to be done at home'. The following comments represent the teacher's own analysis of the lesson written the same evening.

PERIODS 7 AND 8

Form sitting quietly when I arrived late. They went in alone and did not stand when I entered (unusual for them).

No books given out – also unusual.

Exercise books to be distributed. Rest sat quietly while I did this. Made a few comments; a bit more than I can with some forms who need books immediately, but not as long as I would like to spend giving out books and discussing work. Hence comments have to be general (finishing work and filling up

315

pages) when really need to be specific to a third of form perhaps. Can give credit to few (e.g. Karrie: work excellent) but careful not to always credit same people. A good effort by Desmond shown as valid as good work by Steven, Richard, Beryl, etc. With band 1 and 2 lessons, I sometimes pick out pieces of work to read. Don't seem to do it so much in mixed-ability; afraid of too often reading out same people's work, discouraging others. (Yet suspect I often read out only same few from band 1 or 2 forms.)

'Lesson proper'

Had to leave previous card-work; probably should have gone over it a bit before moving on, but forms often restless at doing 'same' work again. Some do not finish, but syllabus dictates time-scale for work-cards. Children do not like to leave things; switching from Saxon Village to Religion straight away. Yet kids adaptable; sooner carry on with work, I feel.

When discussing early religion, trying to bring out evil nature of Saxons, and bravery, foolishness of Augustine to go to Kent. Story/legend of how Augustine chosen (a teacher's hardy annual!). I wonder how many remember. Ask tomorrow. When discussing work, the continual problem of trying to involve everybody emerges. No matter how hard you try, some kids never answer. As they never like to, is it right to ask them? Simon answers because he knows; Richard because he is enthusiastic; Beryl and Barry because they like to get attention. Some occasionally answer (Mandy, Christine, Lennie, Colin, Klarisa, Nicholas, Judith) but a few never do unless asked (Judy, Sharon, Nicki, Paul, John). Should I 'involve' them by asking – what if they get it wrong? Is it better they sit there – Bernice rarely answers but her work is excellent – and so is Karrie's – and write when asked? Too often the same children answer, yet this also happens in band 1 and 2; perhaps you can allow half the form to write and half to discuss more often? As to religions, I could have used the blackboard more for names (Augustine, Ethelbert, Bertha, Pope Gregory) –

316

(rarely use blackboard in first year) – and possibly get an example of a missionary today?

The dates 450–600 AD; 600–1200; very difficult – children rarely comprehend this sort of time-scale. Perhaps a bit more help here by me rather than just saying about Romans, Saxons, Vikings, Normans?

When working a few of the boys made a bit of noise about the calendar dates, etc. They rarely talk – this is their way of talking in class. The girls worked quietly. Beryl asked questions (predictably), Claire gave a very good answer. Such an easy form to handle. I could sit there all lesson if I wanted. Do they act too quietly? They have enthusiasm, though, for things, and do take part in lots of activities. Got annoyed over my losing three books – justifiable – I would be cross with them if they lost theirs. They can do a great deal of good work but as today I sometimes wonder if they are demanding enough as a form.

This review by the teacher highlights some of the decision-making involved in the organization of learning in mixed-ability lessons, and also some of the 'management' constraints that the teacher is confronted with in this situation. He is committed to class-teaching to some extent, but is also aware of the difficulty of differential participation that this raises. When I discussed the lesson-transcript with him in an interview some time later, he commented:

Well, one of my typical lessons, I suppose. I arrived late as I invariably do. A period of confusion which it always is at the beginning of my lessons, at least five minutes which is very bad. I realize I usually do this thing of giving out books and things. It is very difficult, isn't it? I mean it's fairly reasonable, I probably spoke a bit too much. I probably gave them too much information ... probably the next lesson would have been slightly different because they would have been into it, perhaps the books wouldn't have had to be given out. They would have reached a different stage, wouldn't they? I mean, they are all kicking off at the same time, therefore you can talk to a class, can't you? When they're at different levels, that's when it's difficult. . . . Probably next week I would have spent ten minutes talking and then there would have been much more of them.

This was a transition lesson when all the pupils are starting the new worksheet – 'they're all kicking off together'; it was not a time when 'they're at a different stage'. Thus, class-teaching was deemed appropriate because all the pupils were on the same piece of work at the same time. This kind of thinking about the nature of the subject contributed to the feeling that mixed-ability was possible in History. Mr Wright explained:

> Unlike the Sciences it (History) does not involve conceptual learning. It's the sort of subject like other humanities which lends itself to a variety of learning situations. . . . But so does Science, really, with all the super television materials.

However, in History, as in Science, as we shall see, the innovation was implemented primarily in terms of the practical demands of the mixed-ability classroom, and various contextual constraints, rather than in terms of eductional or social objectives.

THE WORKSHEET

For the first- and second-year mixed-ability forms, History was organized almost entirely round the series of worksheets designed by members of the department. The worksheets were usually divided into sections – one or two basic sections which all pupils were expected to complete, and an extra optional section which was designed to cater for and 'extend' the 'faster' pupils after they had completed the basic sections (as was the case in the lesson-extract above). In addition to the worksheets, each pupil would be provided with two or three textbooks. The questions on the worksheets could be answered by reading from the textbooks and specific references were made in each question to the relevant pages in the books. The following example comes from a worksheet on 'Roman Towns'.

Section A

1 Copy into your books the picture showing all the main parts of the Roman town. Explain why the Roman Town was the size and shape you see above. Do you think it was a good idea to have straight streets and buildings in square blocks?

(Read page 63 *Living History*; page 31 *Roman Britain*, Sellman)

Bernstein (1975, p. 29) is highly critical of 'textbooks' and sees their use as epitomizing strong frames and strong classification, thus tacitly transmitting the ideology of the collection code. He argues that:

The textbook orders knowledge according to an explicit progression, it provides explicit criteria, it removes uncertainties and announces hierarchy.

Barnes (1976, p. 317) argues that worksheets are more than anything else devices that teachers use to control what their pupils do, despite the fact that they are

often referred to in books as 'individual learning' or 'individualized instruction'. The name should not prevent us from understanding the sense in which the learning activities are 'individual'. Pupils work at their own pace; the fast worker can complete more calculations, fill more pages with writing, do an extra map or drawing. In no other sense is the work 'individual'; where there are options they are options for all.

While Barnes's comments do suggest that there is some weakening of framing over pacing inherent in the introduction of worksheets, he argues that in other respects framing remains strong. But even with regard to pacing, it is important to make the distinction between long-term and short-term control over the pacing of knowledge. Mixed-ability teaching based on

319

worksheets often appears to give individual pupils more choice in the selection of questions and the speed of working on each worksheet, and sometimes between one worksheet and another, but in most cases it is the teacher who decides when one topic is to be discontinued and another 'begun', and the teacher who also controls the amount of knowledge to be 'got through' in the year. Many of the Beachside teachers maintained in interviews that 'teaching' in the conventional sense would be impossible in a situation where the pupils were given extensive control over the selection and pacing of their work.

The History worksheets were designed in a way very similar to those specifically criticized by Barnes (1976). Many questions merely demanded that pupils should 'rehearse' information which they had obtained from reading the relevant pages in the textbook provided. This demonstrates to the teacher that the pupil has achieved his set task. In the worksheet 'The Spread of Religion in England', which consisted of a total of eleven questions, questions 1, 3, 4, 7 and 8 all required the pupil to read and summarize or repeat information taken from the textbooks being used. As Barnes points out, 'It places little pressure on the pupils to make their learning explicit to themselves'. In addition, questions 10 and 11 were concerned with a similar exercise, but using a wider range of source-books, and numbers 5 and 6 were basically drawing exercises which could be copied from textbook illustrations. Only questions 2 and 9 appeared to call upon more creative skills on the pupil's part (many pupils did not get as far as question 9 or did not choose to do it).

Despite the introduction of worksheets, therefore, in History the social and intellectual hierarchy of teachers as the controllers, transmitters and producers of knowledge and pupils as the consumers remained basically intact.

The worksheet system continued to have the support of the full-time members of the History department, but the strengths and weaknesses of the sheets and the possibility of other methods were discussed. However, most alternatives to the use of worksheets tended only to objectify the constraints within which the teachers' views of mixed-ability teaching methods were set. Mr Card explained:

> I feel that what we have done is that we have reappraised as we've gone along, we haven't just done worksheets and left it. We've not only reappraised the worksheets at History meetings, we've also discussed how they've come across and how we can improve them. And certainly in the third year, there's been much more flexibility and we haven't necess-arily used worksheets for all the topics. We've devised what we're going to do and talked over some ideas and we'll do it our own way and use whatever we want to use ... but no one has had the time, or whatever, to sit down and actually plan and say, 'We must use this and this, and we've got all these resources available.' We could use drama, ideally, but is the room you're in suitable? You know, it's pathetic things like this. It seems pathetic on the surface but you've got the hassle of changing rooms and organizing timetable changes. You've only got the kids for a double lesson a week, and there's a certain amount of work we've got to get through. In the third year, for example, for them to take their exams and choose their options. So if I spend a month and say, 'Well, I'm going to scrap this and do a bit of drama and make it more interesting', which it probably would be – if all the kids muck up their exams and get low marks, where do I stand then? You know, you've always got this dilemma. On the one hand you're torn to do something, on the other you've got certain commitments to the school philosophy. It's a dilemma which is very difficult to solve, probably not solvable unless you say, well I'm going to damn the exams and we're going to go our own way.

Here is a situation where, on the one hand, the teacher is confronted with what he perceives to be the demands and problems of mixed-ability teaching, and, on the other, the field of constraints within which he is obliged to operate, such as the practical difficulties of organizing alternative teaching-methods, the lack of time to organize and prepare resources, the limitations of time in terms of 'a certain amount of work to get through', and, closely linked to this, the demands of the parents and the pupils, which the school philosophy requires be met, that he should produce an acceptable level of academic excellence in terms of examination results.

In relation to their analysis of the organization of learning in the progressive primary classroom, Sharp and Green (1976, p. 218) make the point:

> We have tried to show how these practices are a function of the constraints both ideological and material which influence the practice of the individual teacher. Far from the stratification system being a mere product of interaction patterns at the micro-level, we have suggested that such interactions are socially structured by the wide context of which they are a part of whose major features they reflect and in turn reproduce.

Clearly, it is important to view mixed-ability in the same way. The previous chapter demonstrated how ideological constraints upon the practice of the individual teacher contributed to the emergence of certain views of forms of grouping and methods that are 'necessary' for effective teaching. In this case, the material and physical constraints are also apparent.

Apart from the four full-time members of the History department there was one part-time member, Mr Daniel, who did not find himself in sympathy with the department's approach to mixed-ability teaching. He explained:

> My understanding of mixed-ability teaching is not the same as the rest of the department, having worked in a middle school and having had groups working on different topics. There was no suggestion of a rotation system of different work-cards, so you can have low-ability groups and faster groups or mixed groups. There was no idea that we should move away from class-teaching, it's not mixed-ability, it's just class-teaching with a wide ability range. . . . I don't like these worksheets.

From his middle-school experience, Mr Daniel brought to bear on the mixed-ability classroom a different set of views of what was important and what was possible; he tended to find himself less constrained by the expectation of appropriate ways of working which clearly limited the practice of the other members of the department.

But even among the full-time History teachers there was a range of ways of organizing learning in the classroom subsumed within the notion of 'using worksheets'. The differences between the teachers can be explained in two dimensions, one relating to the extent of the control the teacher exerted over the organization and pacing of classroom knowledge, and the other relating to the extent of the teachers' control over the pupils' conditions of learning. The pupils experience conditions of learning ranging from *socialized* to *individualized*. The relation-

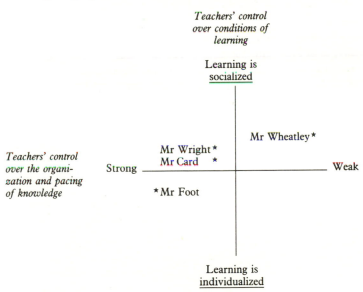

Figure 13.1 Variations in the History teachers' use of worksheets

ship between the two dimensions is shown in figure 13.1. Mr Foot is most easily placed, in that he operates rules of

323

behaviour in the classroom which totally individualize the pupils' learning, and although he does not 'class-teach', there is a strict monitoring of speed of work. Mr Card and Mr Wright can be positioned together on the diagram. They 'class-teach' and monitor their pupils' speed of work quite closely, both of which factors have implications for the pupils' conditions of learning, and for the teachers' control over the pacing and organization of knowledge. However, Mr Card and Mr Wright do allow conversation and interaction between pupils when they are working through worksheets, thus allowing for socialized conditions of learning, at least during these phases of lessons. Mr Wheatley is different again. He does not 'class-teach', nor does he closely control the pupils' speed of work, and he allows the pupils to interact while working. Thus his control over the pacing and organization of knowledge is weak, and conditions of learning in his lessons are socialized.

The term 'using worksheets' thus explains and describes a variety of different classroom practices and ways of organizing learning, and therefore encompasses a range of different kinds of learning experience on the pupils' part.

List of contributors

PAUL ATKINSON is a Senior Lecturer in the Department of Sociology at University College, Cardiff, UK.

STEPHEN BALL is a Lecturer in Education at the University of Sussex, UK.

JOHN BEYNON is a Lecturer in Social Sciences at the Polytechnic of Wales, Pontypridd, Mid-Glamorgan, UK.

B. M. BULLIVANT is a Reader in Education at Monash University, Australia.

SARA DELAMONT is a Senior Lecturer in the Department of Sociology at University College, Cardiff, UK.

MARTYN DENSCOMBE is a Lecturer in the School of Social and Community Studies at Leicester Polytechnic, UK.

JOHN FURLONG is a Lecturer in the Department of Education at the University of Cambridge, UK.

DAVID HAMILTON is a Lecturer in the Department of Education at the University of Glasgow, UK.

ROBERT HULL is an English Teacher at Boundstone School, Sussex, UK.

PAT KEITH teaches sociology of education at Iowa State University, USA.

WARREN A. PETERSON is a Director of the Midwest Council for Social Research in Ageing, based at the University of Missouri at Kansas City, USA.

325

LISA SERBIN is Assistant Professor of Psychology and Co-Director of the Butternut Hill Preschool, State University of New York at Binghamton, USA.

MARTIN SKELTON is Headmaster of Clare House Primary School, Bromley, UK.

LOUIS M. SMITH is a Professor in the Graduate Institute of Education at Washington University in St Louis, Missouri, USA.

LEILA SUSSMAN is a Professor of Sociology at Tufts University, Boston, USA.

ANN SWIDLER is an Assistant Professor of Sociology at Stanford University, USA.

RICHARD TUDOR is a Research Student at the University of Sussex, UK.

References and further reading

The numbers in italics after each entry refer to page numbers in this book.

Adams, R. S. and Biddle, B. J. (1970) *Realities of Teaching*. New York: Holt, Rinehart & Winston. *157*

Aitken, M., Bennett, S. N. and Hesketh, J. (1981) Teaching styles and pupil progress: a re-analysis. *British Journal of Educational Psychology 51*, pp. 170–86. *23*

Amidon, E. J. and Hough, J. B. (eds) (1967) *Interaction Analysis*. Reading, Mass.: Addison-Wesley. *6*

Anderson, J. G. (1968) *Bureaucracy in Education*. Baltimore: John Hopkins University Press. *144*

Atkinson, P. A. (1981) *The Clinical Experience*. Farnborough: Gower.
—— and Delamont, Sara (1984) Bread and Dreams, or Bread and Circuses? In M. Shipman (ed.) *Educational Analysis Monograph* No. 1.: *Educational Research: Principle, Policy and Practice*. Brighton: Falmer Press.

Baily, S. K. (1970) *Disruption in the Urban Public Secondary Schools*. Washington, DC: NASSP. *158*

Ball, S. (1980) Initial encounters in the classroom and the process of establishment. In P. Woods (ed.) *Pupil Strategies*. *257–9*
—— (1981) *Beachside Comprehensive*. Cambridge: Cambridge University Press. *49, 290–324.*

Barnes, D. (1976) *From Communication to Curriculum*. Harmondsworth, Middx: Penguin. *319–20*

Barth, R. S. (1972) *Open Education and the American School*. New York: Agathon Press.

Barton, L. and Meighan, R. (eds) (1979) *Sociological Interpretations of Schools and Classrooms*. Driffield, Yorkshire: Nafferton Books. *000*

Bateson, G. (1958) *Naven* (2nd ed.) Stanford, Calif.: The University Press. *96*

Becker, F. D. *et al.* (1973) College classroom ecology. *Sociometry 36*, No. 4, pp. 514–25.

Becker, H. S. (1953) The teacher in the authority system of the public school. *Journal of Educational Sociology 27*, pp. 128–41.

—— *et al.* (1961) *Boys in White*. Chicago: The University Press.

—— *et al.* (1968) *Making the Grade*. New York: John Wiley.

Bennett, S. N. (1976) *Teaching Styles and Pupil Progress*. London: Open Books. *7, 23*

Berger, P. (1977) *Pyramids of Sacrifice*. Harmondsworth, Middx.: Penguin. *106*

—— and Luckmann, T. (1967) *The Social Construction of Reality*. London: Allen Lane (reprinted by Penguin Books, 1971). *44*

Berlak, A. C. and Berlak, H. (1981) *Dilemmas of Schooling*. London: Methuen. *12*

Bernstein, B. (1971) On the classification and framing of educational knowledge. In M. F. D. Young (ed.) *Knowledge and Control*. London: Collier-Macmillan. *144*

—— (1975) Class and pedagogies: visible and invisible. In B. Bernstein (ed.) *Class, Codes and Control*, Vol. 3. London: Routledge & Kegan Paul. *319*

Beynon, J. and Delamont, S. (1984) The hard and the soft. In H. Gault and N. Frude (eds) *School Violence*. Chichester: John Wiley. *261, 271*

Bidwell, G. E. (1965) The school as a formal organization. In J. March (ed.) *Handbook of Organizations*. Chicago: Rand McNally. *144*

Bird, C., Chessum, R., Furlong, J. and Johnson, D. (1980) *Disaffected Pupils*. Uxbridge, Middx: Educational Studies Unit, Brunel University. *213, 215, 233*

Blackham, G. J. (1967) *The Deviant Child in the Classroom*. Belmont, Calif.: Wadsworth. *152*

Blackstone, T. (1980) Review of M. Rutter *et al.* (1979) *15,000 Hours. British Journal of Sociology of Education 1*, No. 2, pp. 216–19. *12*

Blau, P. (1963) Critical remarks on Weber's theory of authority.

American Political Science Review 57 (June), pp. 305–16. *181*

Borich, G. D. and Madden, S. K. (eds) (1977) *Evaluating Classroom Instruction: A Sourcebook of Instruments*. Reading, Mass.: Addison-Wesley. *7*

Borman, K. (1981) Review of recent case studies on equity and schooling. In R. G. Corwin (ed.) *Research on Educational Organizations*. Greenwich, Conn.: JAI Press. *17*

Bossert, S. T. (1979) *Tasks and Social Relationships in Classrooms*. Cambridge: Cambridge University Press.

Breed, G. and Colaiuta, V. (1974) Looking, blinking and sitting: non-verbal dynamics in the classroom. *Journal of Communication*, pp. 75–81. *157*

Bullivant, B. M. (1978) *The Way of Tradition*. Victoria: Australian Council for Educational Research Press. *9, 18, 81–106*

Burgess, R. (ed.) (1984) *The Research Process in Educational Settings*. Brighton: Falmer Press.

Campbell, H. (1980) Rastafari: culture of resistance. *Race and Class 21*, No. 4. *221*

Castles, S. and Kosak, G. (1973) *Immigrant Workers and the Class Structure in Western Europe*. London: Oxford University Press. *212*

Chamberlin, L. J. (1969) *Team Teaching: Organization and Administration*. Columbus, Ohio: Charles E. Merrill. *158*

Chanan, G. and Delamont, S. (eds) (1975) *Frontiers of Classroom Research*. Slough: National Foundation for Educational Research.

Cicourel, A. (1968) *The Social Organization of Juvenile Justice*. New York: John Wiley.

—— and Kitsuse, J. I. (1963) *The Educational Decision-Makers*. New York: Bobbs-Merrill. *152*

—— (1968) The social organization of high school and deviant adolescent careers. In E. Rubington and M. S. Weinberg (eds). *Deviance: The Interactionist Perspective*. Toronto: Collier-Macmillan.

Cicourel, O. *et al.* (1974) *Language Use and School Performance*. New York: Academic Press.

Cohen, A. (1955) *Delinquent Boys: The Culture of the Gang*. Glencoe, Ill.: The Free Press. *216*

Cohen, L. and Manion, L. (1981) *Perspectives on Classrooms and Schools*. London: Holt Saunders. *6*

Cohen, P. (1972) Subcultural conflict in working-class community. *Working Papers in Cultural Studies 2* (Spring). Birmingham: Centre for Contemporary Cultural Studies, the University. *221*

Coleman, J. S. (1961) *The Adolescent Society*. Glencoe, Ill.: The Free Press. *196, 207*

Connor, J. M. and Serbin, L. A. (1977) Behaviorally-based masculine and feminine activity preference scales for preschoolers. *Child Development 48*, pp. 1411–16.

Corrie, M., Haystead, J. and Zaklukiewicz, S. (1978) *The Classroom Situation: A Study of Teacher's and Pupils' Strategies*. Edinburgh: The Scottish Council for Research in Education. (End of grant Report HR 3012 to the SSRC) Published as:

—— (1982) *Classroom Management Strategies: A Study of Secondary Schools*. London: Hodder & Stoughton for the Scottish Council for Research in Education. *39, 47, 50, 53–4, 57*

Coulthard, M. (1974) Approaches to the analysis of classroom interaction. *Educational Review 22*, pp. 38–50. *4*

Cox, C. B. and Boyson, R. (eds) (1975) *Black Paper 1975*. London: Dent. *152*

—— (1977) *Black Paper 1977*. London: Temple Smith.

Cusick, P. (1973) *Inside High School*. New York: Holt, Rinehart & Winston.

Davies, B. (1976) *Social Control and Education*. London: Methuen. *6*

Davis, H. (1966) *How to Organize an Effective Team Teaching Programme*. Englewood Cliffs, NJ: Prentice Hall. *158*

Dawe, A. (1970) The two sociologies. *British Journal of Sociology 21*, No. 2, pp. 207–18. *6*

Deem, R. (ed.) (1980) *Schooling for Women's Work*. London: Routledge & Kegan Paul.

Delamont, S. (1975a) Participant observation and educational anthropology. *Research Intelligence 1*, pp. 13–22.

—— (1975b) Introduction. In G. Chanan and S. Delamont (eds) *Frontiers of Classroom Research*. Slough: National Foundation for Educational Research.

—— (1976a) Beyond Flanders fields. In M. Stubbs and S. Delamont (eds) *Explorations in Classroom Observation*. Chichester: John Wiley. *8*

—— (1976b) *Interaction in the Classroom* (first ed., second ed., 1983). London: Methuen. *xi–xii, 8, 144*

—— (1981) All too familiar? A decade of classroom research. *Educational Analysis 3*:1, pp. 69–84.

—— (1984) The old girl network: the fieldwork at St Luke's. In R. Burgess (ed.) *The Research Process in Educational Settings*. Brighton: Falmer Press.

—— and Atkinson, P. (1980) The two traditions in educational ethnography: sociology and anthropology compared. *British Journal of Sociology of Education 1*, No. 2, pp. 139–52. *19*

—— and Hamilton, D. (1976) Classroom research: a cautionary tale? In M. Stubbs and S. Delamont (eds) *Explorations in Classroom Observation*. Chichester: John Wiley. *4*

Denham, C. and Lieberman, A. (eds) (1980) *Time to Learn: A Review of the Beginning Teacher Evaluation Study*. Washington, DC: National Institute of Education (Department of Health, Education and Welfare). *7, 13–14*

Dennison, G. (1969) *The Lives of Children*. New York: Random House. *162–3, 165, 174, 181*

Denscombe, M. (1977) *The Social Organization of Teaching*. Unpublished PhD thesis, University of Leicester. *150, 157*

Dhondy, F. (1974) The black explosion in schools. *Race Today* (Feb.), pp. 44–7. *212*

Driver, G. (1979) Classroom stress and school achievement: West Indian adolescents and their teachers. In V. S. Khan (ed.) *Minority Families in Britain*. London: Macmillan.

Dumont, R. V. and Wax, M. L. (1969) Cherokee school society and the intercultural classroom. *Human Organization 28*, No. 3 (Fall), pp. 217–26. *153*

Edgar, E. D. (ed.) (1974) *The Competent Teacher*. Sydney: Angus & Robertson. *147*

Edwards, A. E. (1980) Perspectives on classroom language. *Educational Analysis 2*, No. 2, pp. 31–46. *xiii, 6*

—— and Furlong, V. J. (1979) *The Language of Teaching*. London: Heinemann.

Erickson, F. and Mohatt, G. (1982) Cultural organization of participant structure in two classrooms of Indian students. In G. Spindler (ed.) *Doing the Ethnography of Schooling*. New York: Holt, Rinehart & Winston. *21*

Fagot, B. I. and Patterson, G. R. (1969) An *in vivo* analysis of reinforcing contingencies for sex-role behaviours in the preschool child. *Developmental Psychology 1*, pp. 563–8. *283–4*

Fischer, J. (ed.) (1970) *The Social Sciences and the Comparative Study of Education Systems*. Scranton: International Textbook Co.

Flanders, N. A. (1966) *Interaction Analysis in the Classroom: A Manual for Observers* (revised edition). Michigan: School of Education, The University. *16*

—— (1970) *Analysing Teaching Behaviour*. Reading, Mass.: Addison-Wesley. *7, 10, 19*

Foner, N. (1975) The meaning of education to Jamaicans at home and in London. *New Community 3*, pp. 195–202. *231*

Freeman, K. D. (1973) Bensalem: an analysis. In G. G. MacDonald (ed.) *Five Experimental Colleges*. New York: Harper & Row. *179*

Fuller, M. (1980) Black girls in a London comprehensive. In R. Deem (ed.) *Schooling for Women's work*. London: Routledge & Kegan Paul. *213*

Furlong, V. J. (1976) Interaction sets in the classroom. In M. Stubbs and S. Delamont (eds) *Explorations in Classroom Observation*. Chichester: John Wiley. *259*

—— (1977) Anancy goes to school. In P. Woods and M. Hammersley (eds) *School Experience*. London: Croom Helm.

—— (1985) *Understanding School Deviance: Sociological Perspectives*. Milton Keynes: Open University Press.

Gage, N. L. and Unruh, W. H. (1967) Theoretical formulations for research on teaching. *Review of Educational Research 37*, pp. 358–70. *23*

Galton, M. (ed.) (1978) *British Mirrors: A Collection of Classroom Observation Instruments*. Leicester: School of Education, The University. *7*

——, Simon, B. and Croll, P. (1980) *Inside the Primary Classroom*. London: Routledge & Kegan Paul. *7–8, 11, 13–15, 25*

—— and Simon, B. (1980) *Progress and Performance in the Primary School*. London: Routledge & Kegan Paul. *12, 15–16*

—— and Willcocks, J. (1983) *Moving from the Primary Classroom*. London: Routledge & Kegan Paul.

Gannaway, H. (1976) Making sense of school. In M. Stubbs and S. Delamont (eds) *Explorations in Classroom Observation*. Chichester: John Wiley. *259*

Garfinkel, H. (1967) *Studies in Ethnomethodology*. Englewood Cliffs, NJ: Prentice Hall.

Garner, J. (1972) Some aspects of behaviour in infant school classrooms. *Research in Education 7*, pp. 28–47. *15*

Garrison, L. (1979) *Black Youth, Rastafarianism, and the Identity Crisis in Britain*. Victoria: Australian Council for Educational Research Press. *213*

Geer, B. (1964) First days in the field. In P. Hammond (ed.) *Sociologists at Work*. New York: Basic Books. *255*

Gibbons, M. (1969) The search for a scheme of individualized schooling. PhD dissertation, School of Education, Harvard University. *209*

Goffman, E. (1961) *Encounters: Two Studies in the Sociology of Interaction*. Indianapolis: Bobbs-Merrill.

—— (1971) *The Presentation of Self in Everyday Life*. Harmondsworth, Middx: Penguin. *136, 166*

Gross, N. *et al.* (1971) *Implementing Organizational Innovations.* New York: Harper & Row. *157*

Gussow, Z. (1964) The observer-observed relationship as information about structures in small group research. *Psychiatry 27*, pp. 236–47. *18*

Hall, S. and Jefferson, T. (eds) (1976) *Resistance through Rituals.* London: Hutchinson.

—— *et al.* (1978) *Policing the Crisis.* London, Macmillan.

Hamilton, D. (1974) *The Fieldwork* and *Project Highlands and Islands School Visit: Peerie School.* The Glasgow University Project PH1 Technical Supplements Nos. 13 and 16. Glasgow: The Department of Education.

—— (1976) The advent of curriculum integration. In M. Stubbs and S. Delamont (eds) *Explorations in Classroom Observation.* Chichester: John Wiley. *8*

—— (1977) *In Search of Structure.* London: Hodder & Stoughton. *xiv, 239–254*

—— (1981) Generalizations in the educational sciences: problems and purposes. In T. S. Popkewitz and B. R. Tabachnick (eds) *The Study of Schooling.* New York: Praeger. *19*

—— and Delamont, S. (1974) Classroom research: a cautionary tale? *Research in Education 11*, pp. 1–15. (Reprinted in M. Stubbs and S. Delamont (eds) *Explorations in Classroom Observation.* Chichester: John Wiley) *4*

Hammersley, M. (1980a) On interactionist empiricism. In P. Woods (ed.) *Pupil Strategies.* London: Croom Helm.

—— (1980b) Classroom ethnography. *Educational Analysis 2:2*, pp. 47–74. *7, 17*

—— (1982) The sociology of classrooms. In A. Hartnett (ed.) *The Social Sciences in Educational Studies.* London. Heinemann.

—— and Hargreaves, A. (1982) CCCS gas, *Oxford Review of Education 8, 12*, pp. 139–44.

—— and Woods, P. (eds) (1976) *The Process of Schooling.* London: Routledge & Kegan Paul.

—— and Atkinson, P. (1983) *Ethnography.* London: Tavistock. *17*

Hannan, A. (1978) Unpublished PhD thesis, University of Leicester.

Hanson, D. and Herrington, M. (1976) *From College to Classroom: The Probationary Year.* London: Routledge & Kegan Paul.

Hargreaves, A (1977) Progressivism and pupil autonomy. *Sociological Review 24*, No. 3, pp. 555–621. *43*

—— (1979) Strategies, decisions and control: interaction in a middle school. In J. Eggleston (ed.) *Teacher Decision-Making in the Classroom*. London: Routledge & Kegan Paul. *43*

—— (1980) Review of M. Rutter *et al. 15,000 Hours. British Journal of Sociology of Education 1*, No. 2, pp. 211–16. *13*

Hargreaves, D. (1967) *Social Relations in a Secondary School*. London: Routledge & Kegan Paul. *152*

—— (1979) Whatever happened to symbolic interactionism? In L. Barton and R. Meighan (eds) *Sociological Interpretations of Schools and Classrooms*. Driffield, Yorks: Nafferton Books.

—— (1980) (ed.) *Educational Analysis 2*, No. 2 (special issue on Classroom Studies). *5–6, 12*

—— *et al.* (1975) *Deviance in Classrooms*. London: Routledge & Kegan Paul. *9, 152–3, 157–9, 259*

Harré, R. and Secord, P. F. (1972) *The Explanation of Social Behaviour*. Oxford: Blackwell. *20*

Hartnett, A. (ed.) (1982) *The Social Sciences in Educational Studies*. London: Heinemann.

Hebdige, D. (1976) Reggae, rastas and rudies. In S. Hall and T. Jefferson (eds) *Resistance through Rituals*. London: Hutchinson. *213, 221*

—— (1980) *Sub-culture: The Meaning of Style*. London: Methuen.

Hendrick, C. H. *et al.* (1974) The social ecology of free seating arrangements in a small group interaction context. *Sociometry 37*, No. 2, pp. 262–74.

Hobbs, S. and Kleinberg, S. (1978) Teaching: a behavioural influence approach. In R. McAleese and D. Hamilton (eds) *Understanding Classroom Life*. Slough: National Foundation for Education Research. *7*

Holt, J. (1972) *Freedom and Beyond*. New York: Dell. *179–80*

Hudson, L. (1977) Picking winners: a case study of the recruitment of research students. *New Universities Quarterly 32*, No. 1, pp. 88–106. *3*

Jackson, P. W. (1968) *Life in Classrooms*. New York: Holt, Rinehart & Winston. *137, 144*

Karabel, J. and Halsey, A. H. (eds) (1977) *Power and Ideology in Education*. New York: Oxford University Press.

Karweit, N. (1981) Time in school. In R. G. Corwin (ed.) *Research on Educational Organizations*. Greenwich, Conn.: JAI Press. *10–11*

King, R. (1978) *All Things Bright and Beautiful?* Chichester: John Wiley.

Kohl, H. (1967) *36 Children*. New York: New American Library. *177*

—— (1969) *The Open Classroom*. London: Methuen.

—— (1973) Closing time for open ed.? *New York Review of Books 20* (13 Dec). *179*

Kounin, J. S. (1970) *Discipline and Group Management in Classrooms*. New York: Holt, Rinehart & Winston. *152, 157*

Lacey, C. (1970) *Hightown Grammar*. Manchester: Manchester University Press. *152, 216*

Lambert, A. (1976) The sisterhood. In M. Hammersley and P. Woods (eds) *The Process of Schooling*. London: Routledge & Kegan Paul.

Larkin, R. W. (1979) *Suburban Youth in Cultural Crisis*. New York: Oxford University Press.

Lawton, D. (1973) *Social Change, Educational Theory and Curriculum Planning*. London: The University Press. *157*

Leacock, E. B. (1969) *Teaching and Learning in City Schools*. New York: Basic Books. *134, 145, 149*

Liebert, R. M., Call, R. B. and Hanratty, M. A. (1971) Effects of sex-typed information on children's toy preference. *Journal of Genetic Psychology 119*, pp. 133–6. *283*

Linton, T. E. (1966) *Social and Cultural Factors in Deviant Classroom Behaviour*. Ottawa: Canada's Mental Health Supplement, CMH No. 52. *152*

Lortie, D. C. (1964) The teacher and team teaching: suggestions for long-range research. In J. T. Shaplin and H. F. Olds Jnr. (eds) *Team Teaching*. New York: Harper & Row. *144*

—— (1969) The balance of control and autonomy in elementary school teaching. In A. Etzioni (ed.) *The Semi-Professions and their Organization*. New York: The Free Press. *144*

Lowenstein, L. (1975) *Disruptive Behaviour in Schools*. London: National Association of Schoolmasters. *158*

McAleese, R. and Hamilton, D. (eds) (1978) *Understanding Classroom Life*. Slough: National Foundation for Educational Research.

McHoul, A. (1978) The organization of turns at formal talk in the classroom. *Language and Society 7*, pp. 183–213.

McIntyre, D. (1980) Systematic observation of classroom activities. *Educational Analysis 2*, No. 2, pp. 3–30. *6*

—— and McLeod, G. (1978) The characteristics and uses of systematic observation. In R. McAleese and D. Hamilton (eds) *Understanding Classroom Life*. Slough: National Foundation for Educational Research. *4*

McPherson, G. A. (1972) *Small Town Teacher*. Harvard: The University Press. *148*

Mardle, G. and Walker, M. *Strategies and Structure: Some Critical*

Notes on Teacher Socialization. London: Croom Helm. *157*

Medding, P. Y. (1968) *From Assimilation to Group Survival.* Melbourne: Cheshire.

Mehan, H. (1978) Structuring school structure. *Harvard Educational Review 48*, No. 1, pp. 32–64.

—— (1979) *Learning Lessons.* Harvard: The University Press.

Meister, J. S. (1972) Coming of Age in Counter Culture: Case Study of a free school. Unpublished PhD thesis, Department of Sociology, University of California, Berkeley. *177*

Metz, M. H. (1978) *Classrooms and Corridors: The Crisis of Authority in Desegregated Secondary Schools.* Berkeley, Calif.: University of California Press. *11, 181*

Montemayor, R. (1974) Children's performance in a game and their attraction to it as a function of sex-typed labels. *Child Development 45*, No. 1, pp. 152–6. *283*

Musgrave, P. W. (1973) *Knowledge, Curriculum and Change.* Melbourne: The University Press. *82*

Nash, R. (1973) *Classrooms Observed.* London: Routledge & Kegan Paul.

—— (1976) Pupils Expectations of their teachers. In M. Stubbs and S. Delamont (eds) *Explorations in Classroom Observation.* Chichester: John Wiley. *259*

—— (1977) *Schooling in Rural Societies.* London: Methuen.

Nicolinakos, M. (1973) Notes on an economic theory of racism. *Race 14*, No. 4, pp. 365–82. *212*

Payne, G. C. E. (1976) Making a lesson happen. In M. Hammersley and P. Woods (eds) *The Process of Schooling.* London: Routledge & Kegan Paul.

—— and Cuff, E. C. (eds) (1982) *Doing Teaching.* London: Batsford.

Pollard, A. (1979) Negotiating deviance – and 'getting done' in primary school. In L. Barton and R. Meighan (eds) *Schools, Pupils and Deviance.* Driffield, Yorks.: Nafferton Books. *259–60*

—— (1980) Teacher interests and changing situations of survival threat in primary school classrooms. In P. Woods (ed.) *Teacher Strategies.* London: Croom Helm. *9*

Popkewitz, T. S. and Tabachnick, B. R. (eds) (1981) *The Study of Schooling.* New York: Praeger. *7*

——, Tabachnick, B. R. and Wehlage, G. (1982) *The Myth of Educational Reform.* Madison, Wisconsin: The University of Wisconsin Press. *18*

Rex, J. (1970) *Race Relations and Sociological Theory.* London: Weidenfeld & Nicholson. *212*

—— and Moore, R. (1967) *Race, Community and Conflict*. London: Oxford University Press. *212*

—— and Tomlinson, S. (1979) *Colonial Immigrants in the British City: A Class Analysis*. London: Routledge & Kegan Paul. *212, 230*

Reynolds, D. (1980) Review of M. Rutter *et al.* (1979) *15,000 Hours*. *British Journal of Sociology of Education 1*, No. 2, pp. 207–11. *12*

Rist, R. C. (1970) Student social class and teacher expectations. *Harvard Educational Review 40*, No. 3, pp. 411–51. *16–17*

Rosenshine, B. and Berliner, D. (1978) Academic engaged time. *British Journal of Teacher Education 4* No. 1, pp. 3–16. *7*

Rothschild-Whitt, J. (1976) Conditions facilitating participatory-democratic organizations. *Sociological Inquiry 46* (Spring), pp. 75–86. *181–2*

Rutter, M., *et al.* (1979) *15,000 Hours*. London: Open Books. *7–8, 11–12, 25*

Sacks, H. (1972) An initial investigation of the usability of conventional data for doing sociology. In D. Sudnow (ed.) *Studies in Social Interaction*. New York: Free Press.

Samph, T. (1976) Observer effects on teacher verbal classroom behaviour. *Journal of Educational Psychology 68*, No. 6, pp. 736–41. Reprinted in N. Bennett and D. McNamara (eds) (1979) *Focus on Teaching*. Harlow: Longman. *15*

Schneersohn, J. I. (1962) *The 'Tzemach Tzedak' and the Haskala Movement*. New York: Kehot Publication Society. *89*

Schutz, A. (1972) *The Phenomenology of the Social World*. London: Heinemann.

—— and Luckmann, T. (1974) *The Structures of the Life-World*. London: Heinemann. *44, 47, 49*

Serbin, L. A. and O'Leary, K. D. (1975) How nursery schools teach girls to shut up. *Psychology Today* (December).

—— *et al.* (1973) A comparison of teacher response to the preacademic and problem behaviour of boys and girls. *Child Development 44*, pp. 796–804. *276*

—— *et al.* (1977) Shaping co-operative cross-sex play. *Child Development 48*, pp. 924–9.

Shaplin, J. T. and Olds, H. F. Jnr (eds) (1964) *Team Teaching*. New York: Harper & Row. *158*

Sharp, R. and Green, A. (1975) *Education and Social Control*. London: Routledge & Kegan Paul. *145, 305, 322*

Shipman, M. (1981) Parvenu evaluation. In D. Smetherham (ed.) *Practising Evaluation*. Driffield, Yorks.: Nafferton Books. *22*

Simon, A. and Boyer, G. E. (eds) (1968) *Mirrors for Behavior*.

Philadelphia: Research for Better Schools Inc.

—— (eds) (1970) *Mirrors for Behavior 2*. Philadelphia: Research for Better Schools Inc. *7, 9*

—— (eds) (1974) *Mirrors for Behavior 3*. Philadelphia: Research for Better Schools Inc.

Sindell, P. (1969) Anthropological aproaches to the study of education. *Review of Educational Research 39*, No. 5, pp. 593–606.

Sivanandan, A. (1976) *Race, Class and the State: The Black Experience in Britain*. London: The Institute of Race Relations. *212*

Smith, J. V. and Hamilton, D. (eds) (1980) *The Meritocratic Intellect*. Aberdeen: The University Press. *22*

Smith, L. M. (1978) An evolving logic of participant observation: educational ethnography and other case studies. In Lee Shulman (ed.) *Review of Research in Education 6*. Itasca, Ill.: Peacock Press. *17*

—— (1982) Ethnography. In H. Mitzel (ed.) *The Encyclopedia of Educational Research* (5th ed.). New York and London: Macmillan (4 vols). *16–17*

—— and Geoffrey, W. (1968) *Complexities of an Urban Classroom*. New York: Holt, Rinehart & Winston. *9, 15–16*

—— and Keith, P. M. (1971) *Anatomy of Educational Innovation*. New York: John Wiley. *58–80*

Smith, R. (1980) Scepticism and qualitative research: a view from inside. *Education and Urban Society 12*, No. 3, pp. 383–98.

Snyder, B. (1971) *The Hidden Curriculum*. New York: Knopf. *9, 144*

Solomon, G. (1973) Jewish education in Australia. In P. Y. Medding (ed.) *Jews in Australian Society*. Melbourne: Macmillan and Monash University Press. *91*

Sommer, R. (1967) Classroom ecology. *Journal of Applied Behavioural Science 3*, No. 4, pp. 489–503. *157*

Sorokin, P. and Merton, R. K. (1937) Social time: a methodological and functional analysis. *American Journal of Sociology 42*, No. 5, pp. 615–29. *46*

Spindler, G. D. (ed.) (1982) *Doing the Ethnography of Schooling*. New York: Holt, Rinehart & Winston. *7, 17, 23*

—— and Spindler, L. (1982) Roger Harker and Schonhausen: from the familiar to the strange and back again. In G. Spindler (ed.) *Doing the Ethnography of Schooling*. New York: Holt, Rinehart & Winston. *255–6*

Stake, R. (ed.) (1978) *Case Studies in Science Education*. Urbana-Champaigne: CIRCE.

Stebbins, R. A. (1971) The meaning of disorderly behaviour: teacher definitions of a classroom situation. *Sociology of Education 44*, pp. 217–36. *152, 158–9*

—— (1973) Physical context influences on behaviour: the case of classroom disorderliness. *Environment and Behaviour 5*, No. 3, pp. 291–314. *157*

—— (1975) *Teachers and Meanings*. Leiden: E. J. Brill. *13*

Steinberg, M. (1959) *The Making of the Modern Jew*. New York: Behrman House. *99*

Stinchcombe, A. (1964) *Rebellion in a High School*. Chicago: Quadrangle.

Street, D., Vintner, R. and Perrow, C. (1966) *Organization for Treatment*. New York: Free Press. *181*

Stubbs, M. and Delamont, S. (eds) (1976) *Explorations in Classroom Observation*. Chichester: John Wiley. *xiii*

—— and Hillier, H. (eds) (1983) *Readings on Language, Schools and Classrooms*. London: Methuen.

Sugarman, B. (1967) Involvement in youth culture, academic achievement, and conformity in schools. *British Journal of Sociology 18*, No. 2, pp. 151–64. *152*

Swidler, A. (1979) *Organization without Authority*. Harvard: The University Press. *9, 160–82*

Swift, D. W. (1971) *Ideology and Change in the Public Schools*. Columbus, Ohio: Merrill. *155*

Thompson, E. P. (1967) Time, work discipline and the industrial capitalists. *Past and Present 38* (Dec.), pp. 56–97. *41*

Tikunoff, W. and Ward, B. A. (1980) Conducting naturalistic research on teaching. *Education and Urban Society 12*, No. 3 (May), pp. 263–90. *7*

Tomlinson, S. (1977) Race and education in Britain – an overview of the literature 1960–1977. *Sage Race Relations Abstracts 2*, No. 4, pp. 3–33. *212*

Torode, B. (1976) Teacher's talk and classroom discipline. In M. Stubbs and S. Delamont (eds) *Explorations in Classroom Observation*. Chichester: John Wiley.

—— (1977) Interrupting intersubjectivity. In P. Woods and M. Hammersley (eds) *School Experience*. London: Croom Helm.

Troyna, B. (1978) *Rastafarianism, Reggae and Racism*. London: National Association for Multi-Racial Education. *222*

Vidich, A. J. (1955) Participant observation and the collection and interpretation of data. *American Journal of Sociology 60*, pp. 354–60. *18*

Vierra, A. Boehm, C. and Neely, S. (1982) Anthropology and

educational studies. In A. Hartnett (ed.) *The Social Sciences in Educational Studies*. London: Heinemann.

Walker, R. (1971) *The Social Setting of the Classroom: A Review of Observational Studies and Research*. Unpublished M.Phil. thesis, University of London. *21*

—— (1972) The sociology of education and life in school classrooms. *International Review of Education 18*, pp. 32–43.

—— and Adelman, C. (1975a) Interaction analysis in informal classrooms: a critical comment on the Flanders system. *British Journal of Educational Psychology 45*, No. 1, pp. 73–6. *4, 9, 21*

—— (1975b) *A Guide to Classroom Observation*. London: Methuen.

—— (1976) Strawberries. In M. Stubbs and S. Delamont (eds) *Explorations in Classroom Observation*. Chichester: John Wiley.

Walberg, H. J. (1968) Physical and psychological distance in the classroom. *The School Review*, pp. 64–70. *157*

Waller, W. (1961) *The Sociology of Teaching*. New York: Russell & Russell (originally published 1932). *144*

Warren, R. L. (1973) The classroom as a sanctuary for teachers: discontinuities in social control. *American Anthropologist 75*, No. 1 (Feb.), pp. 280–91. *145*

Wax, M. L., Diamond, S. and Gearing, F. (eds) (1971) *Anthropological Perspectives on Education*. New York: Basic Books.

Werblowsky, R. J. Z. and Wigoder, G. (eds) (1965) *The Encyclopedia of Jewish Religion*. London: Phoenix House. *93*

Werthman, C. (1963) Delinquents in schools. In B. R. Cosin *et al.* (eds) (1971) *School and Society*. London: Routledge & Kegan Paul.

White, M. A. and Charry, J. (1966) *School Disorder, Intelligence and Social Class*. New York: Columbia University Press. *152*

Wilcox, K. (1982) Ethnography as a methodology and its applications to the study of schooling: a review. In G. Spindler (ed.) *Doing the Ethnography of Schooling*. New York: Holt, Rinehart & Winston. *17*

Willis, P. (1977) *Learning to Labour*. London: Saxon House. *42, 145, 215–17, 233*

Wilson, P. J. (1969) Reputation and respectability: a suggestion for Caribbean ethnography. *Man 4*, pp. 70–84. *218–19*

Wolcott, H. F. (1967) *A Kwakiutl Village and School*. New York: Holt, Rinehart & Winston.

—— (1973) *The Man in the Principal's Office*. New York: Holt, Rinehart & Winston. *12*

—— (1977) *Teachers and Technocrats: An Educational Innovation in Anthropological Perspective*, Eugene, Oregon: Centre for Educational Policy and Management, University of Oregon.

—— (1981) Confessions of a 'trained' observer. In T. S. Popkewitz and B. R. Tabachnick (eds) *The Study of Schooling*. New York: Praeger. *12, 17, 23*

—— (1982) Mirrors, models and monitors: educator adaptations of the ethnographic innovation. In G. Spindler (ed.) *Doing the Ethnography of Schooling*. New York: Holt, Rinehart & Winston. *3, 23*

Woods, P. (1977) Teaching for survival. In P. Woods and M. Hammersley (eds) *School Experience*. London: Croom Helm.

—— (1978) Negotiating the demands of schoolwork. *Journal of Curriculum Studies 10*, No. 4 (Oct.-Dec.), pp. 309–27. *43, 56–7, 144*

—— (1979) *The Divided School*. London: Routledge & Kegan Paul.

—— (ed.) (1980a) *Teacher Strategies*. London: Croom Helm. *134–59*

—— (ed.) (1980b) *Pupil Strategies*. London: Croom Helm. *271*

—— (1984) Sociological perspectives on school violence. In H. Gault and N. Frude (eds) *School Violence*. Chichester: John Wiley. *260*

—— and Hammersley, M. (1977) (eds) *School Experience*. London: Croom Helm.

Wragg, E. C. (1974) *Teaching Teaching*. Newton Abbot: David & Charles. *20*

Young, M. F. D. (1971) An approach to the study of curricula as socially organized knowledge. In M. F. D. Young (ed.) *Knowledge and Control*. London: Collier-Macmillan. *144*

Zborowski, M. and Herzog, E. (1952) *Life is with People: The Jewish Little-Town of Eastern Europe*. New York: International Universities Press. *96, 97*

Name Index

342

343

Subject Index

academic: achievement, West Indian boys' attitude to, 214–15, 230–2; engaged time, 7, 13–14; knowledge, 82–4

'achievement orientation', 150–1

acoustics, Kensington School, 72–4

ADI *see* Architectural Design Institute

administrative suite, Kensington School, 75–6

age, teacher's role and institutional setting, 12, 109–33; career research, 110–11; changes in relating to students, 115–22; and extra-curricular activities, 122–8; sampling and interviewing, 110; sponsorship, inter-generational conflict and age-graded cliques, 128–33; teacher in school system, 111–13; young teachers relating to students, 113–15

aggressive behaviour, boys, 276–9

anthropology *see* ethnography

anti-intellectual culture, 196

anti-school culture, 153–4, 216–19, 230–4

appearance of classroom control, 151–4

Architectural Design Institute of America, 59–76 *passim*

artifacts in environment, 104

association, West Indian boys, 225–7

atmosphere, Kensington School, 76

audio-visual aids, 21; Kensington School, 64–7; and noise, 140–2, 156

Australia *see* knowledge in Jewish school

authority: bargaining and, 166, 181; West Indian boys and, 215–16

autonomy, teachers', apparent, 134, 142, 155

bargaining and authority, 166, 181

Basic Skills Division in Kensington School, 58, 60, 62, 64

Beginning Teacher Evaluation Study, 12, 14

345

349

team teaching, 156, 158
textbooks, 319
theatre, children's, 68–70
therapeutic model of education, 160–82
thermal treatments, Kensington School, 72–4
time: private, West Indian boys, 227–30; and task at school, 41–57
Transition department in Kensington School, 58, 64

United Kingdom *see* Britain
United States, 4, 6, 12, 158; age of teachers, 109–33; elementary school, 58–80; free school, intimacy in, 160–82; open classrooms, 185–211; preschool

sex-typing, 273–89

values of Great Tradition, 91–5
visual treatments, Kensington School, 72–4
vulnerability appeal, 165–6

Wales, comprehensive school in, 255–72
women teachers, 109–33, 265, 270, 284
working class pupils, 150, 169, 215, 217, 225–6, 228, 235
'working consensus', 259
worksheets, 295–6, 305, 318–24

young teachers 113–15; *see also* new teachers